TEACHING GRAMMAR, PUNCTUATION AND SPELLING IN PRIMARY SCHOOLS

2ND EDITION

DAVID WAUGH,
CLAIRE WARNER and
ROSEMARY WAUGH

 |

Los Angeles | London | New Delhi
Singapore | Washington DC

Learning Matters
An imprint of SAGE Publications Ltd
1 Oliver's Yard
55 City Road
London EC1Y 1SP

SAGE Publications Inc.
2455 Teller Road
Thousand Oaks, California 91320

SAGE Publications India Pvt Ltd
B 1/I 1 Mohan Cooperative Industrial Area
Mathura Road
New Delhi 110 044

SAGE Publications Asia-Pacific Pte Ltd
3 Church Street
#10–04 Samsung Hub
Singapore 049483

First edition published by Learning Matters/SAGE 2013
Second edition published in 2016

Editor: Amy Thornton
Development editor: Jennifer Clark
Production controller: Chris Marke
Project management: Deer Park Productions
Marketing manager: Lorna Patkai
Cover design: Wendy Scott
Typeset by: C&M Digitals (P) Ltd, Chennai, India
Printed and bound by CPI Group (UK) Ltd, Croydon, CR0 4YY

Library of Congress Control Number: 2015954468

British Library Cataloguing in Publication Data

A catalogue record for this book is available from the British Library.

ISBN 978-1-4739-4225-7 (pbk)
ISBN 978-1-4739-4224-0

TEACHING GRAMMAR, PUNCTUATION AND SPELLING IN PRIMARY SCHOOLS

SAGE was founded in 1965 by Sara Miller McCune to support the dissemination of usable knowledge by publishing innovative and high-quality research and teaching content. Today, we publish over 900 journals, including those of more than 400 learned societies, more than 800 new books per year, and a growing range of library products including archives, data, case studies, reports, and video. SAGE remains majority-owned by our founder, and after Sara's lifetime will become owned by a charitable trust that secures our continued independence.

Los Angeles | London | New Delhi | Singapore | Washington DC

Contents

Acknowledgements

We would like to thank Danielle Knox and Holly Faulkner for writing their own case studies, and all the trainee teachers and teachers who described lessons and planning to enable us to produce case studies.

We would also like to thank Dr Jo Waugh, Lecturer in English at York St John University, for her assiduous proofreading and valuable advice.

Introduction

This book explores the teaching of grammar, punctuation and spelling in primary schools, at a time when the National Curriculum places an increasing emphasis on these important aspects of literacy. Indeed, since 2013, Year 6 children have taken a grammar test (see Chapter 1 and Appendix 3) and teachers are under increasing pressure to prepare children well so that they are successful in the test.

A quick search on the internet reveals a great preoccupation with what are often considered to be the more formal elements of literacy. In 2013, for example, the *Telegraph*'s website included an article entitled 'It's cruel not to teach children grammar' in which the author concludes:

> *At its worst, educational theory that rejects grammar does so because of a mad idea that children are noble savages better left to authenticity and the composition of rap lyrics. That way lies the scrapheap and jail.*
>
> *Grammar sets them free. No one would think it a kindness to give a teenager a car without teaching her to drive, and that includes the rules of the road.*

Wordsworth (2012)

However, there is considerable debate about the most effective way to teach grammar. For some, the words 'grammar' and 'syntax' conjure up images of exercises and formal teaching; but there are alternatives. Myhill, Lines and Watson maintain:

> *The argument underpinning these approaches is that teaching grammar as a discrete, separate topic, where the grammar is the focus of study, is not likely to help writing development because it does not make connections between grammar and writing, or between grammar and meaning ...*
>
> *... a writing curriculum which draws attention to the grammar of writing in an embedded and purposeful way at relevant points in the learning is a more positive way forward. In this way, young writers are introduced to what we have called 'a repertoire of infinite possibilities', explicitly showing them how different ways of shaping sentences or texts, and how different choices of words can generate different possibilities for meaning-making.*

(2011, p.3)

In this book, we stress the importance of contextualised grammar teaching. The examples provided in the chapters, most notably in the case studies, illustrate how children can develop a good knowledge and understanding about language when it is taught through meaningful activities rather than through exercises. Consider two approaches to learning the function of adjectives.

1. Children are shown some examples of adjectives in sentences on the board. They are then given a series of sentences with spaces where they should insert adjectives.

2. Children go outside on a warm spring day and are asked, when they return to the classroom, to discuss and note, in pairs, what it felt like to be outside: what did they see, hear, feel, smell? They then share these descriptions with the class and the teacher writes short noun phrases on the board, such as *warm sunshine, light breeze, damp grass* and *fresh, green buds.* She then creates a short poem comprised only of adjectives and nouns, using the children's ideas. As she does so, she asks the children to suggest a variety of words which describe nouns, telling them that such words are called *adjectives.* The children then return to their tables to write their own adjective–noun poems.

Perhaps you remember the kind of exercises described in the first example. It was easy to fill in the gaps in the sentences because only certain types of words would fit. Try putting words into the gaps in the sentences below.

Jan wore a _____ blouse and a _____ skirt.

Simon drove a _____ car and lived in a _____ house.

It isn't difficult to find words to fit into the spaces, is it? You could happily (or perhaps tediously) complete 20 such sentences, but how much help would this be in understanding and remembering the function of adjectives?

Now look at the sentences below and place pobdrobs in the spaces.

Dave ran _____ towards the goal.

Craig laughed _____ when he heard the joke.

If you completed the sentences, you almost certainly inserted words like *quickly* in the first sentence and *heartily* or *loudly* in the second. You probably wondered what a *pobdrob* was, but this is a book about grammar and you probably expect to find some unfamiliar terms, so you simply completed the sentences anyway. But would you remember what a *pobdrob* is next week? There is actually no such thing as a *pobdrob*, and the missing words were in fact adverbs, but the point we want to make is that a knowledge of terms is meaningless without understanding, and understanding comes through using and discussing language. In the second example, the children learned the term and became familiar with the function of adjectives through discussion and writing; and we would argue that they are more likely to use and be able to name adjectives than those who filled in missing words in sentences. Try completing the following sentence:

The _____ rattled through the _____ at ____ speed.

Easy? Yes, but could you name the parts of speech or word classes of the words you inserted? And why would you want to know them anyway? Apart from the obvious reason that you will have to teach them one day, another strong justification is that you will be able to develop a shared language for discussing language with your pupils. In mathematics, we stress the importance of correct and accurate nomenclature, for example when differentiating between isosceles, scalene and equilateral triangles. Other subjects also teach the use of specialised vocabulary. For some reason, in the past many teachers avoided doing the same for English, using terms such as 'naming words', 'describing words' and 'doing words' rather than nouns, adjectives and verbs. If you want your class to show in a poem just how they felt when walking outside on a warm spring day, it is much easier to use the term *adjective* once they are familiar with it, rather than repeatedly talking about *describing words* or *words which describe things*.

A description of different approaches to Year 3 learning about adverbs suggests that there are advantages to taking a more creative approach to developing children's knowledge about language. Danielle, a PGCE student, worked with groups of Year 3 children as part of her research for an assignment. She describes, below, two different approaches and their outcomes.

Case study: Year 3 learning about adverbs

The basic premise of the task was to determine if *creative* or *traditional* teaching would affect grammatical retention/understanding. Eight Year 3 children were chosen and were divided into two equal groups by their class teacher, based on gender and academic ability, to test their knowledge of adverbs. The children were all taught on the same day (but at different times) and tested the following day. The teaching section for the traditional group involved recapping what verbs and adverbs are (some of the children already knew this). The children then had to identify adverbs (and verbs if they wanted to) in a selection of sentences such as 'The dog ran quickly', and write these on their whiteboards. The sentences were initially read out and written for the children to see, but as the lesson progressed they just heard the sentences.

For the creative group, the same teaching process was followed but when children had to identify adverbs, they used a mixture of drama, music and art to show the adverbs. Both groups were asked to recognise the pattern of the adverbs, i.e. they ended in 'ly' (in the examples provided), and what an adverb was. Overall, both groups generally understood what an adverb was.

$\longrightarrow$

> The groups were tested the next day using a basic reading test where they independently had to identify the adverbs in a list of ten sentences and then define an adverb. Overall, there was no great difference between the scores of the two groups; although the creative group seemed to be more able when defining an adverb and they did comment that they thought the creative aspects helped them to learn during the lesson.

Danielle's small-scale study seems to indicate that there are some benefits to adopting a more creative approach to teaching about language. It certainly suggests that it is worth considering ways of making your lessons interactive and multi-sensory in order to help children to retain knowledge and understanding.

What do children need to know?

The National Curriculum is quite specific about what children should know about grammar and the terminology and states that *they should learn to recognise and use the terminology through discussion and practice* (DfE, 2013, p.74). The glossary (Appendix 1) provides definitions of this terminology and other terms that you will often encounter, and includes brief suggestions for ways of teaching about the terms, as well as an indication as to the chapters where you can find out more. For many trainees and teachers, the terminology may seem quite daunting, and probably includes some terms that you have never previously met.

In Year 1 this includes: letter, capital letter word, singular, plural, sentence, punctuation, full stop, question mark, exclamation mark.

In Year 2 this includes: noun, noun phrase, statement, question, exclamation, command, compound, adjective, verb, suffix adverb, tense (past, present) apostrophe, comma.

It is worth pausing for a moment, before looking at Key Stage 2, to consider how familiar you are with such terms and how confident you would feel about discussing and exemplifying them. It may also be worthwhile looking in the glossary to clarify the meaning of terms that you are unsure about.

The Key Stage 2 terminology will probably have most readers turning to the glossary for some terms.

In Year 3, children are expected to know: adverb, preposition, conjunction, word family, prefix, clause, subordinate clause, direct speech, consonant, consonant letter vowel, vowel letter, inverted commas (or 'speech marks').

In Year 4: determiner, pronoun, possessive pronoun, adverbial.

In Year 5: relative clause, modal verb, relative pronoun, parenthesis, bracket, dash, determiner, cohesion, ambiguity.

And in Year 6: active and passive voice, subject and object, hyphen, synonym, antonym, colon, semi-colon, bullet points and ellipsis.

If you already feel confident that you know and understand all of the terms, we hope that our book will help you to find ways of teaching them. If some of the terms are unfamiliar, you will find explanations and examples, as well as activities and self-assessments, which should enable you to develop confidence in your ability to teach them. The self-assessments sometimes include the kind of exercises we have already criticised in this Introduction, but we hope you will see these as quick checks that you have understood what we hope are more creative examples and explanations. You will find the answers to these self-assessments in Appendix 2.

By reading this book and exploring more creative approaches to knowledge about language, you will not only become more familiar with relevant terminology, but also more confident about teaching it effectively. Chapter 1 provides an introduction to grammar and a rationale for how you might teach it.

We also explore spelling and vocabulary development, emphasising the importance of *teaching* spelling and not simply *testing* it. Perhaps you remember being given ten words to learn on Mondays and being tested on them on Fridays. You may also remember your teacher's frustration that people continued to misspell words that they had only recently been tested upon. In Chapters 2, 3, 4 and 5 you will find guidance on, and examples of, ways of teaching vocabulary and spelling so that children not only remember spellings, but also are able to apply their knowledge of spelling patterns when faced with unfamiliar words.

In Chapter 6 you will find ideas for teaching and learning punctuation, as well as explanations of different punctuation marks. Chapter 7 focuses on one particular punctuation mark: the apostrophe, which seems to cause more problems for writers than all the rest put together!

Chapter 8 looks at the grammar and syntax of sentences, providing examples of ways to teach and learn about phrases and clauses. Chapter 9 draws everything together, examining how we can make our texts cohesive as well as accurate. The requirements for the grammar, spelling and punctuation (GP&S) tests in England are examined in Appendix 3.

We hope that, by reading this book, you will find that acquiring the knowledge and understanding you need to teach children about language in a meaningful and stimulating way need not be too difficult. Indeed, we hope that your curiosity will be aroused and that you will want to take your knowledge and understanding and that of the children you teach further.

David Waugh
Claire Warner
Rosemary Waugh
January 2016

References

DfE (2013) *The National Curriculum in England: Key stages 1 and 2 framework document*. London: DfE. Available from: **www.gov.uk/government/uploads/system/uploads/attachment_data/file/425601/PRIMARY_national_curriculum.pdf** (accessed 25.10.15).

Myhill, D., Lines, H. and Watson, A. (2011) *Making Meaning with Grammar: A Repertoire of Possibilities*. Exeter: University of Exeter.

Wordsworth, D. (2012) It's cruel not to teach children grammar. Available from: **www.telegraph.co.uk/education/educationnews/9381417/Its-cruel-not-to-teach-children-grammar.html** (accessed 25.10.15).

1 Teaching grammar

Learning outcomes

By reading this chapter you will develop:

- an overview of grammar in the National Curriculum for England;
- an understanding of how grammar can help children to become better writers.

Teachers' Standards
This chapter will help you with the following Teachers' Standards.

3 Demonstrate good subject and curriculum knowledge:
- have a secure knowledge of the relevant subject(s) and curriculum areas, foster and maintain pupils' interest in the subject, and address misunderstandings;
- demonstrate a critical understanding of developments in the subject and curriculum areas, and promote the value of scholarship;
- demonstrate an understanding of and take responsibility for promoting high standards of literacy, articulacy and the correct use of Standard English, whatever the teacher's specialist subject.

Introduction

In the book's introduction we considered what grammar is and why it is important. This chapter will look at the grammar you are required to teach, and explore ways of teaching it that are meaningful and effective.

Our starting point is the National Curriculum for English (DfE, 2013) and the knowledge children will be required to have by the end of Key Stage 2. We will consider how we can draw on and extend aspects of children's implicit knowledge about grammar, and help you to develop an understanding of the important concepts that underpin teaching in the classroom. We will draw on recent research that identifies how to teach grammar so that it impacts positively on children's understanding of language.

As you read, you will need to keep in mind the key purposes of teaching grammar. It is not simply for you to be confident about correcting mistakes in children's work, nor is it to pass on tricks and techniques to be replicated in a mechanistic way. This does not make children writers or lead to good writing. Teaching grammar effectively is about making visible what experienced language producers know and do, enabling children to control grammar to express increasingly complex ideas. As they learn how to do this, the range of choices open to them as speakers and writers will be extended. Importantly, this does not need to be dull. Effective grammar teaching takes place in meaningful contexts. It can also be fascinating. Playing with words, investigation, puns, jokes and rhymes can all enrich and inform grammatical knowledge and understanding, and develop a genuine interest in how language works.

Activity

What do you think you know about teaching grammar? You may think you have never seen any explicit grammar teaching, but what is it that you think you know? Try writing it down.

Underline anything that you are not sure about, and turn those uncertainties into questions. By the time you have read this chapter some of your questions will have been answered, and you will also realise that you know a little more than you thought.

Grammar in the National Curriculum for English

The National Curriculum for English highlights the importance of children acquiring a wide vocabulary, an understanding of grammar and knowledge of linguistic conventions for reading, writing and spoken language (2013). It makes clear that children need to know, understand and be able to use a wide range of grammatical terms and features: by the end of Key Stage 2, they should be able to reflect their understanding of the audience for and purpose of their writing by selecting appropriate vocabulary and grammar (DfE, 2013, p.41). To do this they will need to be aware of the variety and complexity of grammatical choices that are available to them, and manipulate language appropriately.

The National Curriculum sets out in great detail the key knowledge that must be taught in primary schools from Year 1 to Year 6. There are three strands: *word structure*, *sentence structure* and *text structure*, and at the end of this chapter (pp. 23–26), you will find an overview to show what this looks like in each year group. Children are tested on their knowledge of grammar at the end of Key Stage 1 and Key Stage 2. You will find further information in Appendix 3.

How to teach grammar

It is important to realise that the teaching of grammar goes far beyond the ability to succeed in end of key stage tests. It is about being able to choose and use language well for a wide range of purposes and audiences, and being able to harness the power that writing offers. Meek (1991) writes about the importance of *confident knowing* (p.23). She describes the *powerful literates* as those who know they will be able to cope with written language, however unfamiliar, *by discovering how it works.* Myhill (2012) stresses how important it is for children to discover how meanings are subtly shaped by lexical and syntactical choices; that language changes in different contexts; that there are differences between spoken and written English, and between standard and non-standard varieties. These discoveries are too important to be left to chance. They need to be planned for.

By this point, you may well have become concerned about your own subject knowledge. However, the good news is that, as an experienced language user, you are already using language flexibly all the time. You will choose your words much more carefully during a job interview than when you are sitting with friends over a drink at the weekend. Similarly, the way that you write your letter of application will be quite different from the note you leave that says 'Dinner in dog – gone out'. The vocabulary you use, the way you construct your sentences, the precision with which you communicate your thinking, and the tone you convey, change to suit the purpose and audience. What you may not yet have is an explicit knowledge of the grammar that informs the choices you make.

Implicit and explicit knowledge of grammar

Children come to school knowing many of the rules of spoken language. This knowledge is implicit – they understand and apply these rules in an unconscious and intuitive way in the classroom to communicate with their teachers and their peers. The rules of oral language will have been learnt from listening to adults talking in a range of contexts, by imitating and innovating. We can see this when young children make generalisations that are inaccurate, such as 'I rided my bike' or 'I goed to the park', which are actually very logical. Many children also cope well with the increasingly complex language in the texts that are read to them, and that they later read for themselves. Our task is to build on the patterns they already know implicitly by making them visible and letting children into the secret of the decision-making process – that is, what goes on in our minds – so that we enable them to become more sophisticated language producers themselves.

Activity

Look at the sentences below. You will know which ones are correct. But can you explain the grammatical knowledge you are applying to make your judgements?

I didn't do nothing.

Me and my dad went to the park.

She was stood at the end of the road.

The reasons is as follows.

I can't hardly believe it.

The childrens' house.

It is quite likely that you found it hard to explain why the grammar in some of the sentences above was incorrect (see our explanations below). This is likely to be because you have implicit rather than explicit grammatical knowledge. Although you will be able to correct the errors in children's writing, having explicit knowledge will allow you to go beyond this to appreciate what they can do and what they need to learn next. It will also allow you to teach and discuss how language works, which is the first step to enabling children to understand, internalise and extend the range of language that they use.

- *I didn't do nothing.* This is a double negative. If you didn't do nothing, then you did do something.

- *Me and my dad went to the park.* 'I and my dad' – you wouldn't say 'me went', because when 'I' is the subject of the verb we use 'I' rather than 'me'. It is also usually considered polite usage to put the other person first, so 'My dad and I'.

- *She was stood at the end of the road.* 'She was standing' – the imperfect tense, used here for describing a situation, uses the present participle (the -ing form) rather than the past participle 'stood'.

- *The reasons is as follows.* 'The reasons' is plural and so the part of the verb to be 'is' needs to be 'are' in order for the subject and verb to agree.

- *I can't hardly believe it.* 'Hardly' means 'with difficulty'. If you have difficulty believing something, then you **can** hardly believe it.

- *The childrens' house.* Apostrophes for possession are placed after the item/person etc. who owns something. Children is the plural of child, so the apostrophe should be placed after n but before s.

Developing a meta-language

It makes sense that it is easier to talk about grammar with children if there is a shared common language. We call this a meta-language. A shared meta-language allows teachers and children to talk together using terms that everyone understands.

Before some less well-known events at the London Olympics, the spectators were told the main rules of the game and some of the tactics that they should look out for. Those watching the diving learnt about *pikes, reverse three and a half somersaults with tuck, rip entries* and *flat hand grabs* as well as the complexities of the scoring system. This basic knowledge made it possible for everyone to understand what was happening and added to their engagement in the drama of the competition. Teachers and children who have a meta-language in common are able to talk together in an inclusive way. There is no need to shy away from using the correct terms consistently and accurately. Indeed, given the demands of the curriculum, it will be unhelpful if we avoid them.

The impact of teaching grammar

Although we have stressed the importance of knowing about grammar and having a shared meta-language, we know that teaching of grammatical knowledge, while interesting in its own right, often has very little impact on the quality of children's talk, reading or writing. Studies such as those carried out by Andrews et al. (2006) suggest that there is little point teaching formal grammar as there is little evidence to indicate its effectiveness. Barrs and Cork (2001) argue that the direct teaching of written language features is no substitute for extensive experience of written language, and demonstrate that the influence of children's reading of literature on their writing at Key Stage 2, when mediated effectively, is significant. Moreover, Bearne (2007) writes about the danger of seeing learning to write as putting together different 'skills' and of reducing writing to a series of formulaic 'this is how to do it' exercises, which research has shown is likely to result in disaffection and a lack of engagement (Packwood and Messenheimer, 2003).

You may have experienced this. You may have noticed children who produce the correct forms on exercises and tests and do not use them accurately or appropriately in the context of their own writing. Using a highlighter to underline all the adverbs in a series of unrelated sentences does not have any intrinsic value beyond knowing what an adverb is. Decontextualised worksheets and exercises do not sit comfortably with the purposes of teaching grammar outlined at the start of the chapter. Grammar teaching is most effective when it is taught in the context of reading and writing, either in the context of the linguistic demands of a particular genre, or the writing needs of a particular child (Myhill, 2012). In the next section we will look at pedagogy and highlight some of the principles that underpin successful grammar teaching in the classroom.

Research focus: pedagogical approaches to teaching grammar

A recent study by Myhill, Lines and Watson (2011) has focused on pedagogical approaches to teaching grammar that make a difference to children's writing. The researchers found that teaching grammar as a discrete, separate topic, where the grammar is the focus of study, was not likely to help writing development because it did not make connections between grammar and writing, or between grammar and meaning. However, they found that actively engaging children with the use of grammar could be a powerful and effective tool for improving their written work. They identified a number of approaches that led to significant improvements in children's writing, including:

- experimentation and playful engagement with language;

- explicit teaching and application using the texts children were already using as part of a unit of work;

→

- explicitly teaching the meta-language – but also the reasons for using it;

- deconstructing how grammar was used in different texts and encouraging children to use this knowledge in their own writing.

The research also showed that:

- teaching grammar out of context as a discrete lesson can teach meta-language successfully, but does not help children to see the use and purpose of the grammar;

- grammar needs to be seen as something to be experimented with and played with rather than labelled and corrected;

- children need to build a repertoire of grammatical skills to experiment with – this does not happen by chance;

- teachers' subject knowledge is an important factor.

Teaching grammar effectively

One of our aims as primary teachers is to open up to children what Myhill called *a repertoire of infinite possibilities*. Knowing the frames and shapes that language uses is part of developing the linguistic competence children need, and allows them to participate in text production, both spoken and written.

The grammatical characteristics of spoken language are quite different from those used in writing. If you listen carefully to a conversation, you will immediately notice how fragmented it is; and how gesture, context and shared understandings influence the nature of the language used. Very few of us talk in sentences all of the time. It would be even stranger to hear the language of most written texts spoken aloud in conversation, unless we are giving a presentation or speaking at a more formal occasion. In these circumstances, we may well craft our words very carefully, and *read a written to be spoken text* (Carter, 2003). If talk is to be an effective bridge between thought and writing, we need to turn this round and look at how we can help children to produce *spoken to be written* texts.

A wardrobe of voices

Recently, a group of children from an inner-city school visited another class in a more 'leafy' part of the city as part of a project that they were involved in. When they were reflecting on their day and the teacher asked what they had learned, one child astutely commented, 'Those children speak like you want me to write, Miss.'

The child who made this observation was commenting on the use of Standard English. Her perceptive remark highlights that children whose dialect is nearest to Standard English may be at an advantage when they write. Mercer and Littleton (2007) have commented that there is no research evidence to show that all children will naturally encounter all the language genres that they might need for taking responsible control over their own lives. However anxious you may feel about expecting all children to add Standard English to their spoken repertoire, particularly when this may be very different from the home language they bring to school, we cannot ignore its importance.

Lockwood (2005) used the metaphor of a *wardrobe of voices* to explore the concept of language variety, and to investigate how Standard English could hang in that wardrobe as one set of linguistic clothing to be worn at certain times. Just as children put on different clothes for different occasions – the clothes they choose when they ride their bikes in the park will be quite different from those they wear to go to a wedding, and would probably not be the same as the clothes they wear for the school disco – so they need to be able to select the right voice from the 'wardrobe'. To do this they need, of course, to have a range of voices available to them, and to know the purpose and the audience for their talk. For example, is it to come to a consensus, to explain, entertain or persuade? Who is it for and where is it going? When they know this, they can begin to make choices about the language they need to select.

Opportunities to use Standard English

Lockwood's analogy is valuable and highlights the importance of providing ample opportunities for children to use more formal language from the beginning. This might include a themed home corner such as a vets' practice or travel agency. Listen to children using such an area next time you are in school, and you will hear them questioning, diagnosing, advising and prescribing. Older children can be given opportunities to take part in debates in role, perhaps as a town councillor when discussing a controversial proposed development; as a newsreader reporting on a historical event; or by presenting findings in assemblies. These provide authentic contexts for the kind of formal talk that tends to be more polished and closer to written English.

Speaking frames to support individual, paired and group talk can also useful. These are often used to support children learning English as an additional language, but they can be beneficial for all children, particularly when you explicitly discuss the differences between formal and informal talk. It is, of course, essential to do this with care. Language and identity are closely intertwined. Our approach needs to be firmly based on how language changes in different contexts.

In the case study below you will meet Kate who is working with a Year 1 class, and is keen to extend the children's language. She makes sure that she always models Standard English in the classroom. When one of the children enthusiastically showed her a photograph and said 'we was at the seaside,' she responded by modelling Standard English, saying 'You were at the seaside yesterday? How fantastic!' Kate is keen to use every opportunity to help children to move beyond their home language and use Standard English in meaningful contexts. When you are reading the case study think about how you might be able to use high quality texts and drama in a similar way with your own class.

Case study: modelling Standard English

The children had been reading *The Lighthouse Keeper's Lunch*. As part of the unit of work, they made freeze frames of events from the story, and Kate used *thought tracking* to interview Mr and Mrs Grinling to extend the children's talk. As they did this, she commented on how well they had taken on particular roles and encouraged them to imitate and innovate on the rich but formal language of the text. Kate set up the role-play area with a seaside theme to provide opportunities for the children to retell the story using props, and others acted as reporters, finding out what had happened using 'magic microphones' and notepads, and reporting back to the news room.

The children wrote their own versions of the story, and Kate was pleased to see that they had started to use the rich language of the text and new vocabulary, such as 'wretched birds' to describe the seagulls. She realised that storytelling was a powerful tool for helping children build a bank of narrative patterns they would be able to use when creating their own stories; and she continued to provide opportunities for children to internalise oral stories and structure their sentences orally. This impacted significantly on the grammatical structures they used in their writing.

Curriculum links

A key aim of the National Curriculum for English (DfE, 2013) is to reflect the importance of spoken language in children's development across the whole curriculum – cognitively, socially and linguistically. It states that *The quality and variety of language that pupils hear and speak are vital for developing their vocabulary and grammar and their understanding for reading and writing* (p.13).

The programme of study for spoken language is for all year groups and includes the need for children to be taught to:

- listen and respond appropriately to adults and their peers;
- ask relevant questions to extend their understanding and knowledge;
- use relevant strategies to build their vocabulary;
- articulate and justify answers, arguments and opinions;

- give well-structured descriptions, explanations and narratives for different purposes, including for expressing feelings;
- maintain attention and participate actively in collaborative conversations, staying on topic and initiating and responding to comments;
- use spoken language to develop understanding through speculating, hypothesising, imagining and exploring ideas;
- speak audibly and fluently with an increasing command of Standard English;
- participate in discussions, presentations, performances, role play, improvisations and debates;
- gain, maintain and monitor the interest of the listener(s);
- consider and evaluate different viewpoints, attending to and building on the contributions of others;
- select and use appropriate registers for effective communication.

In this lesson Kate's objectives related to: becoming very familiar with key stories, fairy stories and traditional tales; retelling them and considering their particular characteristics (Year 1, reading comprehension, p.21); and sequencing sentences to form short narratives (Year 1, writing composition, p.24).

Activity

We all have an accent and we all speak with a dialect. Think about your own language history. Do you speak differently now from the way you spoke as a child? Perhaps you have changed the way you speak on occasions. Can you work out why you think this is?

Think about the children in your most recent school experience. Do you think that some children's dialect – their everyday speech – was closer to a writing style than others? Were they at an advantage? If they were, what strategies were being put in place to make sure that all children could choose from a fuller wardrobe of voices?

Reading aloud and reading as a writer

The links between reading and writing are well known (Barrs and Cork, 2001). If you look at the good writers in the classes you work in you will find that they are almost always good readers. Britton (1982) suggested that the store of language children internalise comes from their reading and being read to. Barrs and Cork explain that what children write reflects the nature and quality of their reading and that it is reading that allows them to *take on the whole feeling and rhythm of a text* (2001, p.116).

A rich experience of reading is important for all children, and a planned read-aloud programme needs to be an integral part of the literacy curriculum. However, being a reader and hearing texts read aloud does not lead to an automatic understanding of what the author has done. If children are going to understand and internalise the more complex grammatical structures of writing, you need to draw their attention to these during shared and guided reading and create opportunities to discuss them explicitly. As we explore children's responses to texts, we can also investigate how writers use language to create particular effects and, as we will see later, use these written texts as models for writing.

Talk for writing

We know how important it is for children to spend time exploring ideas so that they know their material well and can plan effectively. However effectively we do this, it will not automatically lead to good writing. A teacher using the *Talk for Writing* materials (DCFS, 2009) reflected on why, after providing lots of opportunities for speaking and listening, writing outcomes did not reflect the varied and interesting vocabulary used in their talk. She posed the question, 'Can children modify their writing more effectively if they hear it and keep making changes until the talk for writing becomes the writing?' Bridging the gap between high quality talk, high quality texts and high quality writing is not something that you can leave to chance. You need to support the oral rehearsal of the kind of language, vocabulary and sentence structures that can then become the written form.

Shared and modelled writing

We should not be surprised if children find it difficult to write if they have not been immersed in the kind of text and sentence structures they are being asked to produce. An important way of making the writing process explicit is to model writing to the class. Modelled writing is a powerful pedagogy that involves externalising what you do when you write, and is effective whether your focus is on text structure, sentence types, sentence complexity or word structure. As an experienced writer, this will often come to you automatically. You will need to learn to talk aloud to yourself as you write, so that the children can see the decisions you are making. If you are focusing on the use of adverbial phrases to add interest and richness to the text, you may say: 'I think I'll put the phrase there, or perhaps it would make more sense to leave it here. Yes, I'll leave it where it is because then the reader will be wondering what is going to happen next, and I'm trying to keep them guessing.' You will need to prepare this beforehand, so that you can do this confidently. It is not easy to do in front of a class, but it is well worth the effort. As Myhill (2012, p.22) points out, *A writing curriculum that draws attention to the grammar of writing in an embedded and purposeful way at relevant points in the learning is a ... positive way forward.*

Modelled writing plays an important part in ensuring that children have a toolkit of organisational and linguistic structures. Children will, of course, need to try out the techniques for themselves, and apply these in their own writing. It may seem obvious, but if children are to do this, you need to make sure that the context for the writing lends itself to the task. There is no point asking children to practise their use of complex sentences when you are writing haiku.

Language and word investigations

As you have already seen, grammar teaching will be most effective when it arises from the talk, reading and writing that you are already doing in the classroom. However, discrete teaching, when it involves finding patterns and rules through investigations and playing with words, can enrich and inform grammatical knowledge and understanding. What matters is that this is later applied in meaningful contexts. In later chapters, you will discover how to use tongue-twisters and puns, jokes and rhymes, and collections of words to transform texts from non-Standard to Standard English, construct rules and explanations, and simply enjoy language.

A model for teaching grammar in context

The teaching sequence below draws together the key principles discussed above, and provides one model for teaching grammar effectively (see model on p.18).

Key principles for teaching grammar

Knowledge about grammar can make a significance difference to children's literacy development, but it is important to bear in mind seven key principles.

1. **Build up your own subject knowledge.** To teach grammar you need explicit as well as implicit knowledge, so that you are confident about using the correct terms and explaining these. Don't just learn the next term you are teaching. It is important to be able to relate new learning to other features and the text as a whole.

2. **Give talk a high priority in your classroom.** Children need to be able to select from a wardrobe of voices that includes Standard English.

3. **Remember the purpose of teaching grammar.** Grammar is not simply the naming of parts of speech or for teaching the rules of English. It needs to be strongly embedded in classroom talk, reading and writing.

A model for teaching grammar effectively

First, be clear about what you want the children to learn. Remember that there is no point teaching grammatical meta-language unless you can explain how it will make a difference to their writing. Check your own subject knowledge and make sure that you feel confident about this.

Introduce the terms at the point in the teaching sequence that seems most relevant. This may be through discrete teaching, through an investigation, or through interactive grammar games to find patterns, word-play or games, rather like an oral and mental starter in mathematics. Examples can be found throughout this book. Through shared and guided reading, identify examples of the particular grammatical feature you are focusing on in the high quality texts you are reading with the class. Make sure you have identified examples beforehand and can talk about them. Use the correct terminology to make this explicit.

Invite the children to find examples for themselves and to make up some of their own. Remember to remind them of the purpose of the task – they are developing this skill because it opens up all kinds of possibilities for their writing.

Model writing before asking children to write themselves. Make explicit the choices that writers have made. This helps children to know the choices available to them when writing for themselves.

Invite the children to use their new knowledge in the context of an appropriate piece of writing. Encourage the children to be adventurous and to play with language and word choice.

Review the writing as part of the plenary and not just through 'distance' marking.

4. **Teach grammar in context.** By introducing children to grammatical features and language in context, you will be helping them to internalise these principles. Try not to go for the ready-made solution by using a worksheet in a book. It will make very little difference to children's use of language and will be meaningless for those learners who are not yet able to think in abstract ways.

5. **Read aloud and discuss how authors use grammar.** Children who read extensively and are read to will have a 'toolbox' of structures, patterns and rhythms to draw on.

6. **Be systematic.** Make sure you know what the class you are working with have already learned and what they need to learn now. Link new learning with their prior knowledge.

7. **Make learning grammar fun.** Teaching grammar can involve investigation, problem-solving and language play as part of developing children's awareness of and interest in how language works.

In the case study below you will meet Chris, who is in his second year of a three-year degree and is working with a Year 4 class. He had been asked to focus on the children's use of paragraphs so that they can organise ideas around a theme. His first task was to check that he could make his implicit knowledge about paragraphs explicit, so that his discussion with the children would be clear and unambiguous. As you read the case study, think about how Chris helps the children to organise content in a simple but effective way that can support them in their use of paragraphs in other curriculum areas.

Case study: using paragraphs in Year 4

The children had been reading *The Lion and the Unicorn* by Shirley Hughes, a powerful picture book set in World War II. The outcome of the unit of work was for the children to write their own version of the story in role as Lenny, an evacuee and the main character in the story.

Chris modelled how to summarise the key points of a story. He took as an example, Humpty Dumpty, and segmented it into three boxes representing the main stages of the narrative:

Humpty sits on a wall.

Humpty falls off a wall.

Soldiers can't repair Humpty.

He demonstrated how this can be written and organised on the principle of one paragraph per box. As he did this he talked aloud so that the children could see and hear the decisions that he made. The children had already done a lot of work around *The Lion and the Unicorn* and knew it well. This included using a range of drama techniques, visualisation and retelling, as well as more specific work focusing on the language of the text. The children had six strips of paper, and worked in small groups to 'box up' the story. This involved summarising the bare

$\longrightarrow$

bones of the story in six points. Chris worked intensively with a guided group and his TA supported the rest of the class. The children compared their versions and discussed the reasons for the decisions they made.

The next step was for Chris to model the writing of a paragraph before the children did this for themselves, all the time remembering what he wanted the children to be learning.

Chris was surprised that the children found it quite challenging to see the underlying pattern of the story, but his approach was successful and provided a framework that the children later used as a basis for writing their own versions. He was able to use the same approach successfully in other areas of the curriculum, from history and geography to science, and it became a basic planning framework for children when writing non-fiction.

Curriculum links

Effective composition involves articulating and communicating ideas, and then organising them coherently for a reader. This requires clarity, awareness of the audience, purpose and context, and an increasingly wide knowledge of vocabulary and grammar. Chris's lesson enabled children to discuss a text similar to the one they were planning to write, in order to understand and learn from their structure, grammar and vocabulary (Year 3–4, composition, p.39) and focused on the use of paragraphs to organise ideas around a theme (Year 3–4, writing composition, p.39).

And finally – a word of caution

In a discussion about the place of grammar in the curriculum, Myhill (2012, p.22) writes:

> *Learning to label and dissect language into its component parts and learning to underline grammatical errors in artificially generated sentences will not equip young learners to become confident and mature language users. But using grammar to help young writers to see through language, to see how language constructs socially-shaped meanings, to see how great language users break rules – this is where grammar realises its potential as a dynamic and vibrant element of English.*

All children need to know that reading, writing, speaking and listening are powerful. This goes beyond writing accurately and pleasing their teacher. They need to experience the pleasure that having a voice brings, and the opportunities that it offers. Writing can never be taught simply by teaching techniques, and learning about grammar can never be a genuine purpose for writing. Meaning has to be at the heart of all teaching of literacy.

Learning outcomes review

This chapter has highlighted the rewards of teaching grammar. You will be aware of the importance placed on grammar in the new curriculum, and the need to have an explicit knowledge of grammar so that you are confident in your subject knowledge. You will know how to teach grammar effectively, understand the importance of oral language, reading and modelled writing, and explicit discussions about how language works.

Self-assessment questions
1. How can you ensure that all children have a *wardrobe of voices* that includes Standard English?
2. What do you see as they key features of an effective pedagogy for teaching grammar? How can you avoid this becoming a grammar-spotting exercise?
3. Have you observed children having fun and playing with language? Start collecting together word-play activities that you will be able to use in the future.

Further reading

Lockwood, M. (2005) Opening the Wardrobe of Voices: Standard English and Language Variation at KS2, in Goodwin, P. (ed.) *The Literate Classroom*, 2nd edition, London: David Fulton, pp.189–99.

This chapter considers how explicit discussion about dialect, register and Standard English can develop children's knowledge about language. It provides helpful suggestions for strengthening the use of Standard English in the classroom.

Waugh, D., Allott, K., Waugh, R., English, E. and Bulmer, E. (2014) *The Spelling, Punctuation and Grammar app*. Morecambe: Children Count Ltd (available through the App Store).

This app provides guidance and activities on all aspects of grammar, spelling and punctuation.

References

Andrews, R., Torgerson, C., Beverton, S., Freeman, A., Locke, T., Low, G., Robinson, A. and Zhu, D. (2006) The effect of grammar teaching on writing development. *British Educational Research Journal*, 32(1): 39–55.

Barrs, M. and Cork, V. (2001) *The Reader in the Writer*. London: CLPE.

Bearne, E. (2007) *Writing*. Available from: **www.ite.org.uk/ite_readings/writing_20071130.pdf** (accessed 1.10.12).

Britton, J. (1982) cited in Barrs and Cork (2001) *The Reader in the Writer*. London: CLPE.

Carter, R. (2003) Introducing the grammar of talk: Spoken English, grammar and the classroom, in QCA (2003) *New Perspectives on Spoken English*, pp. 5–13. London: QCA.

DCSF National Strategies (2009) *Talk for Writing*. Nottingham: DCSF.

DfE (2013) *The National Curriculum in England: Key stages 1 and 2 framework document*. London: DfE. Available from: **www.gov.uk/government/uploads/system/uploads/attachment_data/file/425601/PRIMARY_national_curriculum.pdf (accessed 25.10.15).**

Lockwood, M. (2005) Opening the Wardrobe of Voices: Standard English and Language Variation at KS2, in Goodwin, P. (ed.) *The Literate Classroom*, 2nd edition, London: David Fulton, pp. 189–99.

Meek, M. (1991) *On Being Literate*. London: The Bodley Head.

Mercer, N. and Littleton, K. (2007) *Dialogue and the Development of Children's Thinking: A Sociocultural Approach*. London: Routledge.

Myhill, D. (2012) The role for grammar in the curriculum, in *Meeting high expectations: Looking for the Heart of English*. Available from: **www.heartofenglish.com** (accessed 1.10.12).

Myhill, D., Lines, H. and Watson A. (2011) *Making Meaning with Grammar: A Repertoire of Possibilities*. Available from: **www.education.exeter.ac.uk** (accessed 1.10.12).

Packwood, A. and Messenheimer, T. (2003) Back to the future: developing children as writers, in Bearne, E., Dombey, H. and Grainger, T. (eds) *Classroom Interactions in Literacy*. Maidenhead: Open University Press.

Progression in vocabulary, grammar and punctuation – Years 1 to 6 in the National Curriculum (DfE, 2013)

Year 1: Detail of content to be introduced (statutory requirement)	
Word	Regular **plural noun suffixes** -s or -es (e.g. *dog, dogs; wish, wishes*), including the effects of these suffixes on the meaning of the noun.
	Suffixes that can be added to **verbs** where no change is needed in the spelling of root words (e.g. *helping, helped, helper*).
	How the **prefix** un- changes the meaning of **verbs** and **adjectives** (negation, for example, *unkind*; or *undoing: untie the boat*).
Sentence	How **words** can combine to make **sentences**.
	Joining **words** and joining **clauses** using *and*.
Text	Sequencing **sentences** to form short narratives.
Punctuation	Separation of **words** with spaces.
	Introduction to capital letters, full stops, question marks and exclamation marks to demarcate **sentences**.
	Capital letters for names and for the personal **pronoun** *I*.
Terminology for pupils	Letter, capital letter
	Word, singular, plural
	Sentence
	Punctuation, full stop, question mark, exclamation mark

Year 2: Detail of content to be introduced (statutory requirement)	
Word	Formation of **nouns** using **suffixes** such as -ness, -er and by compounding (e.g. *whiteboard, superman*).
	Formation of **adjectives** using **suffixes** such as -ful, -less.
	(A fuller list of **suffixes** can be found on page 46 in the year 2 spelling section in English Appendix 1.)
	Use of the **suffixes** -er, -est in **adjectives** and the use of -ly in Standard English to turn adjectives into **adverbs**.
Sentence	**Subordination** (using *when, if, that, because*) and **coordination** (using *or, and, but*).
	Expanded **noun phrases** for description and specification (for example, *the blue butterfly, plain flour, the man in the moon*).
	How the grammatical patterns in a sentence indicate its function as a **statement, question, exclamation** or **command**.
Text	Correct choice and consistent use of **present tense** and **past tense** throughout writing.
	Use of the **progressive** form of **verbs** in the **present** and **past tense** to mark actions in progress (e.g. *she is drumming, he was shouting*).

(Continued)

(Continued)

Year 2: Detail of content to be introduced (statutory requirement)	
Punctuation	Use of capital letters, full stops, question marks and exclamation marks to demarcate **sentences**.
	Commas to separate items in a list.
	Apostrophes to mark where letters are missing in spelling and to mark singular possession in nouns (e.g. *the girl's name*).
Terminology for pupils	Noun, noun phrase
	Statement, question, exclamation, command, compound, adjective, verb, suffix adverb
	Tense (past, present)
	Apostrophe, comma

Year 3: Detail of content to be introduced (statutory requirement)	
Word	Formation of **nouns** using a range of **prefixes** (e.g. *super-, anti-, auto-*).
	Use of the **forms** *a* or *an* according to whether the next **word** begins with a **consonant** or a **vowel** (e.g. *a rock, an open box*).
	Word families based on common **words**, showing how words are related in form and meaning (e.g. *solve, solution, solver, dissolve, insoluble*).
Sentence	Expressing time, place and cause using **conjunctions** (e.g. *when, before, after, while, so, because*), **adverbs** (e.g. *then, next, soon, therefore*), or **prepositions** (e.g. *before, after, during, in, because of*).
Text	Introduction to paragraphs as a way to group-related material.
	Headings and sub-headings to aid presentation.
	Use of the **present perfect** form of **verbs** instead of the simple past (e.g. *He has gone out to play* contrasted with *He went out to play*).
Punctuation	Introduction to inverted commas to **punctuate** direct speech.
Terminology for pupils	Adverb, preposition, conjunction
	Word family, prefix
	Clause, subordinate clause
	Direct speech
	Consonant, consonant letter vowel, vowel letter
	Inverted commas (or 'speech marks')

Year 4: Detail of content to be introduced (statutory requirement)	
Word	The grammatical difference between **plural** and **possessive** -*s*.
	Standard English forms for **verb inflections** instead of local spoken forms (e.g. *we were* instead of *we was*, or *I did* instead of *I done*).

Year 4: Detail of content to be introduced (statutory requirement)	
Sentence	Noun phrases expanded by the addition of modifying adjectives, nouns and preposition phrases (e.g. *the teacher* expanded to *the strict maths teacher with curly hair*).
	Fronted adverbials (e.g. *Later that day, I heard the bad news*).
Text	Use of paragraphs to organise ideas around a theme.
	Appropriate choice of **pronoun** or **noun** within and across **sentences** to aid cohesion and avoid repetition.
Punctuation	Use of inverted commas and other **punctuation** to indicate direct speech (e.g. a comma after the reporting clause; end punctuation within inverted commas: *The conductor shouted, 'Sit down!'*).
	Apostrophes to mark **plural** possession (e.g. *the girl's name, the girls' names*).
	Use of commas after **fronted adverbials**.
Terminology for pupils	Determiner
	Pronoun, possessive pronoun
	Adverbial

Year 5: Detail of content to be introduced (statutory requirement)	
Word	Converting **nouns** or **adjectives** into **verbs** using **suffixes** (e.g. *-ate, -ise, -ify*).
	Verb prefixes (e.g. *dis-, de-, mis-, over- and re-*).
Sentence	**Relative clauses** beginning with *who, which, where, when, whose, that*, or an omitted relative pronoun.
	Indicating degrees of possibility using **adverbs** (e.g. *perhaps, surely*) or **modal verbs** (e.g. *might, should, will, must*).
Text	Devices to build **cohesion** within a paragraph (e.g. *then, after that, this, firstly*).
	Linking ideas across paragraphs using **adverbials** of time (e.g. *later*), place (e.g. *nearby*) and number (e.g. *secondly*) or tense choices (e.g. *he had seen her before*).
Punctuation	Brackets, dashes or commas to indicate parenthesis. Use of commas to clarify meaning or avoid ambiguity.
Terminology for pupils	Modal verb, relative pronoun
	Relative clause
	Parenthesis, bracket, dash
	Cohesion, ambiguity

Year 6: Detail of content to be introduced (statutory requirement)	
Word	The difference between vocabulary typical of informal speech and vocabulary appropriate for formal speech and writing (e.g. *find out – discover; ask for – request; go in – enter*).
	How words are related by meaning as synonyms and antonyms (e.g. *big, large, little*).

(Continued)

(Continued)

Year 6: Detail of content to be introduced (statutory requirement)	
Sentence	Use of the **passive** to affect the presentation of information in a **sentence** (e.g. *I broke the window in the greenhouse* versus *The window in the greenhouse was broken (by me)*).
	The difference between structures typical of informal speech and structures appropriate for formal speech and writing (e.g. the use of question tags: *He's your friend, isn't he?* or the use of **subjunctive** forms, such as *If I were* or *Were they to come* in some very formal writing and speech).
Text	Linking ideas across paragraphs using a wider range of **cohesive devices**: repetition of a **word** or phrase, grammatical connections (e.g. the use of **adverbials** such as *on the other hand, in contrast,* or *as a consequence*), and **ellipsis.**
	Layout devices (e.g. headings, sub-headings, columns, bullets, or tables, to structure text).
Punctuation	Use of the semi-colon, colon and dash to mark the boundary between independent **clauses** (e.g. *It's raining; I'm fed up*).
	Use of the colon to introduce a list and use of semi-colons within lists.
	Punctuation of bullet points to list information.
	How hyphens can be used to avoid ambiguity (e.g. *man eating shark* versus *man-eating shark,* or *recover* versus *re-cover*).
Terminology for pupils	Subject, object
	Active, passive
	Synonym, antonym
	Ellipsis, hyphen, colon, semi-colon, bullet points

2 Words

Introduction

English has always been a vacuum-cleaner of a language.

(Crystal, 2005, p.225)

Crystal expresses succinctly the nature of the English language – it is derived from over 350 other languages and constantly acquires new words, both from other languages and from English speakers who create them. The language is principally Germanic, but has been significantly influenced by French, Latin and Greek, and many other languages. These influences leave us with a rich vocabulary and a language which people all around the world want to learn. However, it also provides us with lots of inconsistencies in spelling, pronunciation and meaning. Look, for example, at the words below:

chef, chocolate, school

sun, roses, sugar

In the first group the *ch* digraph (two letters making one sound) represents three distinctly different sounds due to the origins of the words: *chef* is from French where ch is usually sounded as a *sh* sound (parachute, charade, champagne); *chocolate* comes from a Mexican word in which the original initial x was pronounced *ch*; and *school* is from a Greek word containing the letter χ (chi) which made a sound like that at the end of *loch*.

In the second group of three words, there are similar differences. The *s* in *sun* is what we think of as a 'normal' *s*; the two in *roses* are pronounced with a *z* sound, and *sugar* starts with a *sh* – probably because it used to be said something like 'syugar', which has shifted into a *sh* over time. The *s/z* situation in *roses* is the hardest to explain, because there is no simple consistent rule. Why doesn't verbose rhyme with rose? Why do we speak of a house (with an *s* sound) but say *to house people* with a *z*?

Native speakers meet all of these inconsistencies every day without even noticing them, but we should always be aware that such inconsistencies are one of the reasons why English can be so hard to master for the non-native learner.

English has what is often termed an opaque alphabetical system (Jolliffe and Waugh with Carss, 2015), which means that there are inconsistencies in the way *phonemes* (sounds) match *graphemes* (letters). We can write/represent most of the roughly 44 sounds in more than one way. Look at the examples below to see how.

- The *b* sound in *bag* can also be made with *bb* as in *rubber*.
- The *k* sound in *cat* can also be made by *k* in *king*, *ck* in *kick*, *ch* in *school*, *que* in *cheque*, *q* in *Iraq*, *cc* in *account*, etc.
- The *f* sound in *fan* can also be made by *ff* in *waffle*, *ph* in *graph* and *gh* in *laugh*.

And so on ...

In addition, letters can be used to make different sounds as you can see below (see Waugh and Jolliffe, 2012, p.214).

A	apple, woman, snake, car
B	big, thumb
C	cat, city, ciabatta

This can prove very frustrating for native English speakers when they learn to read and write, and there are many challenges involved in teaching through a phonics programme. Imagine how difficult it must be for people for whom English is a second language to get to grips with our alphabetical system, especially if they come from a country like Finland or Italy, which have transparent alphabetic systems in which there are very consistent correspondences between letters and sounds (see Chapter 4).

However, to learn any language we need to be able to match graphemes to phonemes so that we can read aloud or perform simple tasks like looking at a menu and ordering food and drink in a way that others will understand. Notice how when people impersonate those from other countries they deliberately mispronounce some sounds, for example, 'Can you tell me ze way to ze 'ospital?' (French?) or 'Vot is metter viz you?' (German?). Nevertheless, if we travel to France or Germany we always encounter lots of people who speak English well and are eager to talk to us in our language, sometimes even when we would like to practise our French or German. This can lead to slightly surreal conversations in which the English speak French, only to be answered in English by the French! But everyone is helped by the fact that there are so many similarities in the vocabularies of our languages, partly because English includes strong Germanic and French influences and partly because new words come into the languages and spread across borders. For example, *café*, *croissant*, *crevasse* and *chicane* from French and *hamburger*, *frankfurter*, *blitz* and *hamster* from German.

Activity

Look at the terms related to words which the National Curriculum (DfE, 2013, pp.74ff.) for English states children should learn to recognise and use ... through discussion and practice.

In Year 1 this includes: letter, capital letter, singular, plural.

In Year 2: verb, tense (past, present), adjective, noun, suffix, compound, adverb.

In Year 3: word family, conjunction, adverb, preposition, prefix.

In Year 4: pronoun, possessive pronoun, adverbial.

In Year 5: modal verb, relative pronoun.

In Year 6: subject, object, synonym, antonym.

Most of the terms above are not new to the curriculum and featured in both the National Literacy Strategy (DfEE, 1998) and previous national curricula. How many of the terms could you:

- describe to a colleague;
- explain to children?

Use the glossary (Appendix 1) at the end of the book both to check definitions and see brief strategies for teaching.

What do we really need to know and understand about words?

We need to know how words are constructed using letters, phonemes and graphemes, syllables, and morphemes, because this knowledge helps us when we meet new words. For example, our knowledge that a sequence of letters regularly represents the same sounds helps readers to decode once they have mastered the basic sound-symbol (phoneme-grapheme) correspondences. So we see a word we haven't previously encountered, for example *brandframble*, and we recognise sequences that occur in other words and this helps us to make a reasonable attempt at reading and pronouncing the word.

When we first learn to read in a language we break words down into individual grapheme-phoneme correspondences (c/a/t, b/i/g), but as we become more confident about these we begin to chunk parts of words together (br/and/fr/amb/le). Thus, in English schools there is an emphasis on 'synthetic phonics' in early reading, which involves segmenting words into single sounds or phonemes, but as children develop fluency they begin to be more analytical and often no longer need to break new words into individual sounds.

As children develop as readers, they also discover that there are common affixes (prefixes and suffixes) which can be added to words to modify their meanings. These can range from adding an *s* to *dog* or *-es* to *match* to make them plural, to putting a prefix such as *re-* before a verb to make it mean that the action was performed again (*repaid, regained*). These affixes can also be called morphemes – minimal units of meaning (see Chapter 3). So the word *repaid* has two morphemes: *re-* and *paid*, while *regained* has three: *re-*, *gain* and *-ed*. The morphemes *paid* and *gain* have meaning by themselves and are called **free morphemes**, but *re-* and *-ed* cannot stand alone as words and only have meaning when added or bound to a free morpheme. They are known as **bound morphemes**.

Activity

Look at the words below and separate them into morphemes. Decide which are **free** morphemes and which are **bound** morphemes. Remember that morphemes are units of meaning rather than being syllables, so *market*, for example, is a single unit of meaning and cannot be divided into *mar* and *ket* because these are not units of meaning. Therefore, in *supermarket* the two morphemes are *super* and *market*. The first example has been done for you.

unusually	un (bound) – usual (free) – ly (bound)
disappear	
trigraph	

hypermarket	
minibeast	
antifreeze	
wonderful	
wonderfully	

How did you get on? Below are the answers to the activity.

unlikely – un(bound) + like (free) + ly (bound)

disappear – dis (bound) + appear (free)

trigraph – tri (bound) + graph (free)

hypermarket – hyper (bound) + market (free)

minibeast – mini (bound) + beast (free)

antifreeze – anti (bound) + freeze (free)

wonderful – wonder (free) + ful (bound)

wonderfully – wonder (free) + ful (bound) + ly (bound)

The ending -ee is an interesting morpheme, originally borrowed from the French in words such as *fiancée*, *divorcee*, *employee*, and showing the person to whom something is done. This was followed in English by such coinages as *trainee* and *nominee*, and more recently by *tutee* (one who is tutored). However, since *tutor* is, strictly speaking, a Latin word, there are those who argue that we should rather speak of a *tutatus*, recalling the words of the journalist C. P. Scott in the 1930s: *Television? The word is half Greek, half Latin. No good can come of it.*

Many bus companies in recent years have caught on to the use of -ee, and display signs claiming they can hold '64 seated passengers and 48 standees'. As *standee* should mean 'one who is being stood on', perhaps we should learn to avoid such buses! The correct term would be *standers* or *standing passengers*.

Of course, as language has evolved some bound morphemes have become free in some circumstances, so we have a car called a Mini and *dis* has become a slang verb (*Don't dis me, man!* – originally an abbreviation for 'disrespect'), and some people can be described as being 'a bit hyper'!

Research focus: morphology

The term *morphology* was first used in the early nineteenth century and referred to the form and structure of plants and animals. Crystal (2005, p.236) maintains that its first recoded use in relation to words came in 1869. He describes two main types of morphology: inflectional and derivational.

Inflectional morphology relates to the way we use additions to words, for example to change them from singular to plural – for example, dog becomes dogs, boss becomes bosses.

Derivational morphology refers to the principles governing the construction of new words, for example when we form 'playable' from 'play', 'dislike' from 'like', or 'antifreeze' from 'freeze'.

A feature of language change is that words are often moved from one class to another – for instance, *ask*, *quote* and *invite* are frequently used as nouns nowadays in place of the traditionally correct *request*, *quotation*, *invitation*. Other nouns are made into verbs; the recent Olympics underlined the widespread use of *podiumed* and *medalled*. Busy people are often asked to *diarise* an appointment, or *access* their files.

Over time these new usages become widespread and even pass without notice. In the 1950s, the writer Nancy Mitford was horrified at being told someone would *contact* her, instead of the more formal 'make contact with her'; few people nowadays would raise an eyebrow at the use of contact as a verb. The noun *impact* has recently made the same transition; until very recently, the only use of this word as a verb was in the clinical discussion of *impacted* wisdom teeth, but now it is common to see such phrases as 'this decision impacts on us all'.

Etymology: where words come from

In January 2013 a major company, whose profits had fallen and which had had to make staff redundant, announced in its annual statement that it *degrew* in 2012. This led to much discussion on Radio 4 and among people interested in language and language change about how words are created.

Research focus: neologisms (new words)

Jackson (1995) explained that new words enter our lexicon in different ways. We *borrow* them from other languages (an odd term, since we don't give them back!), so we get *karate* and *tycoon* from Japanese; *boutique* and *discotheque* from French; *anorak* from Eskimo; and *pyjamas* from Hindi. Some words are derived from names, so we often talk about *hoovering* when we use a vacuum cleaner, because Hoover was a major manufacturer, or we say we use a *biro*

→

even when we use a different kind of ball pen, because Biro made such pens. We also get words from authors and characters, including the Marquis de Sade (*sadism*), George Orwell (*Orwellian*), and Cervantes' novel Don Quixote give us *quixotic*.

Jackson also described **compounding** in which we combine existing words to create new ones, such as *double-glazing*, *overcharge* and *lacklustre*. **Derivation** involves adding prefixes or suffixes to create new words. A recent example is *omnishambles*, a neologism first used in the BBC political satire *The Thick of It*. The word is compounded from the Latin prefix *omni-*, meaning 'all', and the word *shambles*, meaning a situation of total disorder: a situation which is seen as shambolic in every way. Real politicians began using it in 2012 and it was eventually named *Oxford English Dictionary* Word of the Year.

Words can be created in other ways, such as **clipping** where we abbreviate existing words (*telly* for *television*, *fridge* for *refrigerator* and *pram* for *perambulator*). It is worth noticing that in such abbreviations, the spelling then changes to reflect the pronunciation of the new word. We also add to the language with **acronyms** where initial letters of a phrase ultimately become used as a word (*laser*, *radar*, *scuba*, etc).

Words can also change their meanings over time, particularly when used by young people. Just consider how the following have acquired new additional meanings in your lifetime: *wicked*, *text*, *wasted*, *hammered*, *sick* and *garage*.

But it is not only recently that words have experienced changes of meaning. Look at the selection below to see how some words which we take for granted have a particular meaning now but have changed over many years.

Awful was once used to mean 'full of awe', i.e. something wonderful, delightful, amazing, but over time it has evolved to mean exactly the opposite.

Manufacture comes from Latin, meaning 'to make by hand'. This originally signified things that were created by craftsmen, but has come to mean made by machines.

Nice comes from the Latin 'not to know', so a 'nice person' used to be someone who was ignorant or unaware.

Prove originally meant 'to test'. So the expression 'the exception which proves the rule' means that exceptions should *test the rule*, as clearly exceptions do not prove things – they cast doubt upon their veracity. In spelling, for example, the 'rule' *that* 'i comes before e except after c' is tested by the fact that there are many exceptions (*their*, *heir*, *being*, *seeing*, *reign*, *rein*, etc). Since we now use the word *prove* to mean something more like 'to establish the truth by using evidence', testing or proving the 'i before e rule' seems to show that it is not very effective (see Chapter 4)!

The change in the meaning of the word *girl* is particularly interesting. In the fourteenth century, *girls* were young people of either gender and had not yet evolved to refer only to females. Males were called *knave girls* (think of the alternative name for a jack in cards); females were called *gay girls*. *Gay*, too, has evolved from meaning happy, bright and merry – 'A gay time will be had by all!' – to a synonym for the cultural expressions of homosexuality.

Activity: nonsense sentences

Look at these nonsense sentences – are they grammatically correct?

1. *Erb buncers skubed diratedly.*

All of the words in the sentence are invented, but which one do you think is the verb and why? What function does *diratedly* have in the sentence? Is *buncers* a proper noun? Is it singular or plural?

Now look at this sentence, which comprises real words but perhaps not in a combination you are ever likely to see them outside this book.

2. *Blue bananas skipped rapidly.*

Which one do you think is the verb and why? What function does *rapidly* have in the sentence? Is *bananas* a proper noun? Is it singular or plural?

Now consider the following.

3. *Awful petals stupidly.*

Is this a sentence? If not, how could it be made into a sentence? What kind of word do you need to add to make it into a sentence?

How did you get on? In the first sentence *diratedly* is probably an adverb describing how the buncers *skubed* (verb). *Buncers* is probably a common noun (it doesn't have a capital b so isn't a proper noun). In the second sentence *bananas* is a common plural noun, *skipped* is the verb, and *rapidly* an adverb. Number three isn't a complete sentence because it doesn't have a verb. You could add *ran*, *drank*, *grew*, etc. to complete it.

Word classes or parts of speech

The activities above were intended to encourage you to think about grammar and to consider the importance of understanding the terminology. You might argue that you could see straight away what was the function of each word in each sentence (or non-sentence in the case of *Awful petals stupidly*). But could you explain this to someone else without using some terminology, even if it involved using definitions rather than terms – *doing word*, *describing word*, etc.?

One of the problems many people encounter when faced with grammatical terminology is that just when they think they have understood something, it emerges that there are exceptions or extensions which add complexity. Take, for example, the most common parts of speech or, as they are now more commonly known, **word classes** (Crystal, 2005): noun, verb, adjective, adverb, pronoun, preposition, conjunction and article. (Note that the English National Curriculum (DfE, 2013) uses the term *determiner* rather than *article*.)

Nouns are the names of things – what could be simpler? All you need do to find examples is look around you and you can find thousands. But then the issue is complicated by the fact that some are **common nouns**, some **proper nouns** and some **abstract nouns**. Most people understand readily that proper nouns are special names (*David, Doncaster, December*) and begin with capital letters, but how can we describe abstract nouns? By their very nature, we cannot see them, since they include words such as *love, hatred, fear, honesty* and *bliss*. Abstract nouns are things we cannot see or touch, and include emotions. So far so good? Look at the words below and decide which are common, proper and abstract nouns:

happiness   joy   Edward   dogs   window   desire   books

Easy? Usually we would say that *happiness*, *joy* and *desire* are abstract nouns since we cannot see or touch them; Edward is a proper noun because it is a special name; and *dogs, window* and *books* are common nouns. However, there is a further subset here – some nouns are **count nouns** (they can be singular but we can modify them to make them plural, as in dogs and books) and some are **non-count nouns** because they represent something that cannot be counted, such as joy and desire. Simple? Yes it is, but there is an added complication: **word class mobility**.

Many words can be different parts of speech in different contexts. Look at these two sentences and decide what part of speech *books* represents in each.

> *I love reading books in bed.*

> *My sister always books a holiday in June.*

In the first *books* is a noun, because it represents the name of some things. In the second it is a verb, because it is the action performed by my sister. Now look at some of the other words cited above and consider which might become different parts of speech according to context. See the end of the chapter for some examples.

In the case study below a trainee uses a game to engage children's interest in vocabulary and encourage word building.

Case study: extending children's vocabulary through cryptic activities

Holly, a second-year trainee teacher, was working with a group of Year 6 pupils. She wanted to expand the children's vocabulary whilst also engaging their interest in language. Holly decided to introduce a competitive element to the learning of new words, and practising spelling, through a fast-paced word game.

→

She based the activity on the game 'Bananagrams', which involves a set of 144 lettered tiles laid face down on the table. Each player must take a quantity of tiles, dependent on the number of players. In this instance, Holly had a group of eight pupils. Each child was given 11 tiles, and these were laid face down on the table in front of them. When the game began, all the children were allowed to turn their 11 tiles over, and begin forming words with the letters. One of the key aspects of this game is that all of the words created must intersect, as in a crossword.

For example, Child A may turn over:

s t o h o e h r a p s

She may then arrange the letters in order to make the following words:

s h o e s
h
a
r
p o t

When a child has created words using all of the letters turned over, he or she may shout 'peel'. This means that every child must pick up one of the overturned letter tiles from the middle of the table, regardless of whether they have used all of their current tiles. This continues repeatedly until all of the tiles in the middle of the table have been used up.

For example, if Child A shouted 'peel' and picked up a 't' they may place it beside the 'a' in their crossword, to create 'at':

s h o e s
h
at
r
p o t

Child A would then shout 'peel' again, and all children would collect another letter.

When the game drew to a close, Holly discussed with the children the meaning of their words. She found that some of the children had created nonsensical words. She used this opportunity to help the children explore words in a dictionary, encouraging them to find out if their word was legitimate. Furthermore, she encouraged the children to spot ways in which they might rearrange a few letters to create a different word, for example rearranging *tap* to *apt*. Additionally, she found that interesting discussions arose surrounding words such as *spot* whereby the letters in reverse order created a new word (*tops*).

Holly found that this game enabled the children to develop their vocabulary through active engagement and competition, and incidental learning also occurred as a result of their discussions.

The competitive element also appealed to some children who might not otherwise have been so engaged in a vocabulary activity.

Curriculum links

In Years 5 to 6 pupils will continue to develop their understanding and application of the concepts of word structure so that they can draw on their knowledge of morphology and etymology to spell correctly. Games such as the one described above will contribute to children's understanding of word structure. They could go on to look at ways of combining words to create compounds (*football*, *headteacher*) and words with prefixes and suffixes.

Activity: word class mobility

Crystal (2005, p.243) provides examples of the word *round* belonging to five different word classes according to how it is used in different sentences. Can you create five sentences which include *round* as respectively: an adjective, a preposition, a verb, an adverb and a noun?

Crystal states that *round* can belong to any of five word classes.

- In the sentence 'Mary bought a round table', it functions as an adjective, like *red*, *big*, *ugly* and many more.

- In the sentence 'The car skidded round the corner', it functions as a preposition, like *into*, *past*, *near* and many more.

- In the sentence 'The yacht will round the buoy soon', it functions as a verb, like *pass*, *reach*, *hit* and many more.

- In the sentence 'The children ran round on the playground', it functions as an adverb, like *quickly*, *happily*, *regularly* and many more.

- In the sentence 'It's your round', it functions as a noun, like *turn*, *chance*, *decision* and many more.

Crystal points out that most words belong to a single word class, but even that doesn't prevent people from changing the way they are used. Nouns, for example, are often made into verbs and while this may be something that excites some people and leads them to write indignant letters to newspapers, it should be noted that this is a feature of language which has been going on for centuries, including many examples from Shakespeare: for example, in *Richard II* the Duke of York cries, 'Grace me no grace, and uncle me no uncles.'

> ## Research focus: changing nouns to verbs
>
> Psychologist Steven Pinker estimates that up to one-fifth of English verbs are derived from nouns, including such ancient verbs as *rain, snow* and *thunder* along with more recent converts like *oil, pressure, referee, bottle, debut, audition, highlight, diagnose, critique, email* and *mastermind*. In fact, Pinker reminds us, *easy conversion of nouns to verbs has been part of English grammar for centuries; it is one of the processes that make English English* (1994, p.379).

Just as nouns include subsets, so do other word classes, all of which seems to make knowledge and understanding of grammatical terms rather complex. In fact, it is often at the point where trainee teachers encounter word class mobility or different types of adverb that they begin to despair and wonder if all of this knowledge is really necessary – especially when they can, often with justification, claim that they have been able to write perfectly well for years without being able to define the word classes which they used so extensively.

Morphemes – inflectional endings

A simple test, called the **wug test**, has been used by linguists to show that even very young children have already internalised systematic aspects of the linguistic system that enable them to produce plurals, past tenses, possessives and other forms of words that they have never heard before. The test and other similar tests show that young children are able to make generalisations about language based upon what they have heard and internalised. Of course, sometimes they get things wrong, for example where plurals or past tenses are irregular (*look at those two sheeps, we wented to town*, etc.) (Berko, 1958).

Try drawing a little cartoon character and tell the child that it is a wug. Draw another exactly the same and say that you now have one wug and another wug so you have two …? Children almost always say *two wugs*, using the regular plural ending of -s. If you modify the creatures so that each is a *gutch*, children will probably tell you there are *two gutches*, using the -*es* ending which is usual for words ending in -*tch* (*matches, watches, stitches*).

Similarly, if you invent a word for an action and perform the action (*I am going to zeck; now I'm zecking*) and then tell the children that you were *zecking* yesterday and asked them what you did yesterday, they are likely to say that you *zecked*, using the regular -ed ending for the past tense. When children are told that a man knows how to *gling* and he does this every day, and are then asked what he did yesterday, they nearly always say *glinged*; adults in the same situation more often offer *glang, glung* or *glought*. The adults are affected by their awareness of irregular patterns in English, which often cause confusion to non-native speakers, in a way that the children are not.

Although there are many exceptions to rules for inflectional endings, certain endings are typical of certain word classes:

- -ed ends many verbs when talking about the past, for example *walked* and *jumped*;

- -er and -est make many adjectives into comparatives or superlatives, for example *taller* and *tallest*;

- -s is often used to make nouns plural, for example *cats*, *boys*, *trains*.

-s is also used at the end of third person singular verbs, for example *I look*, *you look*, *he looks*. There are, however, exceptions:

- Some verbs' past tenses don't end in *-ed*, for example, *swim – swam, run – ran, think – thought*.

- Some words that end with *-er* are not comparative, for example, *swimmer, butter*.

- Some comparatives don't end in *-er*, for example, we don't say *It was difficulter*, we say *It was more difficult*.

All of which makes it easy to understand children's misconceptions about inflectional endings. Emphasis on analogy encourages learners to generalise existing knowledge to new situations. In their learning of grammar, pupils often apply **affixes** incorrectly by analogy: *goed, comed, mouses*.

In the case study below, Joel, a Year 5 teacher, challenges children to build as many words as possible using inflectional endings.

Case study: inflectional endings

Joel wanted to explore the effect that different inflectional endings could have upon words with his Year 5 class. First, he made cards with each of the following suffixes: *-er, -est, -s, -ed, -ing, -es, -ly*. Joel asked the children to look at a selection of words he had written on the board and to discuss which ones could make new words by adding which endings.

Joel then put the children into mixed ability groups of three and provided each group with a dictionary and access to the internet via a laptop. He provided each group with a pack of ten words and challenged the groups to see who could create and write down the most words that were derived from their set of words. To do this, children could use the suffixes *-er, -est, -s, -ed, -ing, -es, -ly*, as well as any others they knew.

At the end of the lesson, Joel used the plenary to share different groups' lists and to make points about spelling conventions. He noted that some groups whose words included those which had a single consonant such as *hit* and *run* had not doubled the consonant when creating hitting, hitter, and running and runner. Joel therefore adjusted his plans for future spelling lessons to explore and reinforce rules for doubling consonants. He was, however, pleasantly surprised by the children's enthusiasm for word-building, even though some had

→

created words that did not actually exist. He reminded them to check their words in the dictionary, but congratulated them on their inventiveness in producing, for example, *carpetly* and *fireness*, and asked the children to suggest definitions (*like a carpet* and *great heat* respectively). Joel explained that words were constantly being created because people added prefixes and suffixes to existing words and they became part of common usage.

Note how Joel adapted future planning once he had spotted that some children had misconceptions about some aspects of word-building. It is important that, while recognising where children *should be* in their learning, you take into account where they actually *are* when you plan lessons.

Curriculum links

There is potential here to develop vocabulary activities related to a nonsense poem such as Lewis Carroll's *Jabberwocky*, the opening verse of which is:

> *'Twas brillig, and the slithy toves*
>
> *Did gyre and gimble in the wabe;*
>
> *All mimsy were the borogoves,*
>
> *And the mome raths outgrabe.*

Children can explore vocabulary and look at inflectional endings to help them determine which word classes are being used, as well as to translate the language into familiar terms. What, for example, might *gyre* and *gimble* mean? Are they verbs? If so, what would you do to put them into a different tense?

Research focus: key elements of vocabulary instruction

Apthorp (2006) maintained that there was strong evidence to support three key elements of vocabulary instruction:

- defining and explaining word meanings;
- ensuring frequent encounters with new words (she recommended at least six exposures to a new word);
- encouraging pupils' active processing of words and meanings in different contexts.

Not only did these activities promote vocabulary development, but they also developed and improved reading comprehension.

Developing children's knowledge about words

It is, then, important that we develop an interest in words in the children we teach, so that they broaden their vocabularies and begin to understand the functions of words. A wide vocabulary is invaluable when reading and can help us to deduce what an unfamiliar word might mean as well as how it might be pronounced.

Even the youngest pupils can play word games such as opposites or antonyms in which the teacher says a word and they have to think of a word which means the opposite (an antonym). (Try starting with *good* and *bad*, *happy* and *sad*, *nice* and *nasty*.) The focus in Reception and Year 1 might be on words which include graphemes and phonemes which children are currently learning, but as they develop their phonological knowledge you can become more adventurous, perhaps discussing the use of prefixes to create antonyms (happy and unhappy, like and dislike).

Further activities could involve making synonym charts (sometimes called semantic maps) to show words with similar meanings. These can be real assets when children are writing, as they can draw upon them to find alternative vocabulary to make their writing more interesting. For example, when writing about snow you might create a synonym chart, with the children's help, for the word *cold* (chilly, freezing, frozen, bitter, shivery, nippy), or you could offer alternatives for the over-used *nice* (pleasant, delightful, lovely), or other words where *nice* applies to food (tasty, delicious), or appearance (pretty, handsome, beautiful).

The English lexicon features many words that can cause confusion because they sound like other words but are spelled differently (**homophones** such as *sew*, *so* and *sow*; *see* and *sea*; *there*, *their* and *they're*). We also have **homographs**, which are spelled the same but may be pronounced differently and have different meanings (*sow* a seed and *sow*, a female pig; *record* your favourite programme and break a *record*; a dog's *lead* and a *lead* weight). Often, both homographs and homophones are referred to under the general heading of **homonyms** (meaning the same name), although more accurately homonyms are words that are both spelled the same and sound the same, but have different meanings (see Chapter 3).

Homophones and homonyms are a strong feature of many jokes in English-speaking countries:

> *What's black and white and red all over?*
> *A newspaper (read all over).*
>
> *Why did the girl take a pen to bed?*
> *Because she wanted to draw the curtains.*
>
> *Why did the Queen draw straight lines?*
> *Because she was the ruler.*

If we encourage children, perhaps with the help of family and friends at home, to make collections of homographs and homophones, we can produce a resource to promote discussion about words, their meanings and their spellings. We might also even create a class joke book with examples children have found and others which they have made up.

Classroom strategies to develop children's vocabularies

There are many simple strategies that you can build into your teaching to develop children's interest in words and their knowledge and understanding of the way words work. For example:

- Have a word of the day. This can be chosen by you initially and might include something related to a topic children are or will be studying, or it could be a word that they might wish to use in their writing. You could choose a word which has recently been added to the *Oxford English Dictionary*, or perhaps one which has recently been used by a celebrity or on the news. Once you have established a display for a word of the day, encourage children to take turns to investigate words and to provide their own words of the day.

- Draw attention to new and interesting vocabulary when reading aloud to children and be sure to write words for display so that children can be reminded of them and can begin to use them in their own speaking and writing.

- Build attention to vocabulary into your planning for all subjects and note key words which children will need to understand. Make a point of discussing how the words are formed and what different parts mean or tell us. For example, in mathematics you could look at prefixes which tell us about the number of sides or angles in plain shapes (*tri-*, *quad-*, *pent-*, *hex-*, etc.), while in art there are opportunities to talk about words from other languages such as French (gouache, papier mâché), and the names of colours (vermilion, crimson, aquamarine, etc.).

- Draw attention to correct usage of vocabulary across the curriculum. In mathematics, for example, when measuring height or weight explain that someone can be taller or heavier than one other person but if there are more than two being compared, we use tallest, heaviest, etc.

- Simple vocabulary games can be introduced. These might include *word snap* in which children turn over word cards and can say 'snap' if they can justify a link between a pair: this might be in meaning (love/like, large/big), structure (a common digraph: read/fear; a common ending: rapidly/slowly; a common initial sound: car/kilt); or a common part of speech/word type: run/jump (verbs), over/above (prepositions). You can make the game as open-ended as you like, providing children understand the concepts.

- More advanced vocabulary games could include 'Call My Bluff', based upon a former TV show in which each of three team members has to provide a definition for an unfamiliar word – you can find thousands in more advanced dictionaries, for example: *bilbo* (a rapier or sword), *cayman* (a Central and South American crocodile) and *harrumph* (make a noise as if clearing the throat). Two people provide invented definitions, which should seem plausible, while the third gives the true definition. The opposing team has to decide who is bluffing and who is giving a correct definition.

- Modelling writing in shared writing gives you the opportunity to show how you make vocabulary choices and the strategies you use when you want to avoid repeating a word and seek a synonym instead. Showing children how to use a thesaurus, both in hard copy and on a computer, is important, as is discussing possible spellings for unfamiliar words and encouraging children to check them in a dictionary.

- Beck (2005) grouped words into three tiers. The first tier comprised basic words which seldom need to be taught e.g. *chair*, *happy*, *tool*. The second tier comprised words frequently used as synonyms for the first tier words, e.g. *settee*, *cheerful*, *implement* and words such as *required*, *vary* and *co-incidence* often used in academic learning and general communication. These words are high frequency in written texts and in the vocabulary of mature language users and important for us to teach. Third tier words include technical and subject specific vocabulary, e.g. *hexagon*, *volcano*, which are interesting in terms of word study.

Conclusion

(a) Through engaging children in meaningful activities and showing that you are interested in words and their usage, you can develop children's knowledge and understanding of words and broaden their vocabularies, enabling them to be more adventurous in their choice of vocabulary and more aware of correct usage. You will also help them to understand how words are structured and this should have consequent benefits for their reading and spelling.

Learning outcomes review

You should now know more about what children need to understand about words, both to meet the requirements of the National Curriculum and to enable them to develop as readers and writers, speakers and listeners. You should also be aware of what you need to know about words if you are to be a successful primary teacher. In developing your own subject knowledge as well as in working with children, you will be increasingly aware of some of the challenges children face as they develop their knowledge and understanding of words.

Self-assessment questions
1. Which of these words have prefixes: ready, reaction, disappear, press, precaution?
2. How many new words can you create from the word *play* (the words must actually exist in a dictionary)?
3. What is a homophone?

4. What is a homograph?
5. *Good* and *nice* are antonyms – true or false?
6. *High* and *low* are synonyms – true or false?
7. In the word *unusually* which parts are bound morphemes?
8. Identify the free morphemes in each of these words: *discoloured, unpainted, bicycle.*
9. What is an inflectional ending? Use inflectional endings to modify these words: *pass, table, plant.*
10. Look at the sentences below and identify in each the verbs and nouns:

    - The chair fell over.
    - Dogs bark at strangers.
    - Girls are clever.

11. Now add an adjective to each sentence.
12. In the sentences below, identify the determiners, prepositions and adverbs:

    - The jolly old man walked slowly along the dusty road.
    - A sneaky snake slithered slyly into the soft sand.
    - Those people who drop litter on the ground carelessly should be put into prison.

Further reading

Berko, J. (1958) The Child's Learning of English Morphology in Natalicio, D.S. and Natalicio L.F.S. (2006) *Learning: A Journal of Research in Language Studies.*

Bryson, B. (2001) *Troublesome Words*, 3rd edition. London: Penguin.

Bryson, B. (1990) *Mother Tongue: The English Language*. London: Penguin.

These two books on language by Bill Bryson are entertaining, readable and packed with information.

Carter, J. (2014) Vocabulary Development, in Waugh, D., Jolliffe, W. and Allott, K. (eds) (2014) *Primary English for Trainee Teachers*. London: Sage.

This chapter provides a wealth of ideas for developing vocabulary.

DCSF (2008) *Teaching Effective Vocabulary: What can Teachers do to Increase the Vocabulary of Children who Start Education with a Limited Vocabulary?* Nottingham: DCSF.

Good, practical ideas to address the needs of children with limited vocabularies when they start school.

Waugh, D., Allott, K., Waugh, R., English, E. and Bulmer, E. (2014) *The Spelling, Punctuation and Grammar App*. Morecambe: Children Count Ltd (available through the App Store).

This app provides guidance and activities on all aspects of grammar, spelling and punctuation.

References

Apthorp, H. (2006) Effects of a supplemental vocabulary programme in third grade reading/language arts. *Journal of Educational Research*, 100(2): 67–79.

Beck, I. (2005). *Bringing Words to Life*. New York: Guilford Press.

Crystal, D. (2005) *How Language Works*. London: Penguin.

DfE (2013) *The National Curriculum in England: Key stages 1 and 2 framework document*. London: DfE. Available from: **www.gov.uk/government/uploads/system/uploads/attachment_data/file/425601/PRIMARY_national_curriculum.pdf** (accessed 25.10.15).

DfEE (1998) *National Literacy Strategy: Framework for Teaching*. London: DfEE.

Jackson, H. (1995) *Words and their Meaning*. Harlow: Longman.

Jolliffe, W. and Waugh, D. with Carss, A. (2015) *Teaching Systematic Synthetic Phonics in Primary Schools*, 2nd edition. London: Learning Matters/SAGE.

Pinker, S. (1994) *The Language Instinct*. London: Penguin.

Waugh, D. and Jolliffe, W. (2012) *English 5–11*. Abingdon: David Fulton/Routledge.

3 Why spelling matters

Learning outcomes

By reading this chapter you will develop:

- an awareness of why spelling matters;
- an understanding of why spelling English is challenging;
- a knowledge of progression in spelling;
- an understanding of key areas of knowledge children need to be good spellers.

Teachers' Standards
This chapter will help you with the following Teachers' Standards.

2 Promote good progress and outcomes by pupils:
- demonstrate knowledge and understanding of how pupils learn and how this impacts on teaching.

3 Demonstrate good subject and curriculum knowledge:
- have a secure knowledge of the relevant subject(s) and curriculum areas, foster and maintain pupils' interest in the subject, and address misunderstandings;
- demonstrate an understanding of and take responsibility for promoting high standards of literacy, articulacy and the correct use of standard English, whatever the teacher's specialist subject.

Introduction

Spelling matters. The parents of the children you teach will worry about their children's spelling and may see it as a barometer of standards of literacy. Government ministers will from time to time criticise the standard of spelling in schools, and have emphasised accurate spelling in the National Curriculum. Employers complain about poor spelling in the workforce generally and will often disregard applications containing spelling errors. Spelling errors cost businesses money. An analysis of website figures (Coughlan, 2011) shows a single spelling mistake can cut online sales in half because of consumer concerns about credibility. A recent advert for a children's educational game that was 'so fun, they won't even know their learning' did not inspire confidence in the product. Even Lord Sugar has a view on spelling. When his young apprentice team produced a cookbook full of spelling errors, he was singularly unimpressed (BBC Television, *Young Apprentice*, 8 November 2012).

We rarely think about spellings when we read a text that is completely accurate, but where misspellings occur in published and official documents they are highly visible. If you have ever had the satisfaction of pointing out a spelling error in a university lecturer's presentation, you will be aware just how much misspelled words can detract from the content. While it has been pointed out that, *Any idiot can tell a genius he has made a spelling mistake* (attributed to Harold Rosen, Institute of Education), poor spelling can completely change the meaning of sentences. The *Times Higher Education*'s annual 'exam howlers' competition (Attwood, 2008) included a sentence that read *Control of infectious diseases is very important in case an academic breaks out.* Spotted on a recent UCAS form was the sentence *My desire to teach has been cremated by recent experiences in EYFS.* In both examples above the writer has used a *malapropism* (the wrong word, but spelled correctly).

The stakes are also high when it comes to end of Key Stage tests. The spelling component of the Key Stage 2 Grammar, Punctuation and Spelling test (GP&S) sets the bar high with 20 challenging words such as 'temperature' and 'immediately'. These are presented to children orally within 20 contextualised sentences. Some argue that this is not the way to judge whether or not someone is literate (Smith, 2008). In a world of 'Kwik-Fit', 'drive-thru', 'Toys R Us' and 'Ye Olde Shoppe', and when computers and smartphones have spellcheckers, is poor spelling really important?

Spelling words with ease and accuracy matters (Alderman and Green, 2011). It is an integral part of writing and without this skill, composition is often constrained. A lack of confidence in spelling can have a paralysing impact on writing. A reluctance to take risks with more adventurous vocabulary often results in safe but dull writing. You may have met young writers who will settle for 'big' in their writing because they are unsure about spelling 'enormous'. Why take the risk of writing a word that you feel bound to get wrong?

Alderman and Green (2011) describe the 'low spellers' as having more anxiety and increased avoidance motivation related to spelling instruction, whereas confident spellers with a fluent handwriting style, who are freed up from the worries of transcription, are much more likely to be able to concentrate on composition (Medwell et al., 2009). A significant number of spelling errors can distract from the content, and make it hard for you, as the teacher, to understand the message being conveyed.

Learning to spell

If you are a good speller, you may barely remember how you acquired this skill beyond perhaps the spelling lists you may have taken home to learn. On the other hand, you may feel anxious about spelling. You may worry when you have to scribe for a group, or model writing to the class. Part of your role as a teacher will be to demonstrate how to spell words as part of modelled and shared writing. You will need to be able to scribe children's ideas without misspelling, and identify the errors that children make in their own writing. You will also need to be able to teach spelling well, and that is our concern in these chapters. In order to do this, you will need to understand why spelling in English is a particular challenge, and know the spelling rules and generalisations that will provide strategies for young spellers to crack our complex written code. In order to teach spelling effectively, you need to know the strategies that children need to use to be confident and effective spellers, and the pedagogical approaches that will enable them to learn and apply these. The next three chapters of this book will address these key issues, but they may also help to support you if you worry about your own spelling, and highlight some key strategies to develop and strengthen your own knowledge.

The challenges of English spelling

I'm lousy at spelling because of my parents. They grew up listening to the Beatles, Monkees and Byrds.

Learning to spell is difficult in English. Our 26 letters are used to make around 44 phonemes (the smallest units of sound) in our spoken and written language. In many countries, spelling is phonetically regular. Words are spelled as they sound. Finnish, Spanish and Italian, for example, have a reliable relationship between their alphabet letters and sounds in speech. In English, this is far less straightforward, as you can see from reading the poem below.

I take it you already know
Of tough and bough and cough and dough?
Others may stumble, but not you,
On hiccough, thorough, lough and through?
Well done! And now you wish, perhaps,
To learn of less familiar traps?
Beware of heard, a dreadful word
That looks like beard and sounds like bird,
And dead: it's said like bed, not bead –
For goodness sake don't call it deed!
Watch out for meat and great and threat
(They rhyme with suite and straight and debt).

A moth is not a moth in mother,
Nor both in bother, broth in brother,
And here is not a match for there
Nor dear and fear for bear and pear,

And then there's dose and rose and lose –
Just look them up – and goose and choose,
And cork and work and card and ward,
And font and front and word and sword,
And do and go and thwart and cart –
Come, come, I've hardly made a start!
A dreadful language? Man alive!
I'd mastered it when I was five!

(Anon)

A brief history of spelling

So just how did our spelling system become so complex?

As you have seen in Chapter 2, English spelling has a history and its peculiarities become easier to understand when we appreciate that words have entered our language in a multiplicity of ways: the many different invaders and settlers brought armies to fight and goods to trade, shaping and changing both spoken and written language. Trade and commerce with countries all over the world have added many **loan words** to English. New inventions and technologies have introduced a whole new vocabulary. These changes can be traced right back to Celtic times.

1. In Celtic times, the words used in conversation were rarely written down. Because of this oral tradition, few words have survived into modern English. Those that have include *brock* (badger), *crag*, and *coomb* (a type of valley), and place names such as *Derwent*, meaning clear water; place names such as *Tredegar* and *Tregaron* from *Tre* meaning hamlet or *Llangollen* and *Llanwrda* from *Llan* meaning church.

2. When the Romans invaded, Latin became the official language. It was only really spoken by those with power and, despite the Romans ruling for around 400 years, Celtic languages continued to be very influential. The words absorbed into our language from this time tended to be those used by Roman merchants and soldiers, such as *wine, candle* and *belt*.

3. As the Romans left, the Anglo-Saxons invaded from Germany. This is the time when what we now call Old English emerged. Many of our basic everyday words such as *food, bread* and *house* come from this time. The Anglo-Saxons bought a runic alphabet with them. A rune is a symbol in a writing system; these were carved onto wood or stone, often to mark objects. The skills of the carvers were highly revered and the runes themselves were considered to be mystical, and to have magical properties – you may know the phrase 'it's written in the runes'. This is relevant because, as you will see, it had a significant influence on the way that English came to be written.

4. When missionaries arrived in the sixth century, Latin became important in English once again. The Church used Latin throughout Europe, and it was the only recorded language for a long time. Latin-derived words from this period include *angel*, *bishop*, *abbot* and *martyr*. Later, the monks began to write Anglo-Saxon down, and because of the association of Anglo-Saxon runes with pagan practices, used Roman letters. However, the Roman alphabet was simply not designed to fit English sounds. There were far more phonemes than letters – 23 Roman letters for about 37 phonemes. For example, Latin had no letters for /th/ which is a very common phoneme in English.

5. Viking invasions added Old Norse to the language and we still use about 2,000 words that originate from this time. The Vikings are responsible for some of our silent letters. They introduced a hard *k* instead of a soft *sh* or *ch* to the language. *Church* became *kirk* – as it still is in Scotland. *Ditch* became *dike*, and they gave us words such as *knife* and *knee*, *gnat* and *gnaw*. If we still pronounced the 'k' and 'g' as the Vikings did, these words would, of course, be easier to spell. But spelling has simply not kept up with changes in pronunciation. Even though some letters became silent, such as the 'e' in *love* and the 'k' in *know*, the spellings stayed the same.

6. After the Norman Conquest in 1066, the vocabulary of English changed enormously. Middle English emerged, mainly a mix of Old English and French, and spelling became more complicated. As well as absorbing French words into the language, the spelling of some English words began to take on French characteristics. For example, in French the letter 'h' is not pronounced when it begins a word: *honest* and *hour* are examples of this. *Cwic* became *quick*, *cwen* became *queen*, and *tung* became *tongue*. Many words containing 'qu', for example *antique*, come from this period. Greek and Latin continued to influence Middle English and had such high status that some spellings were made to fit Latin roots, even when words were Anglo Saxon in origin. This is how we ended up with the letter 'b' in *subtle* and *debt*.

7. The introduction of the printing press led to additional complications. You might think that this would have helped, but many of the printers were Flemish and didn't know English very well. They spelled some words beginning with 'g' with 'gh' – *gost* became *ghost*, and *gastly* became *ghastly*. Not only did they have their own way of spelling words, but they were also paid by the line. As you might imagine, other words gained additional letters from time to time as this increased the typesetter's pay.

8. Over the centuries, trade and commerce all over the world continued to influence the English language. During the Age of Discovery (between the fifteenth and seventeenth centuries), new words were absorbed from languages, including Portuguese, Greek, Spanish, Italian and French, bringing with them different letter patterns and adding to the richness of our language – and the complexity of our spelling.

9. As English expanded, so attempts were made to regulate spelling. Between about 1475 and 1630, English gradually became more standardised. The most famous lexicographer was

probably Samuel Johnson. His *Dictionary of the English Language* took nine years to write. It was completed in 1755 and provided a generally accepted way of spelling. But as new words continued to be added, it became increasingly out of date. In 1879 the Philological Society made an agreement with Oxford University Press to begin work on a new English dictionary. It was finally published in 1928 and later became the *Oxford English Dictionary* (*OED*, undated).

Activity

Look at the list of words below. See if you can work out the origins of the words and sort them under the following headings. You will be able to work out some more easily than others.

German	Italian	French	Greek

kindergarten, fiasco, morpheme, confetti, fest, coup d'état, cuisine, thesis, diameter, photograph, pirouette, regime, lager, antique, delicatessen

---

In the 1,500 years since the Romans left Britain, English has shown an amazing ability to absorb words. It is, as Bryson (1990) suggests, one of the great *borrowing tongues* and has become a global language. All this despite having a spelling system that Bernard Shaw said *can't be spelled*, and which reflects the way words were pronounced 400 years ago.

The answers to the activity above are:

German: *kindergarten, delicatessen, fest, lager*

French: *coup d'état, cuisine, pirouette, regime, antique*

Greek: *morpheme, thesis, diameter, photograph*

Italian: *confetti, fiasco*

An evolving language

English is still evolving. About 800 new words – or neologisms (see Chapter 2) – are added to the *Oxford English Dictionary* every year. Many words are from inventions or new technologies, some of the most obvious being *digital*, *internet* and *bluetooth*. Loan words are absorbed from other languages such as *apartheid* (from Afrikaans), *sauna* (from Finnish) or *elite* (from French). Well-known and used acronyms such as *Ofsted* (the Office for Standards in Education), *Inset* (In-service training) and *scuba* (self contained underwater breathing apparatus) have become words in their own right and no longer need explaining by the words that the letters represent. Blended words such as *motel* (motor and hotel), *smog* (smoke and fog) and *camcorder* (camera and recorder) are all in common usage. More recently, as Crystal (2012) demonstrates, the internet is allowing us all to influence spelling. Taking *rhubarb* as an example, he points out that there were just a few hundred instances of rubarb being spelled without an 'h' in Google searches in 2006. By 2010 there were nearly 100,000 and in 2012 around 750,000. Google recognises this spelling and knows what we are looking for. Interestingly, the original medieval spelling of rhubarb also omitted the 'h'.

Words continue to move in and out of fashion and change their meaning – take *mouse*, *cookies* and *wicked*, for instance. With the advent of text messaging and Twitter, we are adapting spellings to respond to the need for very short message length. The great beauty of 'txt spk' is that it is a *flexible friend* (Shortis, 2007, p.1). It has no dictionary and Shortis suggests that many spellings are widely accepted because they are linguistically coherent, logical and creative. There is also far less time involved and certainly less thumb strain in writing 'c u @ 8' than writing 'see you at eight' in full. Despite worries that its widespread use might undermine children's reading and spelling, this has not been backed up by research (Wood et al., 2011). It can, however, trip us up if we are not careful, as David Cameron found out when he wrote LOL, thinking it meant 'lots of love', in a now infamous text message.

Activity

How standardised has text speak become? List some of the commonly used abbreviations. Are there variations? If there are, does it matter? Reflect on how you learned to use *txt spk*. Was it caught or taught?

What children need to know to be successful spellers

For much of the last century a significant debate raged as to whether children learnt to spell by being 'exposed' to words, particularly through their reading, or whether they needed to be taught how to spell. In the 1980s the view that it was 'caught' led, at its most extreme, to children being expected to learn to spell by 'having a go' and discovering how to spell for themselves. In a highly influential publication, *Spelling Taught or Caught*, Peters (1985) argued that spelling was not automatically absorbed while reading, and couldn't just be discovered. She argued that if children had not 'caught' spelling by the age of seven, they needed to be taught it systematically.

Peters' work also challenged Schonell's (1932) highly influential approach to teaching spelling, which was based on graded word groups and rote learning. Words were sorted according to auditory and visual patterns, but as they were based on adult vocabulary they must have seemed arbitrary to children. Little account was taken of the words that they were likely to use in their writing or those most appropriate for them. Word lists continue to dominate the way spelling is approached in some schools today, and as we will see in the chapter on tricky words, if the right words and the right patterns are carefully taught, they can be useful. If, however, children are simply given spellings and are not told why spellings are as they are, or how the spellings relate to the way words are pronounced, learning them becomes a vast, boring and time-consuming memory task (Crystal, 1985).

For some children, the mark they achieve in the Friday spelling test can cause anxiety, frustration and a sense of failure. It can compound their sense of being a poor speller. Well-known research (Watkins, 2010) has shown that children who develop a 'performance orientation' and are concerned with grades, rather than a 'learning orientation', tend to show greater helplessness, use less strategic thinking, and are more likely to persevere with strategies that are not working.

Perhaps more importantly, giving children spellings to learn may lull us into thinking that we are teaching spelling and need do little more. This is far from the case. Successful spellers, as we will see, are those who are able to draw on and integrate many different kinds of knowledge, and this is the focus of the next section.

Learning to spell: a linear progression?

Research focus: progression in spelling

One of the most influential models of progress in spelling was developed by Gentry (1987), who identified five stages of spelling development:

Precommunicative

At this stage, children are aware that symbols create messages and begin to form invented symbols or letters, and string these together. They will not have the awareness that letters represent phonemes or speech sounds.

Semi-phonetic

Children begin to understand that there is a relationship between letters and sounds. The words they write will usually contain the correct beginning and ending consonants but these are greatly abbreviated, e.g. 'lv' for love, or 'nt' for night.

$\longrightarrow$

Phonetic

At this stage, children use their knowledge of grapheme-phoneme correspondences to make good attempts to represent words, even though the spelling may be unconventional. Gentry cites spellings such as 'monstr' and 'ate' (eighty) as examples of spelling at this phonetic stage.

Transitional

At this stage, children start to move beyond the sound-symbol correspondence and begin to appreciate some of the basic spelling patterns of English. Words are not always spelled as they sound and the visual aspects of words are apparent, even though they are not always employed correctly.

Correct

At this stage, children spell most words correctly. They will have the use of a large 'automatic' spelling vocabulary, be able to distinguish homonyms (words spelled the same way but with different meanings) and homophones (the same sound but different spellings). They can spell contractions such as 'it's' and 'isn't' and correctly use irregular spellings.

Gentry's work is useful since it suggests the kind of progress that is typical of many children. However, learning to spell for most children is not quite as neat as this. More recent work by O'Sullivan and Thomas (2007) has shown that many children do not follow a linear path, but draw on multiple sources of knowledge early on. They provide a sample of writing from a child aged five years eight months to exemplify this.

> *To Mr Gumpy* (these words were provided by the teacher on a flip chart)
> *Sorry for hoppg anbt*
> *Thak you for litg me come on your doat*

Here some words are copied (*Mr Gumpy*); some are known (*for, you*); there are examples of phonetic strategies being used (*thak*) and visual strategies (the *oa* in *boat*, and *pp* in *hopping*).

O'Sullivan and Thomas (2007) also highlighted that children from the earliest stages have individual preferences in their spelling strategies – for example, phonetic or visual. Their research concluded that children need to draw on and integrate many different kinds of knowledge to be effective spellers, and develop a broad range of strategies to make good progress. We can group this knowledge into four main areas that we need to teach – and that children need to learn:

1. phonemic knowledge and analogy making;

2. morphological knowledge;

3. semantic knowledge;

4. visual knowledge.

Phonemic knowledge and analogy making

The ability to work with the sounds of language is crucial to proficient spelling (Brann, 1997). Children need to identify the units of sounds within a word, know the alphabetic code, and know the correspondence between letters (graphemes) and sounds (phonemes). Phonemic knowledge also includes knowledge of syllables, rhymes and analogy; phonics; spelling patterns and spelling conventions. We will explore this in the next chapter.

Morphological knowledge

More experienced readers and writers tend not to rely on phonemic knowledge alone, and draw extensively on their knowledge of morphemes. We have explored morphology in Chapter 2, but include reference to it here because an understanding of morphemes can make a significant contribution to spelling familiar and unfamiliar words (Nunes and Bryant, 2006).

Support for Spelling (DCSF, 2009) identifies five key aspects of morphological knowledge.

1. Root words. They contain one morpheme and cannot be broken down into smaller grammatical units. Examples are words such as *chair*, *man* or *night*. These are sometimes referred to as the stem or base form.

2. Compound words are where two root words combined to make a word. Examples are words like *waterfall*, *tablecloth* and *flowerbed*

3. Suffixes are added after root words, and change the spelling and meaning of a word. Examples are *walk – walking*, *skip – skipped*, *happy – happiness*;

4. Prefixes are added before a root. Examples are *happy – unhappy*; *prove – disprove*; *tie – untie*.

5. Etymology (word derivations) – words in the English language come from a range of sources; understanding the origin of words helps pupils' spelling (e.g. *audi* relates to hearing – *audible, audience, audition*).

Research focus: developing awareness of morphemes

Nunes and Bryant's research (2006) demonstrates that primary school children have difficulties with spelling words that cannot be predicted from the way they sound. However, the morphemic structure of words in English often determines their spelling. They showed that spelling difficulties can be reduced by making children more aware of the morphemes within the words. As well as supporting spelling, this knowledge has a positive effect on children's vocabulary growth.

→

Nunes and Bryant concluded that it was important for teachers to:

- be aware of the role that morphemes play in spelling difficulties and how they can be addressed;

- systematically teach about morphemes and their role in spelling;

- promote spelling and language development by teaching about morphemes.

Helpfully, morphemes have a fixed spelling. 'Form', for example, is always spelled the same whether writing *uniform*, *formation* or *reformation*. It can also help children to see a regular pattern in words that might initially seem irregular. Take the word *unnecessary*. Many children will hesitate over one 'n' or two. When we know that its spelling represents the prefix *un,* meaning not, plus *necessary*, we can be more confident about spelling it *un + necessary*. The same would be true of *unnatural* and *unnerving*, whereas *unimportant* – *un + important* – only has a single 'n'. Similarly, we can work out that that there is only one 's' in *disappear* because it comprises the prefix 'dis', which reverses the meaning of the word, and *appear – dis + appear.* Prefixes rarely change the spelling of the root word.

As children learn to spell parts of words that carry meaning, you can show them that meaning can sometimes be a better predictor of spelling than how a word is pronounced. For example, knowing the meaning of *medic* can help with the spelling of *medicine*; *south* with *southern*; *hero* with *heroism*. Knowing that *government* is linked to *govern* and *governor* may reduce the chances of spelling it as it is said and sometimes written – 'govement' or 'goverment'.

Etymological knowledge

Etymology, the study of the origin and development of words, is fascinating. As we have already seen, the meaning of many English words can be traced back to reveal an intriguing story. Exploring how words have entered the English language and their relationship with other words can offer rich insights into meanings and spellings. Crystal (2012) points out that when unusual spellings turn up in several words, it is likely to be because they all come from the same language. French words such as *beret*, *ballet* and *duvet* are good examples of this. You will find many opportunities to explore origins right across the curriculum. For example, you could try investigating the origins of vocabulary such as *polygon*, *hexagon* and *octagon* as part of developing mathematical vocabulary, or challenge children to discover the meanings of local place names.

In the case study below, you will see how Simon has explored root words with his class as part of a unit of work on Ancient Greece. As you read it consider how you might be able to develop a fascination with word origins across the curriculum.

Case study: finding word origins with Year 6

Simon was teaching a cross-curricular unit of work on Ancient Greece. This provided an excellent opportunity to contextualise some of the children's learning about morphemes. He reminded the children that many root words in the English language derive from Latin and Greek. He provided the children with a set of cards, each containing a morpheme with its origins in Greek: 'graph', 'phone', 'photo', 'tele', 'micro' and 'scope', and set a challenge.

First, children were asked to find as many words as they could make by combining these. Second, they were then set the challenge of working out what they might mean.

Simon then asked the children to work in pairs and choose one of the cards. Their task was to make as many words as they could. He took 'tele' as an example, and asked the children to talk together and come up with words that began with this root. He demonstrated how to create a word web that included *telegraph*, *telephone*, *telepathic*, *telescope* and *television*. This gave the children an insight into its meaning, and they worked out that it must have something to do with 'distance'. They then worked on the word root they had been given.

In the plenary, the children shared their words and definitions. Simon emphasised how understanding word meanings could help spelling.

Curriculum links

The Year 5 to 6 programme of study requires children to use knowledge of etymology in spelling. Simon was keen to use other opportunities across the curriculum to extend and apply the children's developing knowledge and, wherever possible, planned for language work to be threaded through other subjects. He soon found himself bringing this approach into geography, mathematics and science. His working wall became full of examples, and these were regularly added to by the children as their fascination with words grew.

Activity

Use an etymological dictionary to find the origins of:

hippopotamus

hooligan

bungalow

(Continued)

> *(Continued)*
>
> *pram*
>
> *decimal*
>
> How might the origins of some of these words support children's spelling?
> Make sure that etymological dictionaries are among your classroom collection of
> dictionaries, as these will be an invaluable resource for you and the children.

Hippopotamus is from the Greek *hippos* for 'horse' and *potamos* for 'river'. *Hooligan* is from the name of a very rowdy family called Houlihan, who lived in London in the nineteenth century. *Bungalow* is from the Hindi word *bangla* meaning 'belonging to Bengal', where there were thatched one-storey houses. *Pram* is from *perambulator*, which is from the Latin for 'to walk around or travel'. *Decimal* is from the Latin *decem*, ten, and thence *decimalis*, tenth.

Semantic knowledge

Semantic knowledge concerns the meanings of words in sentences and is important for remembering how words are spelled (Ehri, 1987). This is particularly significant in English because of the large number of homophones and homographs that we have. For example, we would use our semantic knowledge to select the correct spelling of homophones in the following sentences:

> *I could see the sea from the hill top.*
>
> *It is so difficult to sow seeds when it is windy.*

The challenge of homophones

We have already seen some of the challenges created by homographs such as *bow/bow*. The words are spelled the same, but have different meanings. Of course, even then there can be confusion. How do you make sense of 'the violinists were bowing'? Or 'the Reading Centre in Reading'? Dombey (2009) suggests that we construct patterns of expectation that prime us to recognise particular words and establish their meaning. For example, if we are scanning a train timetable, we see 'Reading' as a place, not a process, and pronounce it accordingly. If we are writing about an accident, we will use the word *wound* without worrying that it is also the past participle of 'wind'. For spelling, the biggest challenge is not homographs, but homophones (see also Chapter 2). Homophones, from the Greek words *homos*, meaning 'the same' and *phone*, meaning 'sound', are words which are pronounced the same way, but have different spellings and meanings, for example:

- to, two and too;

- serial and cereal;

- meet and meat;

- practise and practice.

English is full of them and younger, less experienced spellers find them particularly challenging (O'Sullivan and Thomas, 2007). In fact, homophones are so numerous in Modern English that jokes and riddles are full of them, for example:

What do you call a pony with a sore throat? A little hoarse.

Spellcheckers often fail because they don't have semantic knowledge. As the poem by Jerry Zar (1992) below demonstrates, correct spelling is no guarantee of accuracy.

I have a spelling checker
It came with my PC
It highlights for my review
Mistakes I cannot sea.

I ran this poem thru it
I'm sure your pleased to no
Its letter perfect in it's weigh
My checker told me sew.

The following case study illustrates a number of different approaches to helping children learn to distinguish between homophones.

Case study: distinguishing between homophones

Shazia was teaching a mixed Year 3 and 4 class. She found that many of the children regularly confused the spelling of common homophones when they wrote. Most notable were *their* and *there*, and *to, too* and *two*.

She began by engaging the children's interest and curiosity in words. She collected together and displayed examples of homophones. The children were encouraged to find more and readily added to these. It became an engaging challenge, and the children were fascinated and competitive. This was one of many ways that she was encouraging a real interest in language.

Shazia knew that it was important to check the children's understanding of the words, and wanted the children to use meaning as a strategy for remembering the different spellings. She invited the

→

children to think about their own ways of remembering the difference between them. The children had time to talk together and came up with the idea of inventing a mnemonic (see Chapter 5) for common pairs of homophones. Shazia gave the example 'pour **u** a drink', and 'rich **or** poor'. She suggested other learning strategies for remembering the difference, such as highlighting different letters and linking them with meaning (e.g. beach – sea/beech – tree).

The children were challenged to work with a partner and come up with cartoons, riddles and sentences using homophones. This required them to think about the spelling and the meaning of the words, and their ideas were collected together and displayed. It was so successful that the children continued to bring suggestions from home for the whole of the following week.

The following day groups of children played 'pairs' using a set of cards matching homophone cards that Shazia had prepared. The cards were placed face down and the children took turns to find pairs. She introduced a rule that they could only claim a pair if they could prove they knew the correct meaning.

Next, the children worked with a partner to look at a list of pairs of common homophones. The children were asked to mark those that they were confident about using accurately in their writing, and to circle one pair they were less certain about.

The final activity was for them to devise a strategy for learning this 'tricky pair' and for each partner to support the other in using it in their own writing.

Curriculum links

Learning about homophones or near-homophones is a statutory requirement in Year 2 of the English National Curriculum (DfE, 2013, p.29). Shazia recognised that children would have different routes into spelling and provided them with a variety of activities that would offer strategies to support their growing knowledge of homophones. The final activity was designed to reinforce the message that the children needed to take responsibility for their spelling themselves and was so successful that spelling partners became an integral part of her classroom routines.

Visual knowledge

Proficient spellers make very good use of visual information when writing. They will see that 'howse' just doesn't look right. This may well be the way you check and modify your own spellings when you are writing. Goswami and Bryant (1990, p.53) explain:

> *Children's invented spelling is often wrong because they seem to be using a phonological code too literally when they spell. This, of course, is not really a surprise, because it is impossible to spell English properly just on the basis of letter–sound relationships. No one who relies just on a phonological code will ever spell 'laugh', 'ache', or even 'have' properly.*

Right from the earliest stages, children will take on some of the visual elements of writing in their home language (Harste et al., 1984). Later on in their spelling, they may write the initial letter and use a mixture of letters that are approximately the right shape and length (O'Sullivan and Thomas, 2007). Children will sometimes remember whole words that are part of their sight vocabulary, or parts of words with significant letter strings. Peters (1985) maintained that *visual recall* was a key factor in spelling development, and stressed the importance of children knowing about the visual aspects of spelling, including drawing children's attention to words that look alike but sound different – for example, *rough*, *though* and *ought*.

Learning outcomes review

You should now know more about why spelling is such an important aspect of writing, the history of our spelling system and why it has become so complex. You should also be aware of the main sources of knowledge that good spellers draw on, know that children often take different routes, phonetic or visual, into spelling, and know that it is not a rote learning exercise.

Self-assessment questions
1. What will your approach be to teaching spelling? Can you justify your reasons?
2. What are the main sources of knowledge that good spellers are able to draw on? What do you think the implications of this are for you as a teacher?
3. How will you try to create a classroom environment where children actively investigate words, their origins and their meanings?

Further reading

Allott, K. (2014) Spelling, in Waugh, D., Jolliffe, W. and Allott, K. (eds) (2014) *Primary English for Trainee Teachers*. London: Sage.

This chapter provides an analysis of how we learn to spell and practical ideas for the classroom.

O'Sullivan, O. and Thomas, A. (2007) *Understanding Spelling*. London: Routledge.

This book is based on a three-year longitudinal study of children's spelling in different primary classrooms. It explores kinds of knowledge that are involved in spelling, how children learn to spell and the kinds of teaching that support them most effectively. There are practical examples of what effective practice looks like in the classroom.

References

Alderman, G. and Green, S. (2011) Fostering lifelong spellers through meaningful experiences. *The Reading Teacher*, 64(8): 599–605.

Attwood, R. (2008) A clear case of 'laxative enforcement policies'. *THES*, 28 August. Available from: **www.timeshighereducation.co.uk/403341.article** (accessed 18.6.13).

Brann, B. (1997) *The Brann Analysis Grid for Spelling: B.A.G.S.* Mordialloc, Vic.: P.J. Developments.

Bryson, B. **(1990)** *The Mother Tongue*. London: Penguin.

Coughlan, C. (2011) Spelling mistakes 'cost millions' in lost online sales. BBC News, 14 July. Available from: **www.bbc.co.uk/news/education-14130854** (accessed 18.6.13).

Cripps, C. (1990) *Joining the ABC: How and Why Handwriting and Spelling Should be Taught Together*. Wisbech: LDA.

Crystal, D. (1987) *The Cambridge Encyclopedia of Language*. Cambridge: Cambridge University Press.

Crystal, D. (2012) *Spell It Out: The Singular Story of English Spelling*. London: Profile Books.

DCSF (2009) *Support for Spelling*. London: DCSF.

Dombey, H. (2009) *Readings for Discussion – The Simple View of Reading*. Available from: **www.ite.org.uk/ite_readings/simple_view_reading.pdf** (accessed 18.6.13).

Ehri, L. (1987) Learning to Read and Spell Words. *Journal of Reading Behaviour*, 19: 5–31.

Gentry, J. R. (1987) *Spel is a Four-Letter Word*. Leamington Spa: Scholastic.

Goswami, U. and Bryant, P. (1990) *Phonological Skills and Learning to Read*. Sussex: Taylor and Francis.

Harste, J., Woodward, V. and Burke, C. (1984) *Language Stories and Literacy Lessons*. Heinemann: New York.

Medwell, J., Strand, S. and Wray, D. (2009) The links between handwriting and composing for Y6 children. *Cambridge Journal of Education*, 39(3): 329–44.

Nunes, T. and Bryant, P. (2006) *Improving Literacy through Teaching Morphemes*. London: Routledge.

OED (undated) *History of the OED*. Available from: **http://public.oed.com/history-of-the-oed/** (accessed 18.6.13).

O'Sullivan, O. and Thomas, A. (2007) *Understanding Spelling*. London: Routledge.

Peters, M. (1985) *Spelling Caught or Taught*. London: Routledge.

Schonell, F. (1932) *The Essential Spelling List*. London: Macmillan.

Shortis, T. (2007) GR8 txspectations: The creativity of text spelling. *English, Drama and Media*, June: 21–26, NATE.

Smith, K. (2008) Just spell it like it is. *THES*, 7 August. Available from: **www.timeshighereducation.co.uk/news/just-spell-it-like-it-is/1/403092.article?Page No=1&SortOrder=dateadded&PageSize=50** (accessed 18.6.13).

Watkins, C. (2010) Learning, performance and improvement. *Research Matters: International Network for School Improvement*, **34.**

Wood, C., Meachem, S., Bowyer, S., Jackson, E., Tarczynski-Bowles, M. L. and Plester, B. (2011) A longitudinal study of children's text messaging and literacy development. *British Journal of Psychology*, 102: 431–42.

Zar, J. H. (1992) *Candidate for a Pullet Surprise*. Available from: **www.bios.niu.edu/zar/poem. pdf** (accessed 18.6.13).

4 Spelling and phonics

Learning outcomes

By reading this chapter you will develop:

- an understanding of the place of phonics in the teaching of spelling;
- an awareness of the interrelationship between reading and spelling;
- a knowledge of English orthography;
- a knowledge of some of the rules and generalisations that govern our spelling.

Teachers' Standards
This chapter will help you with the following Teachers' Standards.

2 Promote good progress and outcomes by pupils:
- demonstrate knowledge and understanding of how pupils learn and how this impacts on teaching.

3 Demonstrate good subject and curriculum knowledge:
- have a secure knowledge of the relevant subject(s) and curriculum areas, foster and maintain pupils' interest in the subject, and address misunderstandings;
- demonstrate an understanding of and take responsibility for promoting high standards of literacy, articulacy and the correct use of Standard English, whatever the teacher's specialist subject.

Introduction

As discussed in the previous chapter, the rich history of the English language has led to a complex and varied matching of phonemes to graphemes. Although it is important to acknowledge that our spelling system is not straightforward, it is actually more regular than it may first appear. Successful spellers know and understand our complex code, and are able to make use of this when tackling unknown words in their writing. This chapter will explain why phonics is important for spelling, and explain the interrelationship between spelling and reading. It will also introduce you to some of the spelling rules and generalisations that young spellers need to know.

The challenges presented by English orthography

Orthography is basically the set of rules that governs how speech is represented in writing. In an alphabetic writing system, successful spelling includes being able to segment a spoken word into individual sounds or phonemes and selecting the appropriate letter or letter group to represent each one. This is the process we call *encoding*. In an ideal world there would be an alphabet where a particular sound is only ever represented by one grapheme. In a language such as Finnish, this is almost the case. There is a consistent one-to-one mapping of sounds to letters and it has a nearly optimal orthography (see Research focus below). This may help to explain why children in Finland, although not formally taught to read until the age of seven, are better readers than children who learn to read at a younger age in the UK (OECD, 2010). Languages such as Spanish and Italian also have an almost consistent match between phonemes and graphemes with few exceptions. Once children are familiar with this one-to-one mapping system of sound–letter correspondences, they are able to do a very credible job when spelling out dictated words or pronouncing written texts.

In English, these processes are readily applied to words such as *pen* and *top*, and such words present relatively little difficulty for young writers. However, as we have already seen, there are many inconsistencies in the pronunciation of letters and clusters of letters, often because many words have retained a pronunciation similar to that used in the language from which they are derived. As Waugh and Jolliffe maintained: *we have 'ch', which teachers have tended to teach makes the sound 'ch' as in 'chip', also making a 'k' sound in words with Greek origins, such as 'chemistry', 'charisma', 'school' and 'character', as well as in names like 'Chloe'* (2012, p.213).

Activity

Take the phoneme 'sh' as an example, and think about some of the different ways in which it can be represented. There are up to 14 different ways.

Here are three to start you off:

shoe, sugar, passion

Now try doing the same with the phoneme 'air'. How many different representations can you find?

The different ways the phoneme 'sh' can be represented include *shoe, potion, passion, ocean, sugar, machine, ancient, pressure, financial, precious, issue, relation, Charlotte*. Representations for the phoneme 'air' include *pair, tear, bare, aeroplane, Claire, yeah, there, mayor, their, they're*.

As we saw in the last chapter, children's spelling can often be wrong because they use the phonological code too literally (Goswami and Bryant, 1990). Indeed, it has been suggested that poor spelling among adults in English-speaking countries may in part be a product of our challenging spelling system. When children build a word by segmenting it into its sounds and then represent these with graphemes, they may make mistakes. You may often have seen 'thay' for 'they'; 'wos' for 'was', 'sed' for 'said' or 'cote' for 'coat'. One commentator has written:

The kee to ending English iliterasy is to adopt a speling that's riten as it sounds (Berger, 1994). George Bernard Shaw famously demonstrated that it can hardly be regarded as a system at all, spelling *fish* as *ghoti*: gh as in *laugh*, o as in *women*, ti as in *motion*.

It is certainly true that the letters and sounds that form our alphabetic code were not designed to go together (Crystal, 2012). Individuals and pressure groups continue to press for the simplification of spelling (Bell, 2004), arguing that until this happens children learning to write English are at a disadvantage when compared to many of their European counterparts. Few would argue with the assertion that teaching segmenting and phonic methods are more suited to transparent and regular orthographies. These demand far less of children's working memory than English (Spencer, 2002). However, English is an international language spoken, read and written by people all over the world. Chomsky and Hale (1968) have even described the orthography of English as a *near-optimal system*. This is not because English spelling is an adequate system for representing sounds but because our spelling system links so well to what words mean. This may seem a little overstated, but it is true that the 'g' in *sign* links it to the 'g' of *signature*, even though it is pronounced differently, and helps us to see what it means. Chapter 2 explains the importance of morphology in more detail.

Research focus: comparing alphabetic codes

A number of studies provide clear evidence of the differences between alphabetic codes. Venezky (1973) studied 240 Finnish children who began reading at seven. In a reading test of nonsense words after a year of tuition, the children scored 80 per cent. College students scored 90 per cent on the same test, showing just how short a time it takes to gain proficiency in Finnish spelling.

Geva and Siegel (2000) studied 245 Canadian children learning to read and write in Hebrew. By the end of the first grade, the children scored 79 per cent correct on the Hebrew reading test, but only 44 per cent correct on the English version.

Cossu et al. (1995) found that young Italian readers achieve 92 per cent accuracy on word reading tests after just six months of tuition. Spencer (2002) found that most pupils in the lowest ability group in Year 2 could successfully spell words using the simple alphabetic code, but that mastering the most difficult common words required an additional three years of schooling.

The importance of phonics for spelling

Despite the many anomalies in English spelling, children still need to learn to spell accurately and they need strategies to help them. Given what we know, is it wise to invest quite so much time teaching phonics to crack our complex spelling code? The simple answer is *yes*. Learning all the words we need by rote is not realistic. The average adult is likely to have a vocabulary of 35,000 to 50,000 words (Crystal, 2009). If you learn 20 spellings a week for a 32-week school year, you will know 640 spellings. Multiply this by the 12 years of being at school and you get 7,680 words. Even if those of us who are considerably older continue to learn words by rote, we would find it hard to learn and remember all the words we use in our writing.

Even with all the complexities and the many debates around the connection between phonics and spelling, it is important to know that the vast majority of English words have some phonic regularity and clues that can help us to spell successfully. Crystal (2005) and Adams (1990) suggest that 80 to 90 per cent of spellings conform to a general pattern. Of those that are left, Crystal suggests that only 400 words or so are so unpredictable they need to be learned by rote. Notwithstanding the exceptions, reliable patterns can be taught and learnt.

The interrelationship between reading and spelling

Children's learning of spelling is closely related to how spoken language is written down, and it is often the case that good spellers read a lot and are curious about language and words (O'Sullivan and Thomas, 2007). However, spelling is not a by-product of being able to read, and being able to read is not the same as being able to spell. We have already seen from Peters' influential work (1985) that children do not simply pick up spelling from their reading. Just because children can decode a complex text it does not mean that they can spell all the words. As an experienced and fluent reader, you decode and understand words at speed. You are unlikely to pay very much conscious attention to the print itself and how the words are written, since you will be attending far more to the meaning. When we construct words from our own resources it is far more demanding, as we need to recall and compose words from memory. You will know this from your own experience. You barely notice the word *accommodate* when you are reading, and you will read and understand it automatically, but you may hesitate when you come to write it.

There are important links between successful spelling and successful reading. Reading informs spelling, and for most children it is when they are beginning to write that they attend particularly closely to letter sounds. Montessori (1912) advised teachers to teach spelling first and use this as a basis for teaching reading, while Huxford et al. (1991) suggested that children's ability to spell phonemically regular words precedes their ability to read them. Frith (1985) maintained that the balance of power shifts from reading to writing when children start to segment the phonemes in their writing. This happens with *such intense concentration* that their attention is also drawn to the phonemes in their early blending (Graham and Kelly, 2003, p.146).

In the following case study you will see how Matthew, an NQT, makes clear links between blending for reading and segmenting for spelling. Look at how Charlie, a Year 1 child, needed to attend particularly intently to his application of grapheme–phoneme correspondences (GPCs) when he was writing.

Case study: quick-write

Matthew worked with a small group of children who had been focusing on the GPCs /ou/ and /se/. He introduced the children to quick-write, an activity that involves children saying a word containing the GPC they are learning aloud, saying the individual phonemes to themselves and writing the word on a phoneme frame or whiteboard. Matthew articulated the word *mouse* slowly and carefully. The children repeated it, and segmented the word, saying the individual phonemes /m/ /ou/ /se/ aloud to themselves. Charlie began to write it on his whiteboard. The initial sound was straightforward and he readily wrote 'm' before pausing. How should he write the phoneme /ow/? He could of course select from 'ow' as in cow, or 'ou' as in loud. He eventually settled on 'ou'. The final sound was also problematical. Should it be 's' or 'se' or even 'ss'? His final spelling was 'mous', a highly creditable attempt as he had written a grapheme for each of the phonemes he could hear. Matthew praised him for a very good attempt, showing him what he had done correctly, and used letter names to draw attention to the 's and e' at the end of the word. The following day as Charlie was reading, Matthew noted that he was able to read *shout*, *ground* and *house* with confidence.

Curriculum links

As Matthew reflected on the children's learning, he began to appreciate how much the children were learning about GPCs as they applied the concepts, skills and knowledge they had been developing, and how it had given him an insight into what the children were able to do.

The main recommendations of the Rose Review (Rose, 2006) were that the knowledge, skills and understanding that constitute high quality phonic work should be taught as the prime approach when learning to decode and encode print. The Review stressed the importance of high quality, systematic phonic work taught discretely, but then applied in the children's reading and writing. Other research has similarly shown that the early and systematic teaching of phonics, extensive use of rhymes in early years, mastery of letter names as well as sounds, and effective early reading all contribute to children becoming confident and effective spellers (Daw et al., 1997).

The curriculum requires that Year 1 pupils are taught to spell words containing each of the 40-plus phonemes already taught and use letter names to distinguish between alternative spellings of the same sound. Matthew went on to plan opportunities for the children to write simple dictated sentences in different curriculum areas as part of their learning, so that they were able to apply and practise their spelling knowledge in a range of contexts.

Understanding phonics

Phonics involves knowledge of the alphabetic code and the skills of segmenting and blending.

The alphabetic code

The alphabetic code is the relationship between the sounds we can identify in speech and how they are represented. It is underpinned by four key concepts that are all important for spelling. The first two concepts, which are taught in the earlier phases of any good systematic synthetic phonics programme, concern the simple code and are relatively straightforward.

1. Sounds/phonemes are represented by letters/graphemes.

2. A phoneme can be represented by more than one letter.

> ### Activity
> No matter whether you teach in the Early Years or at Key Stage 1 or Key Stage 2, it is essential that you know the phonemes of spoken language, are able to segment words into phonemes, and understand the code whereby these are represented by written graphemes. If you are at all unsure about the precise enunciation of phonemes, visit the OUP website and click on the link to the Oxford Owl: **www.oxfordowl.co.uk/Question/Index/3#saysounds**. You will be able to hear how each one is pronounced.

Segmentation for spelling

A key principle when teaching phonics is that decoding and encoding are reversible processes. From the beginning, children need to be taught the relationship between pronouncing and blending individual phonemes into whole words (decoding), and segmenting whole spoken words into phonemes and then selecting letters to represent them (encoding).

Teaching segmentation for spelling involves enabling children to segment a word orally – for example, /sh/o/p/, recalling the graphemes that represent the grapheme–phoneme correspondences (GPCs), and writing the appropriate letters. Knowing GPCs is important from Phase 2 in the phonics programme *Letters and Sounds* (DfES, 2007). Children will typically start segmenting and building the foundations for spelling after the first few GPCs have been taught.

The complex code

Children face an additional challenge when reading and spelling become less easily reversible. What can cause particular difficulty, and is generally less well taught, is the *complex* or *advanced code*. This is where words contain sounds that can be spelled in more than one way, as it involves mastering the multiple spellings for each phoneme. There are two key principles you need to bear in mind when teaching phonics at this stage.

1. The same phoneme can be represented in more than one way.

2. The same grapheme can represent more than one phoneme.

To teach well, you will need to be secure with the alternative sounds for spellings and alternative spellings for sounds yourself, so that you can explain these confidently. Children need to learn the whole alphabetic code and not just the first part of it, or they will only have part of the story and find it difficult to crack the code.

Research focus: three stages in children's developing understanding

Frith (1985) described three stages in children's developing understanding. She suggested that children progress through logographic (whole word), alphabetic (analytical) and orthographic (instant recognition) stages as both readers and spellers.

Logographic

The logographic stage is about children's early encounters with words when they recognise and can spell a small number of whole words, including their names. They may do this by focusing on the shape of the word – some children will recognise the word *elephant* more readily than high frequency words such as *and*, for example. Ehri (1991, p.387) points out that if readers use letters as cues, they do so because their shapes are visually salient, not because the letters correspond to the sounds in the word. When one letter was changed in the Pepsi logo to read Xepsi, 74 per cent of pre-schoolers read the label as Pepsi (Masonheimer et al., 1984). At this stage the children's strategies for reading and writing unknown words are limited, of course.

Alphabetic

The alphabetic stage is where children are developing phonological awareness and start to analyse parts of words. Through spelling, children learn that spoken words can be broken down into speech sounds (phonemes) that map onto letters. At this stage they can pronounce new and novel words, even if they are not always completely correct.

Orthographic

When they have had considerable practice at reading using an alphabetic strategy children learn to recognise words as orthographic units without phonological conversion. By this, Frith

→

means that they are able to recognise and write the whole word. She suggests that orthographic representations used in reading are precise enough to be transferred to spelling and that orthographic reading drives the development of orthographic spelling skills. So spelling shifts from phonetic, to transitional, to correct spellings.

Teaching the complex code

Children following *Letters and Sounds* will typically be at Phase 5 in Year 1 and will be learning about the complex code. They will be segmenting words into phonemes for spelling and many children will be skilled at representing these in a plausible way. The expectation is that children will now be learning vowel digraphs and trigraphs, and will know many of these by the time they enter Year 2. It is at this stage that they will be learning the most complex aspect of phonics and the part you may find most challenging to teach; long vowel phonemes and multiple spelling choices. The key is to be systematic with your teaching, use multi-sensory approaches, and provide plenty of opportunities for children to apply their learning.

Long vowel phonemes and multiple spelling choices

The five short vowel sounds are straightforward – /a/, /e/, /i/, /o/, /u/. But there are also long vowel phonemes, shown in the table below. (Note that some of these may vary according to local and regional accents.)

Phonemes	Graphemes	Common spellings
/ai/	ay, a-e, ae, a	play, take, snail, baby
/ee/	ee, ea, e	feel, heat, me
/ie/	ie, igh, y, i-e, i	tie, fight, my, bike, tiger
/oe/	oa, ow, o-e, o	float, slow, stone, nose
/u/	oo, ou, u	took, could, put
/ue/	oo, ue, ew, u-e	room, clue, grew, tune
/ow/	ow, ou	cow, loud
/oi/	oi, oy	coin, boy
/ur/	u, ir, er, ear, or	fur, girl, term, heard, work
/au/	au, or, oor, ar, aw, a	sauce, horn, door, warn, claw, ball
/ar/	ar, a	car, fast (regional)
/air/	air, ear, are	hair, bear, share
/ear/	ear, ere, eer	ear, here, deer
/ure/	ure, our	sure, tour

(from Jolliffe and Waugh with Carss, 2015)

Other spellings are possible: those listed are the most common representations. You may decide to teach the most common representation of each of the long vowel phonemes first and then later teach all other ways of spelling the phoneme.

To use long vowel phonemes accurately, children need to acquire more word-specific knowledge, and learn that good spelling will sometimes involve choosing the right grapheme from among several possibilities. In the case study below, notice how the teacher supports her Year 2 class to learn new ways of spelling phonemes and to be able to write some words with each spelling accurately.

Case study: spelling vowel phonemes

Sarah worked with a Year 2 class and focused on the long vowel phoneme groups.

Sarah focused on /ai/ and began by inviting the children to suggest words that contain that sound. She collected their ideas together and scribed them on the flip chart. She started them off with *train* and *made*, and they contributed *great* and *gate*. The children soon realised that they could contribute words that rhyme, and the list grew to include *brain, pain, mate, Kate, late*, and so on. Sarah reminded the children that although there are only five vowel letters, the same sound can be spelt in different ways (e.g. *wait, late, great*). She provided examples of words containing a short vowel phoneme: *cat, bat, sat*, and asked the children to repeat the words and identify the short vowel. She gave time for the children to practise oral discrimination and listen to her say the words *cat* and *Kate*. Is the vowel short or long?

Sarah selected a short story with words containing the focus phoneme /ai/. She enlarged the text, displayed it and read it to the children, asking them to listen out for the sound /ai/. Then she took down the story, re-read it while the children listened, and asked the children to indicate (thumbs up) whenever they heard the focus phoneme.

Next, she introduced a *human word sort*. She gave out cards with words containing /ai/. The children had to read the word and find others with the same spelling of the long vowel sound.

Finally she drew three columns on the whiteboard and wrote a different grapheme at the top of each one:

ai – *train*

a-e – *gate*

a-e – *lane*

The children contributed other words and together they sorted them on the whiteboard.

Over the next few days Sarah followed a similar approach to help the children explore and learn other long vowel phonemes, and planned some short complementary investigations.

→

These included:

- giving children copies of a text to highlight a particular phoneme, and writing the words and the phoneme on a separate sheet;

- drawing columns on a large sheet of sugar paper headed with the graphemes and inviting the children to collect as many words as they could for each phoneme;

- providing a pile of sticky notes for the children so that they could list other long vowel phonemes with different graphemes. Children discussed which columns had the most words in them and which had the least.

This allowed Sarah to point out that in English some spelling patterns are very rare and some common words have rare spellings (e.g. *they*).

Sarah was initially concerned about the expected pace of teaching long vowel phonemes but the English subject leader in the school explained that it was important that children learned the whole code and not just part of it. Sarah followed the school's phonics programme and taught alternative spellings for the long vowel phonemes systematically, while continually revisiting and reinforcing the spellings already taught, particularly through modelled and guided writing. She also provided ample opportunities for the children to apply their knowledge in writing across the curriculum.

Curriculum links

Children will begin to meet extra challenges during Year 2 as they learn different ways of spelling the same sound. They need to be able to:

- segment words into phonemes and represent these with graphemes, spelling many correctly;
- learn new ways of spelling phonemes for which one or more spellings are already known, and learn some words with each spelling.

Supporting independent writing

One way of helping children to spell confidently as they write independently is to introduce them to charts that aid their spelling choices. Some schools have devised their own, but there are many available commercially, including those from THRASS (Teaching Handwriting Reading and Spelling Skills) and Read Write Inc. THRASS have produced one chart for consonants and one for vowels. Each phoneme is placed in a separate section with a visual representation for each sound and the spelling choice. For instance, the 'j' sound as in *jam* can be depicted by the graphemes (spelling choice) 'j', 'g' (giant), 'ge' (cage), 'dge' (bridge). Children can be encouraged to discuss plausible possible spellings. For example, English words don't begin with 'dge', so the choices can be narrowed down. The Read Write Inc. simple and complex 'Speed Sounds' charts have a similar function, and support the teaching of sounds and graphemes, as well as providing a quick review of letter–sound correspondences.

You will, of course, need to explain and model how to use these charts, but having ready access to these when writing can help children become more independent with spelling.

Learning exceptions

In the next chapter, we will look in detail at teaching 'tricky' or 'common exception' words, and it is worth noting that there are some word-specific spellings that simply have to be learned. You will need to devote time to learning the common exception words listed in the National Curriculum (p.54 and p.58). Always aim to address the misconceptions children make frequently, as without your intervention they may continue to assume they are correct.

Activity

Peters (1985) collected together the spellings of *saucer* by 967 ten-year-old English children, of whom 62 spelt *saucer* correctly. Given what you have learnt about plausible spellings, which of those that are wrong do you think are logical? Which are worrying? The number indicates the number of children spelling the word in each of the different ways. It does not include examples written by only one child.

67 sauser

23 sorser suacer

20 sacer

18 sorcer

11 soser soucer

10 sucer suser

9 sawser

8 sarser sacar

7 sauce scaucer

6 souser sauer sause

5 caucer sawer socer sorer

4 surcer surser scauer saser saurcer saurser scarcer

2 sosr suar sus susar suse carser causer chocer corcor roce corser

1 curser eswas sacar sacca saccar sacerer sacir sacuere sacuers saer saeucng sancer saose sarce sarear sare saresir sari sarig saroer sarry sarses sarter sary sascaue sasger sasere sasher satard saucere saucor saucing saucher saucter saue saues saught saura saurse saus sauscer sausery sausir sausue sausur savcr sawers sawur sayser seacar scace searces scarsere scarser scaser scasur scauser scocer scoors scorceri scoser scoua scoucel scoue scour scouse scuace scuarcer sciccer scare scuser senrd serner sem ses sesaur sharser shasers shose shower shure sice sinder sined slart sloy smory soc socp splorns soolle sooser sooucer sor sore sorcr sororr sors sorsar sorscur sorb sorur sorus sosa sosed sosar sosiar sosiar sosre sou sourcer sourses sout sowew space spienace sres slous suace suarser suaser sucar succer sucase suce sucger suecher sueer sucur sud suger suier sumser suorser surage surce surer sureer sursar sursur surts susare susas sues

Phonetically plausible spellings of *saucer* will depend on accent, but the most plausible spellings include sauser, sorser, saucor, sorcer, sawser, sarser, sauce, scaucer, sourcer, sorsar, sausur, sauscer.

Spelling patterns and conventions

What rules do you remember from learning to spell? The one rule that is likely to stick in your mind is 'i before e except after c'. We remember this partly because it has a short, memorable rhyme. However, the rule has many exceptions. Just think of some of the words that children meet frequently such as *seeing, being, their* and *weight*. *Support for Spelling* (DSCF, 2009, p.106), a programme designed to follow on from *Letters and Sounds* in Key Stage 2, includes the following advice:

> *The i before e except after c rule is not worth teaching. It applies only to words in which the ie or ei stands for a clear /ee/ sound and unless this is known, words such as* sufficient, veil *and* their *look like exceptions. There are so few words where the ei spelling for the /ee/ sound follows the letter c that it is easier to learn the specific words:* receive, conceive, deceive (*plus the related words* receipt, conceit, deceit), perceive *and* ceiling.

Gentry (1987, p.31) argued that most spelling rules were of little use because of the exceptions, while O'Sullivan and Thomas (2007) refer to spelling patterns rather than rules, and stress the importance of analogy. Whatever terminology your school chooses to adopt, it is important for you and the children you teach to know that there are spelling conventions and guidelines that generalise across many words. The following guidance, which is well worth considering carefully, is taken from *Support for Spelling* (DSCF, 2009).

Position of phonemes

The **ai** and **oi** spellings do not occur at the end of English words or immediately before suffixes; instead, the **ay** and **oy** spellings are used in these positions (e.g. *play, played, playing, playful, joy, joyful, enjoying, enjoyment*). In other positions, the /ai/ sound is most often spelt **ai** or a consonant-vowel, as in *rain, date* and *bacon*. The same principle applies in choosing between **oi** and **oy**: **oy** is used at the end of a word or immediately before a suffix, and **oi** is used elsewhere. There is no other spelling for this phoneme.

O sound following a w sound

When an /o/ sound follows a /w/ sound, it is frequently spelt with the letter **a** (e.g. *was, wallet, want, wash, watch, wander*) – often known as the **w special**. This extends to many words where the /w/ sound comes from the **qu** grapheme (e.g. *quarrel, quantity, squad, squash*).

Ur sound following the letter w

When an /ur/ sound follows the letter **w** (but not **qu**) it is usually spelt or (e.g. *word, worm, work, worship, worth*). The important exception is *were*.

Or sound before a l sound

An /or/ sound before an /l/ sound is frequently spelt with the letter **a** (e.g. *all, ball, call, always*).

Words ending in v

English words do not end in the letter 'v' unless they are abbreviations (e.g. *rev*). If a word ends in a /v/ sound, 'e' must be added after the 'v' in the spelling (e.g. *give, have, live, love, above*). This may seem confusing because it suggests that the vowels should have their long sounds (as in *alive, save* and *stove*) but in fact there are very few words in the *give/have* category (i.e. words with short vowels) – they are mostly common words and are quickly learned.

Using -ant, -ent, -ance or -ence

In deciding whether to use 'ant' or 'ent', 'ance' or 'ence' at the end of a word, it is often helpful to consider whether there is a related word where the vowel sound is more clearly pronounced. When deciding, for example, between *occupant* or *occupent* the related word occupation shows that the vowel letter must be 'a'. Similarly, if unsure about *residance* or *residence*, the word *residential* shows that the letter must be 'e'.

A very real challenge when discussing rules and generalisations is that in order to understand many of these patterns we need quite a sophisticated knowledge of linguistic terminology to understand them. Waugh and Jolliffe (2012, p.219) illustrate this by considering the straightforward principle of doubling consonants when adding 'ing' to verbs containing short vowels.

'Hit' becomes 'hitting', 'bat' becomes 'batting', 'hop' becomes 'hopping' and so on. The rule is widely applicable, although there are some exceptions ('benefiting'), but the terminology may challenge the pupils who need to learn the rule. Of course, they should learn about consonants, vowels and verbs, but combining the three terms in one rule may over-face many children.

Activity

One solution to the problem of learning the principles of spelling is to adopt an investigative approach where children work out the principles for themselves. For example, you might give out a selection of cards with singular words that form plurals by adding 's', adding 'es' or changing 'y' to 'ies', and also cards with the matching plural words and ask them to try and work out the patterns. Try this for yourself. What do you notice?

Look at the following and then explain how to change words ending in -f into plurals:

wolf, wolves

leaf, leaves

thief, thieves

half, halves

knife, knives

scarf, scarves

What happens with words ending in -ff or -fe?

Now try to establish the pattern when:

- adding -ed or -ing to words;
- adding endings to words ending with one l, e.g. *careful*;
- adding a consonant suffix (-ly, -less) to a word with a split vowel (*late, hope*).

Words that form plurals by adding 's', adding 'es' or changing 'y' to 'ies'

If the word ends in -ch, -s, -sh, -x, -z add -es to form a plural, e.g. *torch/torches, gas/gases, dash/dashes, box/boxes, fizz/fizzes*. If the word ends in a vowel and y (for example, *boy, journey*) then just add -s, e.g. *boy/boys, journey/journeys*. If the word ends in a consonant and -y (*baby, ruby*) then it changes to -ies, e.g. *baby/babies, ruby/rubies*.

Words ending in -f, -ff or -fe

Many nouns ending in -f drop the 'f' and add -ves to form the plural (*scarf/scarves*). Words ending in -fe drop the 'fe' and add -ves (*knife/knives*). Words ending in -ff just add 's' (*cliff/cliffs*). However, both *roofs* and *dwarfs* are widely used as alternative to 'rooves' and 'dwarves'.

Adding -ed or -ing to words

Where a word ends with -e, drop the 'e' and add -ed or -ing. There are exceptions to this, including *be* and *see*. Neither drop 'e' when adding -ing. If a base word ends in a single consonant letter preceded by a single vowel letter, double the consonant letter. There need to be two consonant letters between a 'short' vowel and a suffix beginning with a vowel, e.g. *hop, hopping, hopped*.

Adding endings to words ending with one l

For words ending in a single 'l' double the 'l' before adding a suffix: *traveller, carefully, equalling*.

Adding a consonant suffix (-ly, -less, -tion) to a word with a split vowel

When a word with a split vowel spelling has a suffix added that starts with a consonant, it is simply added to the word (*lately, hopeless*).

Learning outcomes review

In this chapter we have considered the place of phonics in the teaching of spelling and the interrelationship between reading and spelling. Despite the complexities of our orthography, the vast majority of our spellings conform to a general pattern, and we need to make sure that our teaching is systematic so that young writers are able to draw on this key strategy. Children also need to know the rules and generalisations that govern our spelling and have ample opportunities to apply their learning in the context of meaningful writing. We will consider this further in the next chapter.

Self-assessment questions

1. Make sure you know the key concepts that are important for teaching the simple and complex code spelling. Look back at pages 69–73 to check that you know and understand these four concepts.

2. Revisit the section on the position of phonemes and check the answers to the following questions.

   a) Which of the following do not occur at the end of English words: ai, oi, ay, oy?

   b) What is the w special?

   c) When an /ur/ sound follows the letter 'w' (but not 'qu') how is it usually spelled? There is one important exception. What is it?

   d) How is an /or/ sound before an /l/ sound frequently spelled?

   e) If a word ends in a /v/ sound, which letter has to be added?

   f) How do you know whether to use -ant or -ent, -ance or -ence at the end of a word?

Further reading

DCSF (2009) *Support for Spelling*. London: DCSF.

This practical guide maps out a sequence for teaching spelling from Year 2 to Year 6 using the teaching sequence above. As well as providing a wealth of suggestions for teaching there are suggestions for strategies to address children's spelling errors in the context of their own writing.

References

Adams, M. J. (1990) *Beginning to Read: Thinking and Learning About Print*. Cambridge, MA: MIT Press.

Bell, M. (2004) *Understanding English Spelling*. Cambridge: Pegasus.

Berger, J. (1994) Struggling to put the 'ortho' back in orthography. *The New York Times*, 23 April, 1994. Available from: **www.nytimes.com/1994/04/23/nyregion/struggling-to-put-the-ortho-back-in-orthography.html?ref=josephberger** (accessed 18.6.13)

Chomsky, N. and Hale, M. (1968) *Sound Pattern of English*. New York: Harper and Row; Cambridge, MA and London: MIT Press.

Cossu, G. Gugliotta, M. and Marshall, J. (1995) Acquisition of reading and written spelling in a transparent orthography: two non parallel processes? *Reading and Writing: An Interdisciplinary Journal*, 7: 9–22.

Crystal, D. (1995) *Cambridge Encyclopedia of the English Language.* Cambridge: Cambridge University Press.

Crystal, D. (2005) *The Stories of English.* London: Penguin.

Crystal, D. (2009) in Gall, C., The words in the mental cupboard. *BBC News Magazine.* Available from: **http://news.bbc.co.uk/1/hi/magazine/8013859.stm** (accessed 18.6.13).

Crystal, D. (2012) *Spell It Out: The Singular Story of English Spelling.* London: Profile Books.

Daw, P., Smith, J. and Wilkinson, S. (1997) Factors associated with high standards in spelling years R-4, *English in Education,* 30(3): 15–27.

DCSF (2009) *Support for Spelling.* London: DCSF.

DfE (2013) *The National Curriculum in England: Key stages 1 and 2 framework document.* London: DfE. Available from: **www.gov.uk/government/uploads/system/uploads/attachment_data/file/425601/PRIMARY_national_curriculum.pdf** (accessed 25.10.15).

DfES (2007) *Letters and Sounds.* London: DfES.

Ehri, L. (1991) Development of the ability to read words, in Barr, R., Kamil, M., Mosenthal, P. and Pearson, P. (eds) *Handbook of Reading Research Volume II.* New York: Longman, 383–417.

Frith, U. (1985) Developmental dyslexia, in Patterson, K. E., Marshall, J. C. and Coltheart, M. (eds) *Surface Dyslexia.* Hove: Lawrence Erlbaum.

Gentry, J. R. (1987) *Spel is a Four Letter Word.* Michigan: Heinemann.

Geva, E. and Siegel, L. S. (2000) Orthographic and cognitive factors in the concurrent development of basic reading skills in two languages. *Reading and Writing: An Interdisciplinary Journal,* 12: 1–30.

Goswami, U. and Bryant, P. (1990) *Phonological Skills and Learning to Read.* Abingdon: Lawrence Erlbaum.

Graham, J. and Kelly, A. (eds) (2003) *Writing Under Control.* London: David Fulton.

Huxford, L., Terrell, C. and Bradley, L. (1991) *The Relationship between the Phonological Strategies Employed in Reading and Spelling.* London: Blackwell.

Jolliffe, W. and Waugh, D. with Carss, A. (2015) *Teaching Systematic Synthetic Phonics in Primary Schools,* 2nd edition. London: Sage.

Masonheimer, P. E., Drum, P. A. and Ehri, L. C. (1984) Does environmental print identification lead children into word reading? *Journal of Reading Behavior,* 16: 257–72.

Montessori, M. (1912) *The Montessori Method* (trans. Anne George). London: Heinemann.

OECD (2010), *PISA 2009 at a Glance.* OECD Publishing. Available from: **http://dx.doi.org/10.1787/9789264095298-en** (accessed 18.6.13).

O'Sullivan, O. and Thomas, A. (2007) *Understanding Spelling.* London: Routledge.

Peters, M. (1985) *Spelling Caught or Taught.* London: Routledge.

Rose, J. (2006) *Independent Review of the Teaching of Early Reading.* London: DfES.

Spencer, K. (2002) English spelling and its contribution to illiteracy. *Literacy*, 36(1): 16–25.

Venezky, R. L. (1973) Letter-sound generalizations of first, second, and third-grade Finnish children. *Journal of Educational Psychology*, 64: 288–92.

Waugh, D. and Jolliffe, W. (2012) *English 5–11.* Abingdon: David Fulton/Routledge.

5 Teaching spelling rules, generalisations and tricky words

Learning outcomes

By reading this chapter you will develop your understanding of:

- effective pedagogies for teaching spelling patterns and rules;
- strategies for teaching and learning tricky words;
- how to address misconceptions in children's own writing;
- strategies to help children correct their own spelling errors;
- a range of classroom routines that support spelling.

Teachers' Standards
This chapter will help you with the following Teachers' Standards.

2 Promote good progress and outcomes by pupils:
- demonstrate knowledge and understanding of how pupils learn and how this impacts on teaching.

3 Demonstrate good subject and curriculum knowledge:
- have a secure knowledge of the relevant subject(s) and curriculum areas, foster and maintain pupils' interest in the subject, and address misunderstandings;
- demonstrate an understanding of and take responsibility for promoting high standards of literacy, articulacy and the correct use of Standard English, whatever the teacher's specialist subject.

6 Make accurate and productive use of assessment:
- give pupils regular feedback, both orally and through accurate marking, and encourage pupils to respond to the feedback.

Introduction

Children meet the challenge of spelling every time they write. Our aim is to ensure that they can spell an increasing number of words with automaticity and accuracy. This is a cumulative process. Children need to practise words that have already been introduced, while they gradually and systematically build their spelling vocabulary.

In this chapter we explore teaching approaches that will support children's spelling, and consider how to strengthen their confidence and independence when tackling unfamiliar words. We will also suggest positive ways of responding to the spelling errors that children make in the context of their own writing.

The spelling curriculum

The National Curriculum has high expectations for spelling in terms of pace and progression. The programme of study is statutory, and set out year by year for Key Stage 1 and two-yearly for Key Stage 2 in English. It outlines:

- pupils should apply simple spelling rules and guidance;
- learn statutory word lists for Years 3 and 4;
- learn statutory word lists for Years 5 and 6.

It also provides examples of words, exemplifying each pattern to be taught.

All schools are required to set out their school curriculum for English on a year-by-year basis and make this information available online, so there will be clarity for you in terms of what you need to teach and what the children need to learn.

Teaching spelling: the role of the teacher

Your role in establishing a rich language environment and a positive classroom ethos for young writers is critical. Children in classrooms where teachers foster their interest in and curiosity about words are far more likely to develop a genuine enthusiasm for language (see Chapter 2). They will be encouraged to experiment with new words, take risks and go beyond the safe vocabulary they know.

Activity

Think about a classroom you have worked in/are working in. How does the teacher create an environment where children develop a genuine interest in and fascination about words? Consider how far the following are in evidence.

- Multiple opportunities for children to use language and explore its possibilities.
- High value given to books and reading.

(Continued)

(Continued)

- Regular opportunities to enjoy word-play – for example, rhymes, jingles, playing with palindromes and puns.
- Teacher demonstrations of different strategies and processes for spelling.
- Time given to exploring words, reflecting on meanings and origins, and finding out why they are spelled that way.
- Engaging displays and interactive working walls that may include labelling in English and community languages, interesting words and examples of writing both by authors and children.
- Active discussion and investigation of words and spelling patterns.
- Opportunities to discuss how words resemble and differ from other words through shared reading and writing.
- Learning about words from other languages.
- Opportunities to write for a wide range of purposes.
- Authentic audiences for writing to encourage children to attend to spelling.
- A range of resources for spelling including dictionaries, thesauruses, sound charts, word banks from investigations, topic words.

What else would you add to this list?

Classroom teaching approaches, routines and organisation

Children need opportunities to apply their learning and to spell confidently when tackling a range of texts for different purposes and audiences. The key teaching approaches for spelling include modelled and shared writing, where you demonstrate how to apply what the children have been learning in the context of continuous text. Articulating the strategies you are drawing on by thinking aloud as you write allows children to see what an experienced speller does. Guided group work provides an excellent opportunity for children to apply their knowledge as part of the writing process. Here, you can scaffold the children's learning and remind them of the knowledge they have about words and their spellings. In addition, it is important to plan for regular, discrete teaching sessions where you can develop phonological, semantic and morphological knowledge and strengthen the children's understanding about how words are constructed. Finally, there need to be regular opportunities for the children to discuss and learn their own 'tricky' spellings so that they see themselves as responsible for their progress.

Regular discrete teaching sessions

From Year 2 onwards, *Support for Spelling* (DCSF, 2009) recommends a flexible four-stage sequence that can be adapted and used according to your specific spelling focus. Underpinning the teaching sequence is an investigative and problem-solving approach that requires children to be actively involved in their learning. The four stages are as follows.

1. *Revisit, explain, use*

The sequence starts with revising and securing prior learning before introducing and explaining new learning. An important aspect of this part of the sequence is for children to be able to use the words orally and in context, so that they have a clear understanding of what they are learning.

2. *Teach, model, define*

This part of the sequence includes direct teaching. You will need to model the new learning and actively involve the children in this.

3. *Practise, explore, investigate*

In the third part of the sequence, children have the opportunity to work independently, in pairs or in small groups, using a range of strategies to practise and consolidate new learning. At this point it is important to consider activities to extend children who would benefit from a higher level of challenge.

4. *Apply, assess, reflect*

This final part of the sequence gives children the opportunity to reflect on what they have learnt and to recognise their achievements. This allows the children to:

- revise the new learning;
- apply the words orally and in writing;
- reflect and assess their progress.

You could provide a further opportunity for the children to apply their learning in writing by a short dictation, by asking the children to compose sentences of their own, or by encouraging them to use some of the words in a particular piece of writing.

In the case study below, you will see how the teaching sequence has been used by one teacher, Sian, with her Year 1/2 class. Children at the end of Year 1 are expected to split compound words into their component parts and use this knowledge to support spelling. Sian was keen to try out an investigative approach to this to ensure that she stretched her more able spellers.

Case study: investigating compound words

Sian wanted to ensure that all the children had a clear understanding that a compound word was two smaller words joined together, so that they could use their knowledge to support the spelling of these words in their own writing.

$\longrightarrow$

1. *Revisit, explain, use*

Sian began by checking that the children understood what a compound word was. She wrote a number of simple words on cards. They included *water, fall, sea, side, sun, shine, week, end, down, stairs*. She held up *water* and then *fall*, and put them together, demonstrating how to make a new word.

2. *Teach, model, define*

She gave out a card to each child and checked that they could read the word they had. This appears spontaneous, but she had thought carefully about differentiation. Each child needed to find a partner to make a compound word and check together that they understood the meaning of the new word. Sian drew two boxes on the whiteboard and demonstrated how to spell the compound word *greenhouse*.

Next, she wrote the compound word *rainfall* and drew boxes around the two words *rain* and *fall*.

The children drew two boxes of their own and were asked to write the word *week* in the first box. They held up their whiteboards so that Sian could check any misconceptions. This was repeated with the second word *day*.

She then invited the children to write *daytime, daybreak* and *birthday*, as a quick-write activity. She reminded them that 'ea' was one way of spelling the long vowel phoneme /ai/ as in *steak* and *break*.

3. *Practise, explore, investigate*

Sian introduced a word chain game. Pairs of children were given domino cards with the last and the first part of a compound word, e.g. *show / sun; day / break; fast / water; fall / play; ground / green; house / birth; day / side*. Sian started off the game by reading out the word *side*. The children needed to look at the first word on their card and see whether it could be added to *side* to make it into a compound word. If it did, they called out the new word – *sideshow*, before reading the second word on their card, which was *sun*. The other children looked to see if their first word could be added to *sun* to make a compound word and so on.

Sian gave each group of children a set of word cards, e.g. *some, any, no, every, thing, one, body, where*. They spread them out and took it in turns to join two together to make a new word. The children needed to read each one aloud and decide whether or not it sounded like a word that they had heard before.

The children were challenged to record the words they made and see how many different combinations were possible. They soon realised that each card could be used more than once to make different words, e.g. *everyone, someone*.

4. *Apply, assess, reflect*

The children completed short dictated sentences on their whiteboards using compound words. As an extension activity for more able spellers, Sian challenged the children to write down the longest word chain they could from compound words, e.g. *goodnight / nightfall / fallout / outside; birthday / daytime / timeout / outdoor / doorstop / stopwatch / watchtower*.

The children were engaged and interested, and most importantly were developing a real interest in words. Sian reflected on this approach and decided to use investigations as a key approach for teaching spelling.

Curriculum links

Compound words are introduced in the Year 1 programme of study. Although they are not mentioned again, you are likely to need to revisit compound words in subsequent years, as they are met more widely in other areas of the curriculum.

Teaching and learning tricky words

Everyone finds some words tricky. It may be that you hesitate over *rhythm* or *separate*, *lightning* or *necessary*. Should it be *spelt* or *spelled*? *Learnt* or *learned*? And can *jail* really be spelled *gaol*?

What counts as a tricky word for the children you teach will depend on their age and experience, what they have been taught and what they know about spelling patterns. Some words will be 'tricky for now'. These may be phonically encodable words that contain grapheme–phoneme correspondences (GPCs) not yet encountered by children. For example, children will encounter the word *could* before knowing that the middle grapheme is a less common spelling for the /oo/ sound.

All children need strategies they can use to learn and recall tricky words and apply them in the context of their own writing. Learning to spell them is not always straightforward – if it was, you would know all your personal tricky words by now. You may well have observed that spelling words correctly in a test on a Friday is no guarantee that they will be applied in a piece of writing on Monday. No matter how high the scores children achieve, unless they can apply their spelling knowledge to their own writing all the effort involved will have been in vain.

Common tricky words

Many of the 100 most common words are 'tricky'. *Letters and Sounds* (DfES, 2007) lists these as:

the	me	said	little	Mrs
to	be	have	one	looked
I	was	like	when	called
no	you	so	out	asked
go	they	do	what	could
into	all	some	oh	
he	are	come	their	
she	my	were	people	
we	her	there	Mr	

The statutory word lists in the National Curriculum (DfE, 2013) contain a mixture of words frequently used in children's writing and words that are often misspelt. These will be quite challenging for some children:

- For Years 3 and 4 the words include *business*, *enough*, *occasionally* and *separate*.
- For Years 5 and 6 they include words such as *cemetery*, *government*, *foreign* and *rhythm*.

Research focus: children's spellings

Research carried out by Oxford University Press while creating dictionaries for children has revealed a fascinating insight into children's spellings (OUP, 2012). They found that when children used unusual words in their writing such as *pterodactyl* and *archaeologist*, they normally spell them correctly. However, they found that commonly used everyday words such as *can't* and *excited* were much more often misspelled.

Does this fit with your observations? Why do you think this may be?

Strategies for spelling tricky words

There will almost always be part of a tricky word that can be segmented using phonic knowledge. Encourage children to use this as a first strategy and then focus on the tricky part rather than the whole word. Start with the graphemes children do know, for example the /s/ and /d/ in said, and then identify the element of the word that is tricky: 'ai'.

There are many tried and tested ways of learning the tricky parts of words and these can be categorised into three main methods:

1. visual strategies;
2. auditory strategies;
3. learning a method for remembering the word.

Visual strategies

Visual strategies include the following:

- The *Look, Say, Cover, Write, Check* routine. Peters (1985) and Cripps (1990) advocated this effective approach to help children see the overall visual pattern of a whole word and memorise it. The routine follows a set pattern. Children:
  - look at the word;
  - say the word aloud to themselves;

- ○ cover the word;

- ○ write the word from memory;

- ○ check that the word has been written correctly.

If the word is misspelled, instead of altering it, the process is repeated. It works, because rather than simply giving a child a spelling to copy a letter at a time, children have to write the whole word from memory. Some teachers apply this approach by writing the words children ask for on a piece of paper or whiteboard and then taking it away. However you decide to implement this in your own classroom, it is important to discourage them from copying one letter at a time, since this achieves very little.

- Some collections of words such as *weight*, *their* and *height* contain a shared visual pattern. Learning these words together, even though they are pronounced differently can help children to remember them.

- Use a highlighter pen to draw visual attention to the tricky part of the word.

- Look for words within words (for example, there's a *rat* in *separate*; *apprehensive* contains *hens*).

- Try rapid writing on mini-whiteboards. Write the word on the board and ask the child to write it three times as quickly as possible. This is one way of committing high frequency words to memory.

Auditory strategies

Auditory strategies include the following:

- Using analogy to support new learning. Goswami and Bryant (1990) demonstrated that children often make analogies with words they know how to spell. If they can spell words such as 'come' they are likely to be able to spell 'some'. As children store common spelling patterns in their memories, they increasingly rely on analogy and remember new words because of their association with words that share familiar patterns.

- Over-articulate the letters or 'spell speak' the silent parts of words, for example *Wed-nes-day*, *bus-i-ness*, *par-li-a-ment*, saying it as it might sound if the vowel was clear.

- Break the word into syllables so that children can hear how it is spelt (or *spelled* – both are correct), for example, *Oc-to-ber*.

- Encourage children to say problem words in their heads, sounding any silent letters.

- Use quick-write – give the children a word at a time to write on their whiteboards (see above). Monitor and record the strategies they are using.

Activity

The *schwa* sound is a short unstressed vowel sound, which is the usual vowel sound in *the*, when it is not before a vowel. Say *'it's for you'*, and *'it's important'* slowly, and then repeat quickly. You will hear the *schwa* as you say *for* and the *a* in *important*.

Giving vowel graphemes their full value can help with the spelling of the *schwa* sound. If children sound out a word such as *tomorrow* in their reading with a clear sound in the first syllable – *to* – this will help them to remember to spell the *schwa* sound in that syllable with the letter *o*.

Underline the *schwa* sound in the following words:

- colour;
- sister;
- picture;
- banana;
- miniature;
- Saturday.

Find five more words with a *schwa* sound. How could you help children to spell these correctly?

The *schwa* sound has been underlined: col<u>ou</u>r, sist<u>er</u>, pict<u>ure</u>, banan<u>a</u>, minia<u>ture</u>, Sat<u>ur</u>day. There are many other words with the *schwa* sound, including *another, dinosaur, doctor, summer*.

Learning a method for remembering the word

Methods for remembering spellings include **mnemonics**. These can be useful memory aids for children when they are remembering tricky spellings. A commonly used mnemonic to help with the spelling of 'because' is **b**ig **e**lephants **c**an **a**lways **u**se **s**mall **e**lephants. This approach can be particularly useful with some of our more confusing homophones. For example, by noting that stationery contains an 'e' for envelopes it is straightforward to recall the difference between this and stationary. Another example would be distinguishing between principle and principal by remembering that 'my pal is the principal'. Mnemonics are most useful when they mean something to the children, so provide opportunities for them to create their own.

Children will have their own preferences and ways into learning spellings. If they are asked which they find most useful and why, and can articulate the strategies they use, they may be more likely to apply them when they are writing independently.

Activity

Look at the following list of spellings. All of them are tricky. Is there one that you think is the correct spelling, or is it something else?

dessicate, dessiccate, desiccate – or something else

sacreligious, sacrilegious, sacreligos – or something else

misspell, misspel, mispell – or something else

cemetery, cemetry, cemetary – or something else

supersede, supercede, superceed – or something else

What were the key strategies that you used to try and spell the word correctly? Did you:

- sound it out;
- write out the word and look to see if it looked right;
- draw on analogy – that is using a known word to help to confirm or spell the word;
- use the word root and your knowledge of the meaning of a word;
- apply a rule;
- use your memory?

Look at the answers below. Some may surprise you. What strategies might you use to remember and write these in the future?

desiccate, sacrilegious, misspell, cemetery, supersede

Supporting independence and risk taking

If children are going to make good attempts at using adventurous and unknown words without developing an unhelpful over-dependence on you or other adults in the classroom, it is important to strengthen independence. If children are continually stopping to ask you how to spell individual words, it can disturb the flow of their composition. You may have had the experience of being about to write a complex sentence when you have been distracted or interrupted. You can easily lose your train of thought.

It can be helpful to set out clear expectations before the children start to write. Remind them that they are very unlikely to get all their spellings right every time and that you value their attempts. Remind them of the strategies, rules and conventions that they can apply. Make sure they know that your marking will focus on the spelling patterns and tricky words they have been taught.

Ways of boosting children's confidence include:

- making occasional spelling errors for children to spot during shared writing – model your thinking and ask for help from the children;
- introducing 'have a go' notepads or whiteboards – these provide children with the opportunity to try out their ideas using their developing knowledge and see what 'looks right';
- writing the initial/final sounds and drawing a line to show what has been missed out;
- encouraging children to write down what they can, using a mix of their knowledge of phonics, probable letter strings and morphology;
- writing a 'temporary' spelling, underlining it and coming back to it at the end: some teachers call these *magic lines* or *squiggles*.

Useful resources to support independence include:

- word banks for particular pieces of writing: for example, when writing about volcanoes you might have a diagram annotated with lava, erupt, magma chamber, flow, ash cloud;
- displays of relevant words and word webs on your working wall;
- small table-top cards with high frequency words;
- charts to aid spelling choices (see Chapter 4);
- a range of dictionaries, including etymological dictionaries and thesauruses.

Make links between spelling and handwriting

Some researchers have noted a link between spelling and handwriting (Peters, 1985; Cripps, 1990). Teaching good handwriting is important for developing a fluent joined style and provides opportunities to practise digraphs as one joined unit, common letter strings, word structures, and words linked to the specific focus in discrete spelling sessions. High-frequency words such as *they* and *said* can also be demonstrated and practised as joined units. Westwood (2005) points out that although we cannot infer *per se* that good handwriting leads to good spelling, it does seem likely that laboured handwriting can inhibit the development of automaticity in spelling.

Proofreading

Good spellers are self-monitoring and self-regulating (First Steps, 2001) and take responsibility for getting spelling correct. As children get older, you will want to encourage them to read their own writing and identify errors and words they are not sure about. This is not an easy skill to develop. Proofreading your own writing is hard because you know it so well.

You may have experienced getting back a piece of work, which you thought you had proofread carefully, with a number of spelling or typing errors marked. As Mark Twain wrote in a letter to Sir Walter Bessant in 1898: *You think you are reading proof, whereas you are merely reading your own mind; your statement of the thing is full of holes and vacancies but you don't know it, because you are filling them from your mind as you go along.*

Proofreading for spelling needs to be taught and modelled by you. One way of doing this is to take a piece of writing and put it under the visualiser as part of a whole-class session. If you are going to use a genuine piece of work, it is essential that you choose carefully and have the permission of the child first. When you start, you may feel more comfortable writing it out and changing it a little so that it is not instantly recognisable. Some teachers take a piece of good writing and say that they have added some errors.

Read through the work with the children – you may want to focus on a particular spelling error, such as words ending in *-ed*. As you identify an error, talk aloud to yourself and say which part looks wrong. You could try out an alternative spelling, or use one of the strategies identified in the chart on page 95. Invite the children to suggest the correct spelling. Challenge the children to proofread their own work and find three misspelled words in their writing. Can they put these right? If you do this on a regular basis, you may well find that children are very keen for their work to be reviewed in this way.

In addition to teaching self-checking, consider establishing writing or spelling partners. Not only does this provide a valuable opportunity for children to hear their writing read aloud, but it is also often easier for them to spot errors in one another's writing. Spelling partners can also test one another on their own tricky words.

Using dictionaries and thesauruses

You will want to make sure dictionaries and thesauruses are readily available, but these are only useful if children are shown how to use them. It is important that children understand alphabetical order as early as possible, if they are to be able to use them successfully and without frustration. They will need to know that they can split the dictionary into sections.

- The first section is A–E.
- The second is F–L.
- The third is M–S.
- The final section is T–Z.

You will also need to teach them how to find words beyond the initial letter. However, here is a word of caution. There are times when children spend so much time looking up words in a dictionary that they may appear very busy, but may not be writing very much.

How you encourage the use of dictionaries will depend on the stage of the writing and the purpose. They may be less important during the drafting process than when writing a final version to be read by others. When children are engaged in the authorial aspects of writing, make explicit that they are free to think about what they are saying and how to say it. Too much time looking through dictionaries or word books or asking for help will interrupt the flow of ideas.

Using word processors, spellcheckers and tablet PCs

Children who are less successful spellers seem to find it easier to detect misspellings on screen than in their handwritten texts (O'Sullivan and Thomas, 2007). Spellcheckers can also be useful if the initial attempt is close enough to be recognised as the intended word. Children need to have an appropriate level of skill in order to use them effectively, and it is wise to make the pitfalls explicit. They may correctly spell the wrong word; for example, 'I was *hopping* for a present'. Inaccurate homophones may not be recognised, with, for example, 'The new breakfast *serial* tasted terrible' left uncorrected. Some commonly used words such as *headteacher* will also come back underlined. Once children know these limitations, they become more useful. It is also important to check that the spellchecker is set for UK and not US English.

In the case study below you will see how one teacher, Carl, is helping the children choose strategies that will help them to spell tricky words. As you read it, consider how he is developing the children's independence so that they start to take responsibility for learning tricky words themselves.

Case study: word of the day

Carl was teaching a mixed Year 3/4 class. He wanted the children to develop strategies that would help them to remember their own tricky words and use them correctly in their independent writing. He created a poster of the four memory strategies (see below) and displayed it on the working wall. Carl showed the children that it contained four good ideas for helping them to remember spellings, and demonstrated two of them by focusing on a word that was proving tricky for several children: *actually*. He wrote the word on the whiteboard, and over-articulated it: *ac-tu-al-ly*. He then invited the children to read it together and clap the syllables.

He asked the children to talk in pairs about anything that they noticed about the word – several commented on the *ll*; others pointed out that it has *act* in it, and Sally pointed out that the last four letters were the same as those in her name. Carl then asked whether there were

→

any features of the word that might make it difficult to remember, and which memory strategy might be helpful. The children decided in pairs which strategy they were going to use, and learned the word.

Carl then rubbed the word off the whiteboard and asked the children to write it themselves. They showed him their spelling and Carl wrote the word again so that they could self-correct. Not all of the children had it completely right, so they looked at where they had made the error, and had another go. Finally, they discussed the strategies that they had used, and how effective they were.

The following day Carl asked them to write the word *actually* in their spelling journals.

Curriculum links

Carl's approach created an interest in how words are spelled, and also drew attention to some of the strategies that could be used. He used this approach regularly to build the children's confidence when attempting unknown words. It also provides a very helpful approach for learning the word lists for Years 3 and 4 set out in the National Curriculum. The programme of study recognises that as children progress through Key Stage 2 they will increasingly need to understand the role of morphology and etymology as well as phonic knowledge.

A poster of memory strategies for spelling

This poster is similar to the one used by Carl and may be a useful resource to display and discuss with children.

Strategies	Explanations
Syllables	To learn my word, I can listen to how many syllables there are, so I can break it into smaller bits to remember (e.g. *Sep-tem-ber, ba-by*).
Base words	To learn my word, I can find its base word (e.g. smiling – base *smile* + **ing**, e.g. *women* = **wo** + *men*).
Analogy	To spell a word, I can use words that I already know to help me (e.g. *could: would, should*).
Mnemonics	To learn my word I can make up a sentence to help me remember it (e.g. *could* – can old ugly lions dance?).

Support for Spelling (DSCF, 2009, p.109)

Approaches to distance marking

In 2012 a *Daily Mail* headline read 'Schools are deliberately failing to correct spelling errors to avoid damaging pupils' self-esteem'. The article described a secondary school's policy of only highlighting three misspelled words in a piece of work as a 'false kindness'.

Marking provides the opportunity to see how well individual children understand and apply what has been taught, and should always relate to the specific focus for teaching. How spelling is marked matters for maintaining children's self-esteem and confidence. It can be dispiriting to be given back work covered in pen. Despite the concerns of the *Daily Mail*, take care that your marking is proportionate. Three errors in a young writer's short sentence is very difference from three errors in an experienced writer's three pages. *Support for Spelling* (DCSF, 2009) recommends that children should learn no more than five of their own target words at a time. You can help by:

- making sure that children know what the criteria for success are for any particular piece of work; if you have been focusing on the rules for adding *-ing* to regular verbs, let the children know you expect these words to be spelled correctly;

- providing feedback to the children; make sure they know that you will be focusing on a manageable number of spellings that they are expected to learn;

- giving the children time for response and clarifying expectations about what they should do next;

- setting mini-targets; these may be individual, for example, 'in my next piece of writing I will spell the word *they* correctly', or you may set targets for a group.

Spelling logs and spelling journals

One helpful way of recording the children's growing knowledge of spelling and supporting individual children with their own personal spellings is to introduce spelling journals. These can be particularly useful from Year 2 upwards. They are very different from the word books that you may be more familiar with, which do not necessarily help children learn strategies for learning new words. They can be used in two main ways:

- First, to record the spelling activities and investigations children have carried out as part of your taught spelling programme. They may also act as *aides-mémoires* of spelling patterns, rules and generalisations.

- Second, to log personal errors from independent writing across the curriculum. The words to be learned will be specific to the individual child. They devise their own strategies for learning them and monitoring their success.

If you introduce spelling journals, do make sure that the children know:

- the purpose of the journal;

- which words go into it – these are likely to be those that you have identified in their writing; be careful not to overload the children;

- how important it is that the words are written correctly;
- strategies for learning the words – introduce the list of memory strategies above and encourage a 'look, say, cover, write, check' approach.

Some teachers find it useful to keep these in the form of a loose-leaf folder that can be added to on a regular basis.

Spelling lists

We have already discussed the value – or lack of value – of sending home spelling lists and rote learning. If you find yourself in a school where this is school policy, the good news is that this routine can be turned into a positive learning experience (Jolliffe and Waugh with Carss, 2015).

Before sending lists home:

- Differentiate the lists for different spelling abilities. Make sure that children are learning words they are likely to meet during lessons and in their reading.
- Consider introducing the test before the children have been given their list of words. They may already be able to spell some of them, but this will also show the children which parts of the words they need to focus on. Remind them of the 'look, say, cover, write, check' approach.
- Spend time talking with children about the spellings in the list. Explain, where possible, why words are spelled in a particular way.
- Relate what they are learning to more general principles about spelling. You might, for example, use lists to reinforce that even when words may appear irregular (as in 'bough', for example) there are usually others that follow the same visual pattern ('though', 'thought', 'bought', 'cough').
- Consider teaching words in families and use them to develop analogy, for example 'could', 'should' and 'would'. Lists can be used to help children strengthen their familiarity with common prefixes and suffixes and understand how these can modify meanings of words.
- Consider sending home children's personal tricky words to be tested the following week by a spelling partner.

Waugh and Jolliffe (2013, p.216) remind us that:

> It is the broadening of knowledge about words that will enable children to develop their spelling abilities rather than simply the memorising of lists. Teachers often complain that children can spell words in a test but seem unable to do so a few days later in their written work. Perhaps if they were to engage children more deeply with the words and take the time to discuss etymology and strategies for learning how to spell those words, their pupils might be better able to work out how to spell them when the test is a distant memory.

Learning from children's errors

Children's spelling errors in their independent writing can help us to see where there are gaps in their spelling knowledge. As you notice and mark errors, look closely at the strategies the children are using. It will give you insights into their understanding. For example, a child using *bode* instead of *body* is successfully using phonological knowledge, but does not yet understand that /ee/ at the end of a word is almost always spelled with a 'y'.

Research focus: learning from children's spelling errors

Peters and Smith (1993) developed a diagnostic grid to analyse children's miscues as spellers, and this was developed further by CLPE (2000). Teachers record all the words in a short piece of writing under five key headings:

1. Standard spelling: words spelled correctly.

2. Developing strategies – misspellings that are linked to word meanings or visual patterns, even though incorrectly spelled: for example, *comeing, strait, befro*.

3. Later phonetic strategies: for example, *ones* (once), *peple* (people), *bode* (body).

4. Early phonetic strategies: for example, *eve* (every), *delsh* (delicious).

5. Early visual strategies: *wal* (wall), *siad* (said).

Try doing this for the first 60 words of a child's independent writing. In which column do most of the misspellings appear? What does that tell you about their predominant spelling strategies?

Learning outcomes review

You will now be aware that learning to spell involves much more than learning words by rote, and that a balanced spelling programme will include some key components:

- the principles underpinning word construction (phonemic, morphemic and etymological);
- how (and how far) these principles apply to each word;
- practising and assessing spelling;
- applying spelling strategies and proofreading.

(Support for Spelling, DCSF, 2009)

You will know interactive and engaging ways of teaching spelling patterns and rules. You will also be aware of some of the strategies you can use to support young writers as they learn tricky words, and have considered classroom routines that will enable them to recognise and address their own spelling errors.

Self-assessment questions

1. Review your current classroom environment. What might you change or add to ensure that it is a positive environment for learning spellings?
2. Revisit the teaching sequence for spelling explained in the section 'Regular discrete teaching sessions' (pp.84–5) and make sure you feel confident about the four key aspects of this.
3. Review the four memory strategies for learning tricky words: using syllables, base words, analogy and mnemonics. Consider how to use them to help children remember the following spellings: *some, their/there, people, resign.*
4. If your school sends spelling lists home each week, how will you make them an effective and worthwhile task for the children? Refer back to the list of suggestions under the heading 'Spelling lists' (page 97) and choose three or four of these to try out.

Further reading

Wray, D. and Medwell, J. (2008) *Primary English: Extending Knowledge in Practice.* Exeter: Learning Matters/SAGE.

For an interesting look at strategies for learning spellings and investigating spellings read Chapter 4.

References

CLPE (2000) Diagnostic Spelling Assessment Grid, in O'Sullivan, O. and Thomas, A. (2007) *Understanding Spelling.* London: Routledge.

Cripps, C. (1990) *Joining the ABC: How and Why Handwriting and Spelling Should be Taught Together.* Wisbech: LDA.

Daily Mail (2012) Schools deliberately fail to correct spelling mistakes. Available from: **www.dailymail.co.uk/news/article-2142547/Schools-deliberately-failing-correct-spelling-mistakes-avoid-damaging-pupils-self-esteem.html#ixzz2KtBKHQG0** (accessed 18.6.13).

DCSF (2009) *Support for Spelling.* London: DCSF.

DfE (2013) *The National Curriculum in England: Key stages 1 and 2 framework document.* London: DfE. Available from: **www.gov.uk/government/uploads/system/uploads/attachment_data/file/425601/PRIMARY_national_curriculum.pdf** (accessed 25.10.15).

DfES (2007) *Letters and Sounds.* London: DfES.

First Steps (2001) *First Steps Spelling Resource Book.* Victoria, Australia: Rigby Heinemann.

Goswami, U. and Bryant, P. (1990) *Phonological Skills and Learning to Read.* Abingdon: Lawrence Erlbaum.

Jolliffe, W. and Waugh, D. with Carss, W. (2015) *Teaching Systematic Synthetic Phonics in Primary Schools*, 2nd edition. London: SAGE.

O'Sullivan, O. and Thomas, A. (2007) *Understanding Spelling.* London: Routledge.

OUP (2012) *New research shows spelling continues to be a challenge.* Available from: **www.ox.ac.uk/media/news_stories/2012/121030.html** (accessed 18.6.13).

Peters, M. (1985) *Spelling Caught or Taught.* London: Routledge.

Peters, M. and Smith, B. (1993) *Spelling in Context.* London: NFER-Nelson.

Twain, M. (1898) *Letter to Sir Walter Bessant.* Available from: **www.twainquotes.com/Proofreaders.html** (accessed 18.6.13).

Waugh, D, and Jolliffe, W. (2013) *English 5–11.* Abingdon: David Fulton/Routledge.

Westwood, P. (2005) *Spelling: Approaches to Teaching and Assessment*, 2nd edition. Victoria, Australia: ACER Press.

6 Punctuation

Learning outcomes

By reading this chapter you will develop your understanding of:

- what children need to understand about punctuation;
- what we need to know as primary teachers;
- some of the challenges we face when we teach children to punctuate;
- approaches to teaching punctuation.

Teachers' Standards

This chapter will help you with the following Teachers' Standards.

3 Demonstrate good subject and curriculum knowledge:
- have a secure knowledge of the relevant subject(s) and curriculum areas, foster and maintain pupils' interest in the subject, and address misunderstandings;
- demonstrate a critical understanding of developments in the subject and curriculum areas, and promote the value of scholarship;
- demonstrate an understanding of, and take responsibility for, promoting high standards of literacy, articulacy and the correct use of Standard English, whatever the teacher's specialist subject.

Introduction

Within two years of publication, Lynne Truss's (2003) book about punctuation, *Eats, Shoots & Leaves: The Zero Tolerance Approach to Punctuation*, had sold three million copies. Even though the book you are reading covers spelling and grammar too, we would not dare to dream of selling even 5 per cent of that figure! But why should a book about commas, colons and apostrophes attract such interest? One reason was that the title held an appeal, being based upon a misunderstanding caused by a missing comma, as explained on the back cover of the book:

> *A panda walks into a café. He orders a sandwich, eats it, then draws a gun and fires two shots in the air.*
>
> *"Why?" asks the confused waiter, as the panda makes towards the exit. The panda produces a badly punctuated wildlife manual and tosses it over his shoulder.*

> *"Well, I'm a panda," he says, at the door. "Look it up."*
>
> *The waiter turns to the relevant entry in the manual and, sure enough, finds an explanation.*
>
> ***Panda**. Large black-and-white bear-like mammal, native to China. Eats, shoots and leaves."*

Another reason for the book's appeal was that it was well written, entertaining and full of humour. Nevertheless, many people were taken by surprise by the book's success, and it certainly provided plenty of prompts for discussion in educational establishments and among the wider public.

That punctuation should be such a topic for discussion and debate is interesting, particularly given that we managed quite well without it for many centuries. The word *punctuation* derives from the Latin *pungere*, 'to prick' (think of 'puncture'); this gives *punctus* – 'pierced' – as the participle. Until 300 years ago very little punctuation was used in texts, and then its main function was to help actors when reading aloud. The marks showed suitable places to pause, breathe, and change the emphasis or tone of voice. Gradually, punctuation marks began to be used more widely, and during the eighteenth century they started to look and be used as they are today (Crystal, 1987).

In this chapter, you will look at the range of punctuation used in English and consider ways in which we might develop children's understanding. You will also see that punctuation can be a very powerful tool when we write, enabling us to express ideas in different ways and often substituting for the tone, volume and expression we are able to use in speech. You will find out more about all major punctuation marks, but you will need to look at Chapter 7 for details about apostrophes. Such are the problems associated with correct usage of apostrophes that we have devoted an entire chapter to them!

Why is punctuation important?

Choosing punctuation well is about communicating meaning precisely. When we speak, we can rely on gesture, tone of voice and body language to make ourselves understood. There is often a shared context; those involved are usually present, unless it is a phone or conference call. Everyday speech will often be fragmented and rarely be in complete sentences, and if the meaning is unclear it can be immediately clarified.

The distinction between speech and writing is, of course, more blurred than this. Take, for example, a lecture or presentation; or the rehearsed speech you give when you have something difficult to communicate; or a message left on voicemail. These will be less spontaneous and may be carefully prepared. They can also be dynamic and can be altered and changed by content, tone and gesture in response to the reaction of the audience. Answerphone messages can be re-recorded. Writers, of course, do not have the same opportunity to change what they have written, unless they are publishing on the web. Once a piece of writing is printed, there is little opportunity for revision.

The careful use of punctuation is one of many skills that writers need if they are to communicate clearly in writing: it is more than memorising and applying a set of rules. Used well, punctuation allows certain words, phrases and clauses to be emphasised and can make subtle or major changes to meaning. Thus, the same words may be given different meanings through varying the punctuation marks.

Look at the sentence below. What does it tell you?

Charles the First walked and talked half an hour after his head was cut off.

Now look at the same sentence, but with a semi-colon and a comma added:

Charles the First walked and talked; half an hour after, his head was cut off.

Without accurate punctuation, the same words can convey different meanings. Look at the two sentences below:

I saw a man eating tiger.

The host stood at the door and called the guests names.

As they stand, the sentences are grammatically accurate, but if we change the punctuation we can make them mean something quite different:

I saw a man-eating tiger.

The host stood at the door and called the guests' names.

Punctuation can be used to separate items and to draw them together. In the first example, the insertion of a hyphen between *man* and *tiger* brings the two words together and changes the meaning of the sentence. In the second, the apostrophe after *guests* shows that the names belonging to the guests were announced, rather than that the host insulted his visitors. Crystal (1996, p.151) explains:

> *Punctuation marks are the main means of showing the grammatical organisation of what you write. Hide the punctuation and you hide the grammatical structure. And if you hide the grammatical structure, you hide the meaning of what you are trying to say.*

Put another way, punctuation can help us to resolve some of the ambiguities in a text. Graddol et al. (1996, p.63) describe punctuation as *guiding the reader's interpretation of a text.* Using it accurately is an integral part of ensuring that the reader understands what you are trying to convey. It tells us who is speaking, and exactly what they say. It indicates the status of the writing: a sentence ending in an exclamation mark is read very differently from a sentence with a question mark.

The rules of punctuation are, however, not completely fixed. Just as spelling and pronunciation have changed over the years, so has punctuation. While some punctuation is correct or incorrect, more sophisticated uses can be a matter of choice or style. There will be times when we can choose between full stops, commas, colons and semi-colons; we can choose when to use exclamation marks, or decide to substitute brackets for dashes.

Text messages are rarely punctuated, and sophisticated punctuation is actively discouraged. A number of blogs suggest that using a semi-colon in a text shows that the message has been too thought-out, revised, and over-edited. Or to put it another way, *a semi-colon in a text message is the equivalent of putting on makeup to go to the gym* (Greenspan, 2011).

Research focus: rules and conventions

Bunting (1997, p.44) maintains that there are two main aspects of punctuation: *rules which must be used and conventions which are more open to interpretation.* She provides the following examples of rules in English.

- Capital letters at the beginning of sentences.

- Full stops to end sentences.

- Question marks at the end of sentences which are questions; apostrophes to mark elision (*don't*) and possession (*John's*). (*Its* is the possessive exception).

What we know about young children learning to punctuate

As we saw in Chapter 1, children come to school with a lot of intuitive knowledge about grammar and how to make meaning. Graham and Kelly (2003) draw attention to examples of young children's earliest writing attempts that contain punctuation-like symbols, although they are clear that there is a significant difference between using a symbol and understanding its significance.

Research focus: children's attitude to punctuation

In his study of children learning to punctuate, Hall (2005) compares two young writers. One of the children saw punctuation as serving no function other than being demanded by the teacher. Without a grasp of what punctuation was for, the child had omitted punctuation marks or randomly interspersed them within the text. The child's explanation for the placement of full stops included 'because it's a bit long' or 'I didn't put one in that line so I put it there'. The other child was curious about punctuation and was noticing it in her reading. She had worked out the basic relationship between punctuation and the structure of written language. Punctuation was used to demarcate units of meaning: it was an intrinsic part of the writing process. Hall points out that appreciating the basic relationship between punctuation and the structure of written language is the first major conceptual leap for children.

Hall writes that punctuation must be *a very strange object for beginning writers* (2001, p.141). His research into how young children learn to write also suggests that punctuation may be fairly low down their list of priorities, and hard for them to focus on, particularly as it is *the least visually salient aspect of writing* (2001, p.144).

However, the National Curriculum for English requires children in Year 1 to be introduced to the use of capital letters, full stops, question marks and exclamation marks to demarcate sentences. By the time they are assessed at the end of Year 2, the knowledge they need to demonstrate includes the use of commas in lists and apostrophes to mark contracted forms. When children sit the Grammar, Punctuation and Spelling test (GP&S) the end of Year 6 they will need to have a sophisticated understanding of punctuation, including the accurate use of semi-colons, colons and dashes and hyphens. The broad progression for what needs to be covered in each year group is outlined below (DfE, 2013, pp.75–9).

Year	Punctuation
1	Separation of **words** with spaces.
	Introduction to the use of **capital letters, full stops, question marks** and **exclamation marks** to demarcate **sentences**.
	Capital letters for names and for the personal **pronoun**.
2	Use of **capital letters, full stops, question marks** and **exclamation marks** to demarcate **sentences**.
	Commas to separate items in a list.
	Apostrophes to mark where letters are missing in spelling and to mark singular possession in nouns (for example, *the girl's name*).

(Continued)

(Continued)

Year	Punctuation
3	Introduction to **inverted commas** to punctuate direct speech.
4	Use of **inverted commas** and other punctuation to indicate direct speech (for example, a comma after the reporting clause; end punctuation within inverted commas: *The conductor shouted, 'Sit down!'*).
	Apostrophes to mark **plural** possession (for example, *the girl's name, the girls' names*).
	Use of commas after **fronted adverbials**.
5	**Brackets, dashes** or **commas** to indicate parenthesis.
	Use of **commas** to clarify meaning or avoid ambiguity.
6	Use of the **semi-colon, colon** and **dash** to mark the boundary between independent **clauses** (for example, *It's raining; I'm fed up*).
	Use of the **colon** to introduce a list and use of **semi-colons** within lists.
	Punctuation of **bullet points** to list information.
	How **hyphens** can be used to avoid ambiguity (for example, *man eating shark* versus *man-eating shark*, or *recover* versus *re-cover*).

Teaching punctuation – what primary teachers need to know

Full stops and question marks

The most basic concept in punctuation is the sentence. Kress (1982) reminds us that this is a key element of learning to write, but, as we have seen, this is not the basic unit in which children – or most adults – speak.

If you have taught at Key Stage 1, you may frequently have come across children putting a capital letter at the beginning of every 'sentence', but a full stop at the end of every line. As we have seen from Hall (2001), the basic relationship between punctuation and the structure of written language is not yet clear to them. This practice also mirrors some of the texts young learners read, comprising short sentences and just one line to a page. Even towards the end of Key Stage 2, you may find children who are still struggling with demarcating sentences correctly. We recently came across a Year 5 writer who had been set a target for his writing: 'Remember capital letters and full stops.' He was a keen writer and when he had the opportunity, he would write pages of rushed narrative packed full of action, but with no punctuation. He had kept the same target for the whole of Year 4. Not only was this enormously dispiriting, but it was also likely to remain the case throughout Year 5 unless something significant happened to change the situation.

The case study below shows how one teacher used a novel approach to encourage her class to focus on the functions of punctuation marks.

Case study: Year 6 children who use very little punctuation

Zafira's Year 6 class included several children whose punctuation, apart from full stops, tended to be erratic or absent. She found that asking the children to go back and check their work before they handed it in was ineffective: most seemed content to add a random comma or two and then submit their writing again. Zafira decided that she would get children to read aloud and record their work, so that they could listen to it and follow the text to see where punctuation might be needed. She provided two voice-recorders and a quiet space for children to do this. She found that not only did many children develop a greater awareness of where they had missed punctuation when they listened to their recordings, but that many also paused as they were recording to insert punctuation. As a result, Zafira decided to make time for children to read their work aloud to each other more often, and to encourage them to help each other to add and correct punctuation.

Try reading your own writing aloud. If you have ever written a story for children, you may well have checked it carefully, but you will probably discover when you read it aloud that there are mistakes, repetitions and omissions which your proofreading didn't reveal.

Curriculum links

Children should indicate grammatical and other features by:

- using commas to clarify meaning or avoid ambiguity in writing;
- using hyphens to avoid ambiguity;
- using brackets, dashes or commas to indicate parenthesis;
- using semi-colons, colons or dashes to indicate a stronger sub-division of a sentence than a comma;
- punctuating bullet points consistently.

Asking children to look at a list of sentences and identify which require full stops and which need question marks may help to reinforce the use of punctuation. An alternative to this is to provide the children with answers and ask them to write their own questions in as creative a way as possible. You might even show them the well-known *Two Ronnies* sketch in which Corbett specialises in answering the question before last (www.youtube.com/watch?v=BvmRI6K8TS8).

Children could be asked to think of questions that might produce answers such as:

Half past nine.
Yes, but only on Saturdays.
Florida.

They also need to know that when the question is indirect, the sentence does not need a question mark:

> *She wondered what he was thinking of.*
>
> *He asked whether the train was on time.*

Capital letters

Historically, capital letters have been used to portray formality. In the forum of Ancient Rome, the emperors' deeds were written in capital letters. Until the nineteenth century it was common for all nouns to be capitalised in English (they still are in German). Today, however, dropping the initial capital letter from a company name can be seen as a mark of significant success. The move from *Hoover* to *hoover*, now a generic term for vacuum cleaners, and *Google* to *google*, now often a generic term for search engines (despite the Google company's efforts to resist this), demonstrates how influential these companies have become.

The rules for using capital letters are generally quite straightforward.

- A sentence always begins with a capital letter.
- A proper noun, such as your name, always begins with a capital letter.
- A proper noun, such as a country or place and words relating to them, begins with a capital letter: Portugal, Portuguese. You do not capitalise these words when they are part of a fixed phrase such as 'french windows'; this has no direct connection with France.
- Titles of special days, books, plays and films begin with a capital letter: Diwali, *The Tempest*, *Mission Impossible*. A capital letter is needed for all the main words, but not for connecting words such as 'a', 'of', 'the': *The House at Pooh Corner; The Curious Incident of the Dog in the Night-time.*
- Use capital letters at the beginning of an abbreviation if the original form starts with a capital letter: Doctor, Dr. If you are using the first letter of abbreviated words, every letter should be a capital: MP (Member of Parliament).
- The pronoun 'I' is always capitalised.

There are some interesting exceptions.

- Although the names of the days of the week and the months of the year are written with a capital letter, the seasons (spring, summer, autumn, winter) are not.
- Whether or not you capitalise the main words in the title of a book at the end of an academic assignment will depend on the referencing system being used. The American Psychological Association (APA, 2010) style, for example, only requires you to use a capital letter for the first word of a title: *Grammar, punctuation and spelling in primary schools.* The referencing system used in this book does require capital letters for main words.

The comma

The use of the comma can only be understood when children have an understanding of the nature of a sentence. Brien (2012) writes that this is one of the most difficult pieces of punctuation to teach, because writers need to make judgements about when it is helpful. She points out that *many writers have a quirky approach to commas because they want to depict idiosyncratic speech or distinct authorial voice*, citing Jane Austen's lavish use of commas as an example (2012, p.113). Truss suggests that the comma, more than any other mark, *requires the writer to use intelligent discretion* (2003, p.96). There is a well-known story about Oscar Wilde arriving exhausted at a dinner party. When asked why, he said: *I spent the entire morning putting a comma in and the afternoon taking it out* (Harborough Sherard, 1902, p.72).

A comma is generally used in one of two ways: to help the reader by separating parts of a sentence; or to separate items in a list. Both are intended to make the sentence clearer. For example, 'Let's eat Dad' is decidedly worrying without a comma before 'Dad'.

Children are regularly taught that commas are not used before 'and'. We may be wiser to include the word **normally** in the sentence, as there are times when commas before 'and' can be useful. Take a look at this sentence:

> *My favourite jacket potato toppings are tuna, beans and bacon and cheese.*

This sentence doesn't make clear whether 'bacon' is a favourite and 'cheese' is another favourite, or whether it is 'bacon and cheese' together or beans and bacon together. Adding commas clarifies things:

> *My favourite jacket potato toppings are tuna, beans, and bacon and cheese.*
>
> *My favourite jacket potato toppings are tuna, beans and bacon, and cheese.*

Using semi-colons (see later in the chapter) might clarify things still further so that there can be no misunderstandings:

> *My favourite jacket potato toppings are tuna; beans; and bacon and cheese.*
>
> *My favourite jacket potato toppings are tuna; beans and bacon; and cheese.*

Avoiding the comma splice

The comma splice occurs when a comma is used to connect two independent clauses or a clause and an independent phrase. Here is an example:

> *Jenny threw open the door, she was in a bad mood.*

A simple rule of thumb to tell whether a comma is being used to 'splice' main clauses together is to see if you could substitute a full stop. In this example, the two clauses make sense separately.

Jenny threw open the door. She was in a bad mood.

In this case a full stop works well, but it can lead to very staccato sentences and you may want to suggest a closer link between the clauses. If you want to show that some sentences are more closely linked in meaning than others, you could substitute a dash or a semi-colon:

Jenny threw open the door – she was in a bad mood.

Jenny threw open the door; she was in a bad mood.

It would also be possible to link the clauses by inserting a conjunction such as 'and', 'but', 'although', 'even though', 'yet' or 'because'.

Jenny threw open the door even though she was in a bad mood.

Activity

Some **comma-splicers** will be good punctuators in many other respects. You may even be known to comma-splice when you are under pressure. Look at the following sentences and identify which sentences are correct, and where there is a comma splice. Choose ways of correcting them.

I hate writing assignments, I always leave them until the last minute.

Sally loves to keep fit, she runs a marathon at least once a year.

The team was determined to win, they had lost the last four matches.

Walking round Windermere, we saw a beautiful rainbow.

This is a lovely cheesecake, you must give me the recipe.

Despite the bad weather, the village fete was a great success.

The following sentences are correct as they each have a main clause and a dependent phrase:

Walking round Windermere, we saw a beautiful rainbow.

Despite the bad weather, the village fete was a great success.

The other sentences have two clauses which could be linked, but a comma is not sufficient for this. They could be punctuated as follows:

> *I hate writing assignments: I always leave them until the last minute.*
>
> *Sally loves to keep fit: she runs a marathon at least once a year.*
>
> *The team was determined to win: they had lost the last four matches.*
>
> *This is a lovely cheesecake: you must give me the recipe.*

Alternatively, you might use a dash rather than a colon.

Exclamation marks

Cut out all those exclamation marks, F. Scott Fitzgerald wrote. *An exclamation mark is like laughing at your own jokes* (cited in Clandfield, 2011).

Despite Fitzgerald's exhortation, the exclamation mark is having something of a renaissance. Texts, tweets and e-mails in particular are often littered with exclamation marks; sometimes to the extent that they have become a replacement for the full stop.

'Hiya!! Look at this!!'

and the reply 'Thanks!!!!'

This may simply be because the exclamation mark feels like a friendlier and more informal form of punctuation. An e-mail that says 'Thanks for the tickets!!' has much more emotion than 'Thanks for the tickets'.

An exclamation mark is conventionally used at the end of a sentence. It can be:

Exclamative: *What a nightmare!*

Imperative: *Go away!*

Declarative: *It's a wrap!*

An interjection to show strong emotion: *Oh no!*

We can draw on a wealth of material when children are learning about exclamation marks. They are highly visible in environmental print: tabloid newspaper headlines provide a rich source and collecting these can be a helpful addition to your working wall, or classroom display.

As with other aspects of punctuation, once you have taught children how to use them you are likely to find that they are overused as they are tried out in different contexts. This is quite usual, but do remind the children to beware of this!! Using exclamation marks too often reduces their power!!! Used judiciously, they have greater impact.

Inverted commas

Truss (2003, p.150) recalls a conversation with Nigel Hall when he described the writing of a small boy who regularly peppered his work with inverted commas. When asked to explain this, he replied, 'Because it's me who is doing all the talking!'

The placement of inverted commas when writing dialogue demands a lot of young writers:

- placing inverted commas around the words being said;
- starting each piece of speech with a capital letter except when the speech is broken up: 'If you think I've forgotten,' said Suzy firmly, 'you are very much mistaken.' Direct speech which is split into parts may only require a single capital letter (think of the direct speech as a sentence within a sentence);
- punctuating the speech before we close it;
- starting a new line for each new speaker.

You may find that children have a better understanding of inverted commas if they are introduced to them through texts with speech bubbles, and comics. Speech bubbles could be blanked out and children invited to compose dialogue. Subsequently, they could write their own comic strip using speech bubbles, before changing this into direct speech and adding text to show the identity of speakers. Take full advantage of the wonderful picture books you may be reading to model the use of direct speech, such as Lauren Child's *Beware of the Storybook Wolves* where direct speech is shown in a different font. Wordless picture books with rich, complex plots and narrative structures invite opportunities for children to freeze-frame scenes and add dialogue. When you are using freeze-framing to explore texts, you might ask two children to stand either side of the children in the frame and to hold up cards with inverted commas as each character explains his or her thoughts.

In the case study below, note how the teacher makes use of texts rather than exercises to focus children's attention on punctuating direct speech.

Case study: learning to use inverted commas

Lloyd, a final year BA student, found, when listening to children in his Year 3 class read during shared and guided reading, that many seemed to ignore inverted commas and failed to change tone or expression when speech began or ended. He decided to use shared reading to focus children's attention on the function of inverted commas.

→

Lloyd chose a passage of dialogue from Roald Dahl's *Matilda* and read it to the children, changing his voice when Miss Trunchbull, Matilda or other characters spoke. He then allocated roles to children and asked them to read only the words their characters said, while everyone else read all of the words which were not direct speech. Occasionally, a few children either read beyond their speech or read into other people's speech, but almost everyone quickly grasped the idea that inverted commas surrounded the words spoken.

Lloyd went on to develop a shared writing activity in which children used mini-whiteboards to write suggested dialogue for an invented episode involving Matilda at school as a conversation progressed. Lloyd asked for examples of what characters might say and wrote some on the board. He then asked children for suggestions as to how words might have been said, for example, *shouted Miss Trunchbull loudly*; *whispered Amanda nervously*. As the dialogue developed, Lloyd drew attention to punctuation, discussing the use of commas, full stops, question marks and exclamation marks.

There are many other ways in which you might develop children's understanding of correct usage of inverted commas. You might follow up an activity such as Lloyd's by giving children short extracts from playscripts and asking them to rewrite them as direct speech. This is best done on a computer so that children can focus on the key learning by cutting and pasting, rather than having to write everything out by hand.

Curriculum links

Children should learn how to use inverted commas in direct speech from Year 3 and learn that they are also known as inverted commas. It is important to explain that inverted commas can be single or double (increasingly they tend to be single). As children develop their writing, they may sometimes need to use inverted commas within inverted commas, as below:

> *"I asked her to tell me where it was and she just said 'I don't know!' in a really grumpy way," said James angrily.*

On these occasions, we use whichever version of inverted commas we didn't use around the main speech to indicate the quotation within it.

Some teachers show classes how to remember the correct punctuation for direct speech with the mnemonic: *66 Capital One of 4 99*, which translates as:

- 66 – open inverted commas;
- capital: speech begins with a capital letter (unless it is the second part of a sentence broken by 'he', 'said', etc. – see below);

(Continued)

(Continued)

- one of 4 (? ! , .);
- 99 (close inverted commas).

Of course, they might equally well teach them 6 *Capital One of 4* 9. If you use this mnemonic it is important to remind children that the inverted commas are not really numbers at all, but just have the same shapes as 6 and 9.

Activity: punctuating direct speech

Use inverted commas and other punctuation in the following examples of direct speech. You should not change any of the words, but sometimes you may need to change a letter from lower to upper case. See below for answers.

1. He called loudly I want you to hurry up and get ready.
2. I will not she said put up with any more of this.
3. Before Christmas she said I was a happy person.
4. What do you mean by I don't like it?
5. He asked do you know what the expression too many cooks spoil the broth means?
6. John said, David I do not like you.
7. John, said David, I do not like you.
8. Please let me go pleaded Sue I will wash up for a week if you do.
9. Don't cried Bob let me catch you doing that again.
10. I like She Loves You best of all the Beatles' songs said Paul.

Please note that some punctuation, such as the use of exclamation marks rather than, say, full stops, may vary from author to author.

1. He called loudly, 'I want you to hurry up and get ready!'

2. 'I will not,' she said, 'put up with any more of this.'

3. 'Before Christmas,' she said, 'I was a happy person.'

4. 'What do you mean by "I don't like it"?' asked Jo.

5. He asked, 'Do you know what the expression "too many cooks spoil the broth" means?'

6. John said, 'David, I do not like you.'

7. 'John,' said David, 'I do not like you.'

8. 'Please let me go,' pleaded Sue.' I will wash up for a week if you do.'

9. 'Don't,' cried Bob, 'let me catch you doing that again!'

10. 'I like "She Loves You" best of all the Beatles' songs,' said Paul.

Colons and semi-colons

In Year 6, children are introduced to the use of the colon and semi-colon.

The winner of the 2013 Booker Prize, Hilary Mantel, says she is addicted to semi-colons (cited in Truss, 2003). Rosen (2012) blogs that he tries to avoid them altogether, and expresses a concern that children might think that they *have* to use them. He writes, *I like short sentences. I like to punctuate them with full stops and not semi-colons. I got this from a writer I like. His name is Charles Dickens. Moral of the story: don't read Charles Dickens, you might pick up bad habits.*

The 'rules' governing the use of colons and semi-colons are flexible. Their purpose is to indicate a stronger sub-division of a sentence than a comma, but less final than a full stop. The following guidelines may be helpful.

Colons

The colon can be used to indicate that an example is following or to introduce a list, such as:

> *All students undertake to: attend all lectures and seminars, submit assignments on time, and meet their tutor each term.*

The use of the colon separates and highlights the list showing that each separate item is a requirement.

A colon is often preceded by a complete sentence and may also be used before a second clause that expands or illustrates the first.

> *She was very tired: it was three in the morning.*

> *He pulled back the curtains: bright sunlight lit up the room.*

Semi-colons

A semi-colon can be used to separate two main clauses in a sentence instead of a conjunction or comma. It is most suitable when the clauses are closely related in meaning. The following sentences make perfect sense when joined together in this way.

> *I enjoyed the concert; it was a pleasure to be there.*

> *Some students are well organised with assignments; others leave them until the last minute.*

There may also be times when the semi-colon indicates the relationship between two sentences.

> *Sam vacuumed the floor for the third time.*
>
> *The party had been a great success.*

If this becomes *Sam vacuumed the floor for the third time; the party had been a great success*, the relationship between the two can be inferred.

Semi-colons can also be used to separate items in a list, usually when these items consist of longer phrases or where commas would not make separations clear enough, as in our earlier example of jacket potato toppings.

> *He packed a large jar of yeast extract; a jar of his favourite marmalade; several tins of baked beans; the largest box of tea he could find; and a packet of digestive biscuits.*

Once children know how to use them, semi-colons can add a level of sophistication to their writing.

Dashes and brackets

Dashes and brackets perform similar functions and can be used to replace colons, semi-colons and commas. While colons and semi-colons often suggest a link between the two parts of the sentence, dashes and brackets can be less connected. They are useful for separating off parts of a sentence which introduce information or ideas that are new, or are not essential to an understanding of the rest of the sentence.

Dashes

Dashes tend to be used in more informal writing such as personal e-mails or blogs, and can often be seen in newspaper reporting. They are often, but not always, used in pairs.

> *Several hundred residents – like the couple in this photograph – have been left homeless by the floods.*

Dashes can also introduce after-thoughts, particularly those that are surprising or unexpected:

> *Everyone turned up for the wedding – even Sally.*

They tend to be more conversational, and it is hard to use them inaccurately. Just remember to use them sparingly when you are writing formally.

Brackets (parentheses)

A parenthesis is a word or phrase inserted into a sentence to explain, clarify or elaborate. It may be placed in brackets or commas.

The English planning was due in (along with everything else) but it was nowhere near completion.

The lead singer (despite being well into his seventies) was amazing.

They can also be used to enclose a comment by the person writing.

Jas is (I believe) the best child for this role.

He was clearly furious about it (not that I blamed him).

The term parentheses can also refer to the brackets themselves.

Activity

Find different ways of punctuating the following to give very different meanings:

Go slow children

Private no fishing allowed

Shoot Jones

Scream a silly word every day

Go slow children: *Go slow, children. Go, slow children. Go slow – children.*

Private no fishing allowed: *PRIVATE! No fishing allowed. Private? No, fishing allowed. Private – no fishing allowed. Private, no fishing allowed.*

Shoot Jones: *SHOOT, Jones! Shoot Jones?*

Scream a silly word every day. *Scream a silly word every day. Scream a silly word – every day.*

Hyphens

A hyphen can be used for a wide range of purposes.

- To join the different parts of a compound noun (see Chapter 2), such as *city-centre*, although it is more usual for compound nouns to be written as single words:
  - *football*
  - *playground*
  - *greenhouse*

- In compound adjectives and longer phrases used as modifiers before nouns:
  - *the bad-tempered ladybird*
  - *a well-known singer*
  - *a five-year-old boy*

- In compound nouns where the second part is a short word like *in, off, up* or *by*:
  - *drive-in*
  - *kick-off*
  - *top-up*
  - *passer-by*

- With certain prefixes including *co-, non-,* and *ex-* that traditionally require hyphens:
  - *co-construct*
  - *ex-teacher*
  - *non-viable*

- It is quite a common mistake for people to write 'non' as if it were a word in its own right (it should be *none* when we use it as a word) by failing to hyphenate it to another word. *Non* is, of course, a word in French (no), but in English it is a **bound morpheme** (see Chapter 2).

- When a compound formed from two nouns is made into a verb:
  - *risk-taking*
  - *I am going strawberry-picking.*

- When a compound verb form is made, either by adding a noun to make the original verb more specific:
  - *I am going strawberry-picking.*
  - *They enjoyed mountain-climbing.*

  Or by coupling two verbs together:
  - *She always blow-dries her hair.*
  - *It is illegal to drink-drive.*

- To add clarity:
  - *Deice and reignite are much harder to read than de-ice and re-ignite.*

- To divide words at the end of a line of print. If children need to do this, encourage them to divide the word between syllables to help the reader: for example *sur-prise* rather than *su-rprise.*

June Crebbin's poem 'River' (in Foster, 2009) uses hyphens to create evocative compound nouns.

boat-carrier

    bank-lapper

        home-provider

           tree-reflector

      leaf-catcher

    field-wanderer

stone-smoother

    fast-mover

        gentle-stroller

          sun-sparkler

          sea-seeker

Try finishing her 'City River' poem (in Corbett, 2006, p.254) in the same way:

wall

    factory

        backstreet

           bridge

      steps

    park

summer

    ducks

        choppy

          crows

         onward

Bullet points

Bullet points are useful when we want to present a list, especially of items with several words, as information can be easier to read than in a sentence. There are different ways to present bullet points and the key is to be consistent.

1. Bullet points that follow a colon

If there is an introductory sentence, a colon should follow the sentence and each bullet should begin with a lower-case letter. Put a full stop after the last bullet point.

Bullet points can be used in different texts, including:

- *essays;*
- *information texts;*
- *presentations.*

When bullet points consist of more than one sentence, start each bullet point with a capital letter and end it with a full stop. For example:

Before you hand in your work:

- *Check that you haven't made any spelling mistakes. You can use a computer spellchecker to check your spelling.*
- *Look carefully for any missing capital letters. Ask a friend to help you.*
- *Make sure that your writing is easy to read. If in doubt, cross the word out and write it again.*

2. Bullet points that follow a heading

Bullet points that follow a heading should start with a capital letter and end with a full stop. For example:

Rules

- *Always be polite.*
- *Walk when you are in school.*
- *Open doors and hold them for other people.*

Activity

In the two quotes from *Winnie the Pooh* below, the punctuation has been changed for symbols and the capital letters have been removed. It will not take you long to work out what the symbols stand for, but this can be an active way of encouraging children to engage with and talk about the punctuation marks on the page.

1. #it*s snowing still~# said eeyore gloomily ☐ #so it is ☐ #and freezing ☐#

   #is itᵃ # #yes~# said eeyore ☐ #however~# he said~ brightening up a little~ #we haven*t had an earthquake lately ☐#

2. #it is more fun to talk with someone who doesn*t use long~ difficult words but rather short~ easy words like #what about lunch[a] #

1. 'It's snowing still,' said Eeyore gloomily. 'So it is.'
'And freezing.'
'Is it?'
'Yes,' said Eeyore. 'However,' he said, brightening up a little, 'we haven't had an earthquake lately.'

2. 'It is more fun to talk with someone who doesn't use long, difficult words but rather short, easy words like, "What about lunch?"'

Another investigative approach is to present children with a short, unpunctuated passage. Ask them to read it through and then read it again, walking as they read. Invite them to pause briefly where the text seems to indicate that a comma is required, and pause for longer when a full stop might be required. They could begin working individually and go on to discuss with partners where other punctuation may be needed. Avoid asking them to write it out in their best handwriting, unless you are focusing on handwriting rather than punctuation.

Teaching punctuation

Learning to punctuate is something we continue to do as we become more sophisticated writers. It is a hard skill to master, because it is not discrete but an integral part of effective writing. Exercises and worksheets are unlikely to succeed in helping children to punctuate well, no matter how engaging and colourful they are. Developing a sophisticated knowledge of punctuation needs to occur in the context of children's deepening understanding of the craft of writing, and the importance of making meaning clear to the reader.

Consider trying the following tried and tested approaches.

- Explicitly draw attention to punctuation in reading. Help children to see the power of punctuation and how it helps writers to convey meaning.

- Think aloud as you model writing, so that children are able to see and hear the choices you make as you punctuate writing.

- Make writing meaningful. If children write for authentic purposes and audiences, making sense will genuinely matter.

- Draw children's attention to how changes in punctuation impact on meaning. Include the use of word play, puzzles and investigations to do this.

- Provide opportunities for children to write for a wide range of purposes: challenge them to think about their use of punctuation and talk about what is most appropriate to make the meaning clear to the reader.

- Establish writing or response partners, so that all children have the opportunity to hear their work read aloud and see and hear where punctuation needs adding, changing or deleting.

- Provide opportunities for children to discuss punctuation in their writing with you and their peers.

Learning outcomes review

You should now be confident about what you need to know as a primary teacher to teach punctuation well, and be confident in your own subject knowledge. Punctuation is complex, and you will know that we cannot simply teach children how to punctuate and expect them to apply this knowledge accurately throughout their writing. Demarcating simple sentences is the first building block (Hall, 1999). You will also be aware that although there are some rules governing punctuation, other things are a matter of choice, and this is one of the many challenges we face when we teach children to punctuate. Most importantly, you will know that teaching punctuation is integral to teaching good writing and is never an end in itself.

Self-assessment questions

Punctuate the sentences below. You may need to change some lower-case letters to upper case, and you may even wish to use italics for some words or phrases.

1. david julie rosemary and gill sat in trafalgar square
2. sam who was thirty two had thinning blond hair
3. oh no cried sue as she saw the damage bill had done to her new bmw
4. you shouted the teacher have the manners of a two year old
5. rimmer sat miserably in the control room of red dwarf

Select the punctuation mark that is used for each of the following purposes.

1. To separate the different parts of a sentence and provide clarity for the reader.
2. To separate two main clauses in a sentence.
3. Before a second clause that expands or illustrates the first.
4. At the end of an interjection to indicate strong feeling or emotion.
5. In informal writing to replace brackets and other punctuation marks.

Choose from the list below:

full stop	question mark	exclamation mark
semi-colon	colon	dash

Further reading

Jeffries, S. (2009) *The Joy of Exclamation Marks!* Available from: **www.guardian.co.uk/ books/2009/apr/29/exclamation-mark-punctuation**

A light-hearted and interesting viewpoint on the use of exclamation marks.

Truss, L. (2003) *Eats, Shoots & Leaves: The Zero Tolerance Approach to Punctuation*. London: Profile Books.

For an entertaining and interesting look at punctuation, with lots of examples, Lynne Truss's book is ideal.

Waugh, D., Allott, K., Waugh, R., English, E. and Bulmer, E. (2014) *The Spelling, Punctuation and Grammar app*. Morecambe: Children Count Ltd (available through the App Store).

This app provides guidance and activities on all aspects of grammar, spelling and punctuation.

References

APA (2010) *Publication Manual of the American Psychological Association*, 6th edition. Washington, DC: APA.

Brien, J. (2012) *Teaching Primary English*. London: Sage.

Bunting, R. (1997) *Teaching about Language in the Primary Years*. London: David Fulton.

Clandfield, L. (2011) *Online writing is great!!!* Available from: **www.macmillan dictionaryblog.com/online-writing-is-great** (accessed 18.6.13).

Corbett, P. (2006) *The Works Key Stage 1*. London: Macmillan Children's Books.

Crystal, D. (1987) *The Cambridge Encyclopedia of Language*. Cambridge: Cambridge University Press.

Crystal, D. (1996) *Discover Grammar*. Harlow: Longman.

DfE (2013) *The National Curriculum in England: Key stages 1 and 2 framework document*. London: DfE. Available from: **www.gov.uk/government/uploads/system/uploads/attachment_ data/file/425601/PRIMARY_national_curriculum.pdf** (accessed 25.10.15).

Foster, J. (2009) *The Works 8*. London: Macmillan Children's Books.

Graddol, D., Leith, D. and Swann, J. (1996) *English History, Diversity and Change*. London: Routledge with the Open University.

Graham, J. and Kelly, C. (2007) *Writing Under Control*. London: David Fulton.

Greenspan, S. (2011) *11 Secret Meanings Behind Punctuation in Text Messages*. Available from: **www.wired.com/underwire/2011/06/secret-meanings-text-message- punctuation/** (accessed 18.6.13).

Hall, N. (1999) *Punctuation in the Primary School*. Reading: Reading and Language Information Centre.

Hall, N. (2001) Developing understanding of punctuation with young readers and writers, in Evans, J. (ed.) *The Writing Classroom: Aspects of Writing and the Primary Child 3–11*. London: David Fulton.

Hall, N. (2005) *The Development of Punctuation Knowledge in Children Aged Seven to Eleven*: ESRC Full Research Report, R000238348. Swindon: ESRC.

Harborough Sherard, R. (1902) *Oscar Wilde: The Story and an Unhappy Friendship, with Portraits and Facsimile Letters*. London: Hermes Press.

Jeffries, S. (2009) *The Joy of Exclamation Marks!* Available from: **www.guardian.co.uk/ books/2009/apr/29/exclamation-mark-punctuation** (accessed 27.10.15).

Kress, G. (1982) *Learning to Write*. London: Routledge and Kegan Paul.

Rosen. M. (2012) *Punctuation: semi colon terrorism from the DfE*. Available from: **http:// michaelrosenblog.blogspot.co.uk/2012/07/punctuation-semi-colon-terrorism-from. html** (accessed 18.6.13).

Truss, L. (2003) *Eats, Shoots & Leaves: The Zero Tolerance Approach to Punctuation*. London: Profile Books.

7 Apostrophes

Learning outcomes

By reading this chapter you will develop:

- an understanding of the correct use of apostrophes for both contraction and possession;
- an appreciation of children's possible misconceptions about apostrophes;
- an understanding of how to teach apostrophes effectively.

Teachers' Standards
This chapter will help you with the following Teachers' Standards.

3   Demonstrate good subject and curriculum knowledge:
- have a secure knowledge of the relevant subject(s) and curriculum areas, foster and maintain pupils' interest in the subject, and address misunderstandings;
- demonstrate a critical understanding of developments in the subject and curriculum areas, and promote the value of scholarship;
- demonstrate an understanding of and take responsibility for promoting high standards of literacy, articulacy and the correct use of Standard English, whatever the teacher's specialist subject.

Activity
Try the exercise below before you read this chapter, and then try a similar exercise in the self-assessment questions at the end of the chapter. The sentences below do not have any apostrophes. Can you place apostrophes in appropriate places? (Answers are provided in Appendix 2.)

1. The dogs arent used to their kennels.
2. The snows been falling all day but there still isnt enough to make snowballs.
3. Jacks mother didnt send him out to swap the cow for some beans.
4. The mens team lost to the womens team by three goals to two.
5. The Joneses roof had a hole in it.

How did you do? If you got everything right, congratulations: you probably already understand how to use apostrophes correctly. However, even if you did, look again at your answers and consider how and why children might make mistakes and how you would address their misconceptions.

Introduction

This book includes a chapter on punctuation, and apostrophes are usually discussed under that heading. However, we have devoted a whole chapter to apostrophes because this little punctuation mark seems to cause more problems than any other. A walk through almost any market will reveal misplaced apostrophes on stalls (carrot's, potato's, bean's, etc.), and even major retailing chains sometimes struggle to place apostrophes correctly: a leading supermarket in York, for example, had 'childrens' books' for sale over the Christmas period in 2012, while the Stockton branch of a well-known department store recently had a sign pointing to 'Ladie's Toilets'. You will also often see misplaced apostrophes on vans which have been commercially painted with details of a company – painter's and decorator's, etc. So why does the apostrophe cause so much confusion?

Part of the problem, as you will see later in this chapter, is that the way apostrophes are used has changed over time so that what was once acceptable is no longer considered so. For instance, until the 1960s it was common to see aeroplanes referred to as *'planes.* These days this is very uncommon, and *planes* has become the normal usage. Another problem for children and people learning English is that they so often encounter misplaced apostrophes that they may be confused about what is correct. The research focus below shows how some writers have responded to frequent misuse of apostrophes.

Research focus: controversial apostrophes

Ian Mayes, a journalist, provided a definition for a strange insect (2005, p.118):

> **Apostrofly:** *an insect that lands at random on the printed page, depositing an apostrophe wherever it lands.*

The tendency for some people to use apostrophes almost at random has also led to some rather obsessive pieces of journalism. For example, the *Sydney Morning Herald* has a regular column by Apostrophe Man (George Richards), which has been emulated in Boston, USA, where a retired journalist, John Richard, formed an Apostrophe Protection Society. John and his son Stephen send letters to businesses in Boston which misuse apostrophes:

> *Dear Sir or Madam. Because there seems to be some doubt about the use of the apostrophe, we are taking the liberty of drawing your attention to an incorrect use [they insert the misuse here]. We would like to emphasise that we do not intend any criticism, but are just reminding you of correct usage should you wish to put right the mistake.*

→

One of the *Guardian* newspaper's top-selling T-shirts, incidentally, proclaims the wearer to be a member of the Apostrophe Preservation Society.

However, there are also people who have campaigned to get rid of apostrophes, including the late George Bernard Shaw, and the organisation Kill the Apostrophe, which can be found at: www.killtheapostrophe.com/. Shaw called the apostrophe an *uncouth bacillus* – a reference either to its shape or its infectiousness! – and refused to use it in many words, such as *hes*, *wont*, or *shant*. These look strange to us, but they are unambiguous and may provoke the reader to wonder why this did not catch on.

As one might expect, the history of the apostrophe is as long, complicated and contentious as are the rules for its use. The origins of the apostrophe being used to show a dropped *h* may come directly from ancient Greek, which has no letter for *h*. Any word that started with a vowel had a little sign over the first letter to show whether or not it should be *aspirated* (pronounced with an 'h'). So Ἰχθυς (*ichthus – a fish*) starts with an unaspirated vowel, while Ἵππος (*hippos – a horse*) sounds different. A very similar mark is used today to show the lack of an h-sound in such phrases as *'orses 'ooves*, when the writer is conveying the accent or dialect of a character, so it seems likely that when writers first wanted to show this effect, they chose the Greeks' way of marking it.

So apostrophes have a long, if not always distinguished, history, but do they serve any useful purpose? Marsh and Hodsdon (2010) justify the use of apostrophes by using an example of four phrases with identical words but different placements of apostrophes, so that each means something different depending on the positions of the apostrophes:

- *my sister's friend's books* (refers to one sister and her friend);
- *my sister's friends' books* (one sister with lots of friends);
- *my sisters' friend's books* (more than one sister, and their friend);
- *my sisters' friends' books* (more than one sister, and their friends).

The author Kingsley Amis, given the challenge of producing a sentence in which an apostrophe was necessary for clarity, came up with:

- *Those things over there are my husband's.*
- *Those things over there are my husbands'.*
- *Those things over there are my husbands.*

The first of these is quite unproblematic – it clearly suggests a woman with an untidy partner. The second could be spoken by, perhaps, an elderly lady who has been widowed two or three times. The third is, frankly, somewhat disturbing.

Why are apostrophes such a problem?

Even some teachers are not always confident in their own ability to use apostrophes, and this is evident in some classroom displays and letters sent to parents. Like many other people, they may not appreciate that apostrophes have two uses: they are used either to show omission or to show possession. No one is helped by the fact that there are lots of incorrect examples all around us, or that some possessive words like *yours*, *his*, *hers*, *ours*, *theirs*, and *its* are not written with an apostrophe, while *someone's*, *everyone's*, *no one's* and *one's* are. And then there are further complications such as what to do when words end in 's', and how to deal with words that have irregular plurals. A plethora of websites offer often quite clear guidance on using apostrophes, but a search will also reveal many which provide a forum for people to grumble about other people's misuse of apostrophes and to share examples of this. However, it seems that even one of the groups who are often derided for their use of apostrophes may have some historic justification for their errors.

Research focus: greengrocers' apostrophes

Apostrophes used incorrectly to form plural words are sometimes known as 'greengrocers' apostrophes' because, traditionally, they were often seen on fruit and vegetable market stalls (Truss, 2003). Because the plural form of most nouns used in English sounds, when spoken aloud, like the possessive form (for example, 'the apple's core' and 'a bag of apples'), people sometimes give both versions an apostrophe.

It is thought that the term 'greengrocers' apostrophes' was coined in the mid-twentieth century by a teacher in Liverpool, England (Apostrophes, www.supaproofread.com). So, far from being a modern phenomenon, incorrect use of the apostrophe to make words plural was apparently common on the advertising signs of greengrocers in the UK around 60 years ago.

Indeed, Crystal (2005) shows that using an apostrophe for plurals was actually quite common in the eighteenth century, especially for words ending with a vowel. Johnson's dictionary (1755) includes the plural *vulcano's* rather than *volcanoes* (notice, too, in the definition, how an apostrophe is used in place of an 'e' in *calcin'd* (calcined).

> *Vulcáno. n.s. [Italian.] A burning mountain; volcano.*
>
> *Earth calcin'd, flies off into the air; the ashes of burning mountains, in vulcano's, will be carried to great distances.*

Apostrophes were seen as a solution to the problem of pluralising words ending with 'o', since merely adding an 's' could lead to confusion over pronunciation (*potatos, tomatos*). Crystal concludes that *to condemn someone for using such forms as potato's is actually to display linguistic ignorance – an ignorance of the logic behind such forms which the modern users are subconsciously manifesting* (2005, p.455).

However, while Crystal may be linguistically and historically correct, you should certainly not revert to the eighteenth-century usage of apostrophes, either in your writing or your teaching. Our language changes constantly, but it is hard to envisage a time when the 'greengrocers' apostrophe' will be acceptable in schools or other educational institutions.

The apostrophe exists in other languages and can be found, for example, in French, where monosyllabic words which are formed of a consonant followed by an unaccented *e* (a *schwa* – the sound of, for example, the second syllable of *sofa* in English, or *je, te, ce* and *ne* in French) is contracted with an apostrophe when in front of a word that begins with a vowel sound, for example, *j'ai, c'est, n'a pas*. The French, however, are not immune from greengrocers' apostrophes, as you can see if you look at T-shirts and some shop signs, especially where these are translated into English. The English on many T-shirts often comprises familiar words but presented in an unfamiliar order (*Static Line in Athletic's Ass!* was seen recently) and these are rivalled by some of the translations of food items on menus.

An interesting phenomenon recently was the craze in France for small enamelled lapel pins, which could be bought on market stalls throughout the country. The French have several serviceable words for pins, brooches and similar items, but these were called *pin's*. One of them was *un pin's*, while en masse they were *les pin's*. The combination of an English word and an apostrophe apparently conferred a great glamour on these little articles. This effect is comparable, perhaps, to the use of exotic but superfluous inflection marks in the name of the group Motörhead, the unnecessary apostrophe in the band Hear'say, or the umlaut in the ice-cream company Häagen Dazs (this name, incidentally, was invented in the 1950s by an American wanting a Danish-sounding name for his brand: the Danish language actually contains neither an 'ä' nor a 'zs' combination!)

Speakers of other languages sometimes seem to assume that the apostrophe gives a particularly British air to their writing – Japanese T-shirts often bear cryptic slogans such as 'My flowers' garden', or 'Team sunshine play's sport', and translated menus are also a rich source of this kind of error. Tourists in France, Spain or Italy are often offered lamb's chops (or lamb's chop's), spare rib's, or apple's pie. (The French phrase 'de maison', meaning homemade, is not infrequently translated as 'house's', though here at least the apostrophe use is correct.)

Essentially, apostrophes are used to show that something is missing. For omission or contraction this is relatively simple: 'has not' becomes 'hasn't', 'did not' becomes 'didn't', and so on. To understand the use of the possessive apostrophe, we need to go back a few hundred years. Although English has developed from many different languages, it is essentially a Germanic language which has much in common with modern German. Older versions of English used a genitive case ending to show possession. This was normally *-es*. For example, *The man's car* in German is *Das auto des mannes* (*The car of the man*). The ending *-es* on *mann* shows possession.

Chaucer's *Canterbury Tales*, written in the fourteenth century, included *The Knyghtes Tale* (*Knight's Tale*), *The Clerkes Tale* (*Clerk's Tale*) and *The Nonnes Priestes Tale* (*Nun's Priest's Tale*) and featured phrases such as *Kynges court* (*King's court*) and *Goddes love* (*God's love*). *The Millere his tale* also appears instead of *The Miller's Tale* in the original, suggesting that Chaucer had two ways of showing possession.

Given the examples from earlier versions of English and from modern German, it is often argued that we no longer use the *-es* possessive form in English and have replaced it with *-'s*, so that apostrophes always replace missing letters for possession as well as for omission.

Using apostrophes correctly

In this section, we have taken frequently asked questions about apostrophes and have answered them with answers and explanations. You will find further explanations in the glossary.

- I understand that I need to add *'s* to singular nouns to show possession, but what should I do when a word already ends with 's'?

    For singular possessives like Jess, Charles and Burns add *'s* to get *Jess's bike*, *Charles's book* and *Burns's poetry*.

    For French names which end with a silent 's', the same applies – *Rabelais's ideas, Louis's palace*.

    For names like Hodges, Bridges and Moses, where the name ends with -es pronounced -iz, just add an apostrophe – *Paul Hodges' coat, Mrs Bridges' kitchen, Moses' followers*.

    Polysyllabic names like Nicholas can have just an apostrophe, but it is also correct to add an 's' after the apostrophe; this is a rare example where it is a matter of personal choice. The 's' is generally pronounced – we would say *Nicholas's*.

    Classical or historical names like Ceres, Mars and Jesus are usually made possessive with an apostrophe but no 's'. This can lead to problems – St James, for instance, is a historical or classical figure, so by this convention we would write *St James' Church*, but when talking of a child in the class, *James's book*. As you will see later in the chapter, there are many inconsistencies to be found.

    For plurals ending with -es, add an apostrophe but not 's' to the normal plural, so that we get *the buses' routes*, *the Joneses' house*, and *the horses' stables*.

- What about expressions like a week's holiday and two days' break? Why do they get apostrophes?

    This is because they represent a shortening of the phrase 'a holiday *of* one week', and so on; the usage is similar to the possessive – *of* meaning 'belonging to'. *Three days' work* means 'the work of, or assigned to, three days'.

- Why don't pronouns have apostrophes when they are possessive?

It's not necessary to add an apostrophe because possessive pronouns already show ownership, for example, hers, his, ours, theirs and its.

The only personal possessive pronoun with an apostrophe is *one's*, which extends to *everyone's*, *someone's* and *no one's*.

The pronouns in *who's*, *it's* and *they're* are contractions of *who is* (or *who has*), *it is* (or *it has*), and *they are* respectively, and are not possessive pronouns.

However, we do add an apostrophe plus 's' to form the possessive of some indefinite pronouns:

○ somebody's car

○ nobody's fault

○ one's corgis.

Probably the most common error is to confuse *it's* (meaning 'it is') with the possessive pronoun *its*:

○ **It's** time you learned this.

○ The cat licked **its** paws.

• Why do many shops have apostrophes in their names?

Originally, the shop would have been a possession of the owner – the pharmacy owned by Jesse Boot became Boot's Chemists, then simply Boot's, just as we might talk of *going over to Tom's* when referring to a friend's house.

Many businesses have now dropped the apostrophes which once showed who owned them (*Barclays* is no longer *Barclay's* and *Currys* no longer *Curry's*, and *Chambers English Dictionary* has no apostrophe). Waterstones bookshop attracted much press attention by deciding to do this in 2012, claiming this made the name more versatile in online use. The press reacted with much lamentation and talk of falling standards of literacy and so on, and a *Guardian* journalist simply suggested that that one should carry a felt-tip pen and some correcting fluid around to correct errors wherever they are spotted, claiming *This will make you feel much better* (Mayes, 2005).

Curriculum links

What are we expected to teach at Key Stage 1? Year 1 children should read words with contractions, e.g. *I'm*, *I'll*, *we'll*, and understand that the apostrophe represents the omitted letter(s). Year 2 children should understand how spoken language can be represented in writing by learning how to use both familiar and new punctuation correctly (see Appendix 1), including full stops, capital letters, exclamation marks, question marks, commas for lists and apostrophes for contracted forms.

More on inappropriate uses of apostrophes

Some time around Years 2 to 4, most teachers experience an outbreak of apostrophes from many of their pupils. This usually coincides with children developing as independent readers and noticing that in some words an apostrophe precedes the final 's'. Joseph, a third-year undergraduate trainee, found this happening in his Year 3/4 class and, after discussion with the class teacher, devised a series of lessons to show the children how to use apostrophes correctly.

Case study: an outbreak of apostrophes

Joseph decided, after discussions with the literacy coordinator, who was also the usual teacher of his class, that he would use two main approaches to develop children's understanding of apostrophes.

He focused on apostrophes in shared reading, using a passage from a short story he had written for the class. He chose a section in which there was dialogue which included words such as *can't, won't* and *wouldn't,* and in which there were three examples of apostrophes being used for possession (*Tom's, the girls' changing room,* and *the car's headlights*). The initial focus was very much on the text and its content, but then Joseph asked the children about the apostrophes:

- Why were they there?

- What did they tell us?

He then spent a few minutes writing some examples of both possession and omission, with the children's help, all the time discussing where to place apostrophes and why they were needed.

Next, Joseph asked children in two of his literacy groups to collect and classify apostrophes by looking in pairs at different photocopied texts which he provided. First, the children used highlighters to show where the apostrophes were, using green for possession and yellow for omission. Where they were unsure about why an apostrophe was used, they used a pink highlighter. The highlighted sheets gave Joseph a quick and easy way of assessing children's knowledge and understanding and helped him to plan for further lessons to address misconceptions and explain usage. He also made extensive use of shared writing to model correct usage and looked for opportunities to discuss apostrophe usage when children were engaged in guided or independent writing.

The case study shows the importance of assessment in informing our planning for children's learning. By analysing children's errors and misconceptions you can tailor your teaching to their needs.

> ## Curriculum links
>
> In the National Curriculum (2013), Year 2 children are expected to be able to use apostrophes to mark where letters are missing in spelling and to mark singular possession in nouns (for example, *the girl's name*).
>
> Year 4 children should be able to use apostrophes to mark plural possession (for example, *the girls' names*).

Clearly, children could use a range of texts to collect and classify apostrophes, but they will usually find more examples in fiction texts, especially those which include dialogue. This is because informal versions of *do not* (*don't*), *could not* (*couldn't*) and so on are often a feature of dialogue, but tend to be used less in non-fiction or in more formal pieces of writing. In the next section, you will see how apostrophes are also used in dialogue to indicate how a speaker pronounces words.

Apostrophes in dialogue

When teaching children about apostrophes, many teachers focus on omission through examples such as *can't*, *don't* and *isn't*. These are relatively easy to understand for most children, but as their reading develops they will begin to encounter other examples, in dialogue, in stories, and on road signs, posters and lists.

> ## Activity
>
> Look at the dialogue below and decide why each apostrophe has been used:
>
> Bill turned to Jo and said, "'old on a minute! What's goin' on 'ere?'
>
> 'I 'aven't a clue,' replied Jo, 'but if 'arry doesn't 'urry up we'll get caught!'
>
> 'Too blinkin' right we will,' grumbled Bill, 'and then we'll all end up goin' t'nick.'
>
> Jo's face turned red with anger. 'It'll be 'arry's fault if we do!'

The dialogue above provides an example of the way in which authors make use of apostrophes to show the reader how characters speak. Dropped aitches (and they are aitches and not 'haitches', otherwise the word might have been written as 'aitches – see Research focus below) are signified by omitting the aitch and replacing it with an apostrophe; in two cases a final 'g' is replaced by an apostrophe to show it wasn't sounded by the speaker; and *t'nick* replaces *to the nick* (prison). The final line includes *it'll*, which is short for *it will*, and *'arry's,* which has one apostrophe to show there is a missing *h* at the beginning, and another to show that the fault belongs to Harry.

For other examples of apostrophes being used in dialogue, look at Sergeant Samways' dialogue in Roald Dahl's *Danny the Champion of the World* or at Frances Hodgson Burnett's *The Secret Garden*, in which the author reproduces the Yorkshire dialect spoken by some of her characters.

Research focus: aitch vs haitch

The dropping of aitches in dialogue is a common feature of many novels, but the name of the letter often causes confusion. The BBC has a pronunciation unit responsible for advising presenters on pronunciation and offers the following on aitch:

British English dictionaries give aytch as the standard pronunciation for the letter H. However, the pronunciation haytch is also attested as a legitimate variant. We also do not ask broadcasters who naturally say haytch to change their pronunciation but if a broadcaster contacted to ask us, we would tell them that aytch is regarded as the standard pronunciation in British English. People can feel very strongly about this and this pronunciation is less likely to attract audience complaints.

Haytch is a standard pronunciation in Irish English and is increasingly being used by native English-speaking people all across the country, irrespective of geographical provenance or social standing. Polls have shown that the uptake of haytch by younger native speakers is on the rise. Schoolchildren repeatedly being told not to drop Hs may cause them to hyper-correct and insert them where they don't exist.

(Jo Kim, BBC Pronunciation Unit, BBC 2010)

All of which might lead to a thought-provoking pub quiz question: Which is the second letter of the alphabet to be defined in the *Oxford English Dictionary*? (Answer: *aitch.*)

Apostrophes are also often used in names, particularly on road signs and lists where space is limited. However, they are increasingly disappearing from names of streets and villages as signs are replaced, and some councils, like Birmingham in 2009, have made a conscious decision to omit them. Badsey-Ellis (2008) even studied the history of London Underground to find out about apostrophes in station names.

Apostrophes on the London Underground

Badsey-Ellis found that there are currently eight station names with apostrophes:

- Earl's Court
- King's Cross St Pancras

- Queen's Park
- Regent's Park
- Shepherd's Bush (two stations)
- St James's Park
- St John's Wood
- St Paul's.

Three stations started out in life with apostrophes, but lost them many years ago:

- Parson's Green – last used around 1909
- Golder's Green – lost around 1919
- Rayner's Lane – lost around 1921.

Badsey-Ellis also found that maps of the Tube system have sometimes been produced with no apostrophes, for example in 1913, 1928 and 1933. The last station to lose its apostrophe was Collier's Wood in 1987. All of which you may either find fascinating or dull, or you may even be provoked to wonder why the saints and the aristocracy have kept their apostrophes while Messrs Parson, Golder, Rayner and Collier have been downgraded. However, the example shows how apostrophe usage has fluctuated for more than a hundred years; there is, perhaps, small wonder that people are confused.

Abbreviations on road signs continue to include apostrophes so that lettering can be large and easy to see when travelling at speed. The presence of such abbreviations led children in one class to ask their teacher questions about the use of apostrophes in abbreviated place names and surnames, during a coach trip from Durham to Scarborough.

Case study: researching apostrophes for omission in names with Year 5

Laura, an NQT, had been working with her Year 5 class revising the use of apostrophes in the days before the coach trip took place. She was delighted that on the journey some children were sufficiently aware of apostrophes that they asked her about some of the place names they noticed on road signs, such as H'pool. M'b'ro' and S'boro'. Fortunately, Laura had brought some inexpensive road atlases with her so that children could follow their route, and she asked them to look at the atlases to find out which places might be represented by the abbreviations.

Back at school in the following days, the children explored road signs and abbreviations further and looked at other names and words which were commonly abbreviated using apostrophes, including *o'clock*, *O'Neill*, *D'Artagnan*, *D'Arcy* and *John O'Groats*.

→

Through exploring books and websites, and with Laura's help, the children discovered that *O'* in names came from Irish names where *O'* was short for 'of', and showed who the person's father was ('Martin of Neill' becomes 'Martin O'Neill' over time). *D'*, they discovered, also indicated parentage in France, with *de* meaning *of*, being shortened to *d'* before a vowel. This also led to discoveries about the ways in which surnames have been created in other countries (*son* was added in many northern European countries, regardless of whether the offspring was a boy or girl, except in Iceland where females acquired *dottir*; and *Mac* preceded names in Scotland: *MacDonald, McNeill*, etc.).

Children also looked at *o'clock*, which they found was short for *of the clock* ('the time is seven of the clock').

Laura also drew children's attention to football league tables, especially those shown as a narrow strip at the side of a television screen, in which teams' names were shortened using apostrophes (for example, T'ham, B'ham, M'c'r City and B'pool).

The children's heightened awareness of apostrophes led them to ask questions about other examples they found in books, newspapers, websites and on signs and posters. Laura found that she was unsure what to tell the children about the use of apostrophes for things like 1960's (or is it 1960s?), minding your P's and Q's and even SAT's (or is it SATs?), and this led her to explore these herself (see later in this chapter for an explanation).

The case study above illustrates one of the problems associated with developing an understanding of apostrophes: not only are they widely misused in places where children see them, but there continues to be debate about their usage, with conventions changing over time and apostrophes often ceasing to be used by councils and companies for names which had previously included them on fascias, in company logos and so on.

Curriculum links

An exploration of maps to find places which include apostrophes in their names, as well as those which perhaps ought to but no longer do, can help develop children's awareness of the functions of apostrophes. Where they find place names which they think ought to have apostrophes, they could use the internet to find out more about the places and to see if they had ever had apostrophes in the past. Children could look at both atlases with maps of large areas and street maps. There should be no shortage of examples, even including some school names: *St John's, St Andrew's, Our Lady's*, etc.

Interestingly, the English football club Queen's Park Rangers no longer has an apostrophe in its name, while the Scottish club, Queen's Park, does. Newcastle United play at St James' Park, while Exeter City play at St James Park – and a park in Central London is called St James's Park. In Birmingham, residents of the suburb of Kings Norton campaigned for the restoration of an apostrophe in its name.

Residents voted 80 to 8 in favour of returning to being called *King's Norton*, but the local council refused to make the alteration, claiming that this would be costly as stationery would have to be changed.

You may not wish to turn your classes into apostrophe hunters on the lines of the Apostrophe Protection Society, but with ready access to cameras in mobile phones and a range of apostrophe-focused websites, it should be easy for you and them to bring examples to school for display and discussion. You might also like to read Lynne Truss's (2003) chapter in which she cites some of her favourite errors, which include a giant financial institution announcing 'Prudential were here to help you' rather than 'Prudential we're here to help you', and the BBC website, which advertised a grammar course for children: *Next week: nouns and apostrophe's.*

Other (mis)uses of apostrophes

It is quite common to see apostrophes used for plurals of abbreviations such as SAT's, MOT's, CD's, MP's and 1960's. These apostrophes are unnecessary and do not show that anything is omitted or owned (unless you wanted to talk about the CD's box – the box belonging to the CD – or the MP's constituency). Nevertheless, children see so many examples of apostrophes used in this way that there can be little surprise when they copy from such examples.

When lower-case letters are being used, it is common practice to use an apostrophe for clarity – in the phrase, 'dotting the i's and crossing the t's', for example, it would look strange and ambiguous to refer to 'the is and the ts'. However, there is no need to do this when the letters are upper case. So *CDs, MPs* and *1960s*, then, are perfectly correct. And when minding your manners, you can refer to p's and q's or Ps and Qs.

In the case study below, note how a teacher provides a visual aid as a reference for children as they learn about contractions, and then reinforces children's understanding through meaningful activities.

Case study: apostrophes for contraction in Year 2

Pippa, a Year 2 teacher who had recently taken up her post for the summer term, found that her new class often missed out or misplaced apostrophes in contractions, writing things like *did'nt, should'nt* and *was'nt*. She decided to create a chart which showed which letters were missed out of each contraction and used this at the beginning of a series of literacy lessons.

→

Words in full	Contracted form	Missing letters
let us	let's	u
should not	shouldn't	o
could not	couldn't	o
do not	don't	o
we are	we're	a
I am	I'm	a
you are	you're	a
it is	it's	i
that is	that's	i

Pippa asked the children to look for examples of apostrophes in texts which she prepared specially, in which all apostrophes were for contractions, and added to the table several new words. She then asked some children to look at books in the class library to find more examples. The contractions *you'd* and *shan't* required careful explanation, as more than one letter is missed in each (*woul-* is omitted when *you would* becomes *you'd*, and *ll* and *o* when *shall not* becomes *shan't*). *Won't* presented a greater challenge, given that *will not* changes to *won't* and the vowel changes from *i* to *o*, as well as the letters *ll* and *o* being omitted. Examples discovered by the children were added to the chart, which became a reference point for them in future lessons.

As children looked for examples in books they also encountered possessive apostrophes and this led Pippa to discuss these and work with a higher ability guided group to develop the children's understanding.

In subsequent lessons, Pippa asked children to write dialogue for short presentations and to include contractions with apostrophes wherever appropriate.

Most errors in using apostrophes for contractions arise because children are unaware of the reason for the placement of the apostrophe. By providing a chart and discussing its content, we can offer children a reference point when they are writing, as well as a focus for discussion.

Curriculum links

Children should learn about apostrophes for contracted forms and possessive apostrophes for singular nouns in Year 2 and possessive apostrophes for singular and plural nouns in Year 4. However, where children are capable of understanding concepts from the curriculum for the next age group, it is often valid to teach them, especially when they encounter them in their reading and wish to find out more.

Could we do without apostrophes?

In many cases: yes, as Shaw showed in his writing. Take this extract from Act 1 of his play, *Pygmalion* (1912): *Dont start hollerin. Whos hurtin you? Nobodys going to touch you. Whats the good of fussing?*

It may look strange, but we can read it quite easily. We would soon get used to the changed look of the text, and learn not to miss the apostrophe when one would have been used to show the omission of letters. Even the distinction between singular and plural possessives is often superfluous:

> *Johns books the red one over there.*
>
> *Johns books dustjackets are all torn.*

However, an official decision to do away with the use of the apostrophe in written English is not likely to be made law in any of our lifetimes, so it is important that our children should learn to use it correctly! There are many situations, as suggested earlier in this chapter, where a correctly used apostrophe can add precision or avoid ambiguity in writing.

Conclusion: what do you need to know about apostrophes?

- Apostrophes have two functions: to show possession and to show omission of letters.

- Apostrophes of omission are found in informal writing or in dialogue.

- You need to understand how children's misconceptions come about. For example, it is understandable that they might put apostrophes in possessive words like *yours*, *his*, *hers*, *ours*, *theirs* and *its*, but they need to understand that these words already show possession and do not, therefore, need apostrophes.

- You need to be aware that children will see examples of apostrophes, both correctly and incorrectly placed, and that they may be confused about their purpose and may consequently place them before every 's', especially as words can sound the same when they need and don't need apostrophes (for example, *the potato's skin* and *the skins of the potatoes*).

- You need to understand that many people confuse *it's*, which is short for *it is* (it is time for bed) and *its*, which is possessive (the elephant flapped its ears).

- You need to show children that apostrophes for omission replace letters, but that sometimes they replace more than one letter (*you've*, *we've*, *shan't*) including in place names on road signs, etc.

- When using an apostrophe for possession, we save words by writing things like *Jo's book* instead of *the book belonging to Jo*.

Learning outcomes review

You should now have an understanding of the correct use of apostrophes for both contraction and possession. In addition, you should be aware of children's (and adults') possible misconceptions about apostrophes, and have an understanding of how to teach apostrophes effectively. Use the self-assessment questions below to check your own understanding.

Self-assessment questions

Look at the sentences below and remove misplaced apostrophes and insert missing apostrophes.

1. The childrens' work was'nt as good as that of their teachers.
2. Jills shoe's were covered with mud and the twin's jackets were little better.
3. The pupil's desks were dreadfully untidy and their attitude to the teachers' instruction's was poor.
4. The Governments' concern for education is illustrated by it's commitment to maintaining teacher's salaries at their present level.
5. The boy's toilets' were a haven for smokers' nefarious activities.
6. The ladys' cloakroom was full of expensive fur coat's belonging to the party's guests.
7. The greengrocer's shop window bore signs advertising potato's, carrots', tomato's and onion's.
8. 'It's unlikely that you will pass your course if you miss my lectures',' announced the balding academic.
9. The Rover's goal was being bombarded by shots from Uniteds' eager forwards'.
10. The trouts' eye seemed to be looking at me as I prepared to take a forkful of his body.

Further reading

Truss, L. (2003) *Eats, Shoots & Leaves: The Zero Tolerance Approach to Punctuation*. London: Profile Books.

Lynn Truss's chapter on apostrophes is not only entertaining but also informative.

Waugh, D., Allott, K., Waugh, R., English, E. and Bulmer, E. (2014) *The Spelling, Punctuation and Grammar app*. Morecambe: Children Count Ltd (available through the App Store).

This app provides guidance and activities on all aspects of grammar, spelling and punctuation and has a section on apostrophes.

References

Apostrophes: an introduction. Available from: **www.supaproofread.com** (accessed 29.1.2013).

Badsey-Ellis, A. (2008) *The Underground and The Apostrophe*. Available from: **http://lurs.org. uk/documents/pdf%2008/nov/The%20Underground%20and%20the%20Apostrophe. pdf** (accessed 18.6.13).

Crystal, D. (2005) *How Language Works*. London: Penguin.

DfE (2013) *The National Curriculum in England: Key stages 1 and 2 framework document*. London: DfE. Available from: **www.gov.uk/government/uploads/system/uploads/attachment_ data/file/425601/PRIMARY_national_curriculum.pdf** (accessed 25.10.15).

Johnson, S. (1755) *Dictionary of the English Language*. London: J. & P. Knapton.

Kim, J. (2010) BBC Pronunciation Unit, *BBC News Magazine*, 28.10.2010. Available from: **www.bbc.co.uk/news/magazine-11642588** (accessed 18.6.13).

Marsh, D. and Hodsdon, A. (2010) **Guardian Style**, 3rd edition. London: Random House.

Mayes, I. (2005) **Only Correct**. London: Guardian Books.

Shaw, G. B. (1912) *Pygmalion*. London: Constable.

Truss, L. (2003) *Eats, Shoots & Leaves: The Zero Tolerance Approach to Punctuation*. London: Profile Books.

8 Phrases, clauses and sentences

Learning outcomes

By reading this chapter you will develop your understanding of:

- definitions of phrases, clauses and sentences;
- the concepts of simple (single), compound and complex (multi-clause) sentences;
- ways of working with children to help them to compose and refine sentences.

Teachers' Standards
This chapter will help you with the following Teachers' Standards.

3 Demonstrate good subject and curriculum knowledge:
- have a secure knowledge of the relevant subject(s) and curriculum areas, foster and maintain pupils' interest in the subject, and address misunderstandings;
- demonstrate a critical understanding of developments in the subject and curriculum areas, and promote the value of scholarship;
- demonstrate an understanding of, and take responsibility for, promoting high standards of literacy, articulacy and the correct use of Standard English, whatever the teacher's specialist subject.

Introduction

In this chapter, you will look at sentences and their component parts. Before you begin to read the chapter, look at the activity below.

Activity
Which of the following are complete sentences? Complete those which are incomplete:

1. My cat is up a.
2. My neighbour's dog barks.
3. Dawn broke and the birds.
4. Dean picked the wrong.
5. Water flows.

When you looked at the examples above, you probably found it quite easy to decide which were sentences and which needed something else to make them complete. You almost certainly decided that numbers 2 and 5 were complete, although you may have wanted to add something to them. Number 1 (*My cat is up a*) clearly needs something to make it complete – up a what? Similarly, numbers 3 and 4 seem to need more words for them to become complete sentences. They could become:

3. Dawn broke and the birds sang.

4. Dean picked the wrong answer.

But what is a sentence? (You may have been told not to begin them with words like but, but your teachers were wrong! For example: But for the fact that you were told you couldn't begin sentences with 'but', you might have varied your writing more over the years.) When asked to define a sentence, many trainee teachers say things like: It begins with a capital letter and ends with a full stop. This is a description of some of the features of most sentences (they can also end with question or exclamation mark), but does little to explain what actually constitutes a sentence. The National Curriculum's glossary defines a sentence as: *a group of words which are grammatically connected to each other but not to any words outside the sentence* (DfE, 2013, p.94).

It may be helpful to look at an example of children learning about how to use sentences as we work towards a definition. In the case study below, a trainee teacher works with her Year 1 class on composing sentences orally before they work together to write them down.

Case study: oral sentence composing

Natasha, a first-year trainee, was asked to work with her Year 1 class to help them develop their understanding of sentences. Some of the children still inserted full stops in a rather random way, often at the end of lines rather than at the ends of sentences, and the class teacher was concerned that they should practise composing sentences orally before writing, in order to get a better 'feel' for the nature of a sentence. Some of the children's reading scheme books included many sentences that were a line long, and Natasha felt that this might account for the children's misconception about placement of full stops. Therefore, she decided to work with children not only to compose single sentences, but also to create pairs of sentences so that when these were written on the board she could make teaching points about placement of full stops.

Natasha brought in a large sack which included several of the toys she had played with as a child and produced them one by one, asking children to think of a sentence to describe each one and then share it with a neighbour. She then invited children to share their sentences with the class and wrote some on the board. She made sure to include two or three sentences about the same toy and then asked children where full stops were needed. For example:

$\longrightarrow$

The doll has a sad face. The doll has brown hair. She is wearing a green dress.

Sometimes when she wrote the sentences on the board, Natasha either omitted the full stops or deliberately put them in the wrong places and encouraged the children to 'catch her out' and help her get them right.

Some children were quick to spot that many sentences could be combined by using conjunctions, so Natasha asked them to help her to do this and discussed the placement of full stops. For example:

The doll has a sad face and brown hair and she is wearing a green dress.

In subsequent lessons, Natasha asked children to create sentences in pairs to tell a story which was circulated around the class. First, they listened to Natasha telling them the story of *Goldilocks and the Three Bears*. With the children's help, Natasha wrote key points from the story as a list, in note form, on the board:

1. In forest

2. Sees house

3. Goes in

4. Tries porridge – Mummy bear's

5. Tries porridge – Daddy bear's

6. Tries porridge – Baby bear's

7. Tries chairs – Mummy bear's

8. Tries chairs – Daddy bear's

9. Tries chairs – Baby bear's

10. Tries beds – Mummy bear's

11. Tries beds – Daddy bear's

12. Tries beds – Baby bear's

13. Bears return

14. Runs away

She then allocated a number from 1 to 14 to each pair of children and asked them to compose sentences orally, before taking turns to say them aloud as the class told the story in sequence. They then they wrote their sentences on mini-whiteboards and refined them, before retelling the story. Natasha used the children's sentences to write the story on the board and asked children to help her to refine and develop the story as she wrote.

By composing sentences orally before writing them down, children are liberated from concerns about transcription at the first stage of writing. They can, therefore, often produce more interesting sentences, which can then be developed and punctuated when written with guidance from a more experienced writer. Interestingly, children's author Michael Morpurgo has stated that he spends a lot of time thinking about his stories before writing them by hand, and does not worry about spelling, grammar or punctuation at the initial stages of composition. This comes later as he refines and edits the stories, with help from his wife.

Curriculum links

Year 1 children should be taught to write sentences by:

1. saying out loud what they are going to write about;
2. composing a sentence orally before writing it;
3. sequencing sentences to form short narratives;
4. re-reading what they have written to check it makes sense.

Oral composition of sentences can be a valuable strategy for older children too, across the curriculum. For example, Year 5 children learning how to write up science experiments might consider, with partners, how to phrase their description of events and try their ideas orally before committing them to paper. Oral composition can also be used for different genres of writing within literacy work, and can be followed by children working in pairs using mini-whiteboards.

Types of sentences

There are different kinds of sentences, and in this chapter you will find definitions, as well as examples of case studies in which teachers and trainees have taught children about different types of sentence. A sentence can be *simple*, *compound* or *complex* and these terms are in common use in schools. However, the National Curriculum recognises that these terms may suggest that there is a hierarchy of sentence types and states:

> *Classifying sentences as 'simple', 'complex' or 'compound' can be confusing, because a 'simple' sentence may be complicated, and a 'complex' one may be straightforward. The terms 'single-clause sentence' and 'multi-clause sentence' may be more helpful.*

(DfE, 2013, p.94)

It is certainly true that children think that there is a hierarchy of sentence types and that writing full of complex sentences will always be of a high quality. This is, of course, not the case. What does matter is that young writers are able to choose appropriately and know when to use different kinds of sentences to have the intended effect on their reader. We have used the terms *simple*, *compound* and *complex* sentences in the examples below as the terms are still in common use, but you may prefer to follow the DfE's recommendation.

Simple (single-clause) sentences

A simple sentence has one clause: *I ate lunch.*

Clauses include verbs, and simple sentences comprise, as a minimum, a subject (a noun – what the sentence is about) and a verb. Often there is a second noun, which is the object of the sentence (the person or thing to which something happens). Look at the simple sentences below and decide which have objects, and what the subjects and verbs are:

1. Rob kicked the ball.

2. Yesterday I ran.

3. The car skidded.

4. David left Hull.

Only numbers 1 and 4 have objects. In the first sentence, *Rob* is the subject and *the ball* the object. In the fourth sentence, *David* is the subject and *Hull* the object. You could add an object by inserting, for example, *to work* for number 2. The verbs in 1 and 4 are *transitive* verbs, which means they have a direct object which is directly affected by the action of the verb. Most verbs in English are transitive. See below for examples:

I read – is a sentence, because it has a subject and a verb.

I read enthusiastically has added an adverb to tell us more about the action.

I read the newspaper has added an object, which answers the question, 'What did I read?', so in this sentence the verb is being used transitively.

Activity

1. Add an object to the following:

   a) The children ate
   b) Suddenly he saw
   c) My teacher had
   d) Yesterday James bought

2. Which could be sentences without an object?

Your answers could include:

a) The children ate (biscuits, burgers, apples).

b) Suddenly he saw (the way home, a large dog, the light).

c) My teacher had (good manners, measles, good ideas).

d) Yesterday James bought (a new car, socks, a book).

The children ate could stand alone without an object. In some contexts, c) could also stand alone: *Who had eaten all the pies? My teacher had!*

Most verbs in English can be used either with or without an object:

> *Sami collapsed.*
>
> *Sami collapsed the tent.*

There are only a few, like *die*, which can never be used transitively.

For instance, can you add an object to the following sentences?

> *The crowd reacted.*
>
> *The team's manager despaired.*
>
> *The train arrived.*

You can react *to* something, despair *of* something or arrive *at* something, but none of these sentences can have a direct object which receives the action of the verb.

There are different kinds of simple sentence and the National Curriculum defines these as statements, questions, commands and exclamations.

- **Statements** (or declarative sentences)

  John stepped back in amazement.

  Perhaps we could go to town.

- **Questions** (or interrogative sentences)

  Do you know the way to San Jose?

  Can you tell me how to get to Carnegie Hall, please?

- **Commands** (orders and instructions, or imperatives)

  Stop it at once!

  Put the kettle on.

- **Exclamations** (sentences with exclamation marks)

  You must be joking!

  What a brilliant idea that is!

Simple (single-clause) sentences are very useful and enable us to give information concisely, but they are not always short as in the following example.

> *The young boy in the blue jumper hit the ball with his new cricket bat.*

The sentence is still simple because it has one verb and one clause.

When we want to include more than one piece of information in a sentence, we often combine simple sentences to create compound sentences.

Compound and complex (multi-clause) sentences

Compound sentences

A compound sentence has two or more clauses of equal weight (they are both main clauses) joined by a coordinating conjunction such as *and, or, but* or *so*, or by a comma, semi-colon or colon. For example:

> *Rob kicked the ball but he missed the goal.*
>
> *Durham is a beautiful city and Doncaster is very pleasant.*
>
> *As Jo left the room, her head was held high.*
>
> *Mike covered his ears: the music was deafening.*
>
> *Nick looked under the table; he found nothing.*

Sometimes we need to write sentences in which some clauses are more important than others and so create complex sentences, but before you explore them it is important to find out more about what is meant by the term *clause*.

Clauses

The word *clause* comes from a word meaning 'closed' (think of *closet* and *closure*). A clause presents a complete thought, or a statement about an action. A *main clause* is a simple sentence; other clauses can be added to it to make a compound or complex sentence.

- *The door opened. Mr Wilson came in.* – two short sentences, each consisting only of one main clause.
- *The door opened and Mr Wilson came in.* – a compound sentence, in which both clauses are equal in importance.

- *When the door opened, Mr Wilson came in.* – the first clause has been subordinated by the addition of 'when', and is now a *subordinate* clause, telling us more about when the main action happened.

If we need to say more to children about subordinate clauses, we can divide them into different categories by looking at what job they are doing in a sentence:

- An **adverbial clause** often tells us more about the time, place or manner in which the action happened:

  When the door opened, Mr Wilson came in.

  Kim danced beautifully *although she was only seven.*

- An **adjectival clause** describes a noun in the main clause.

  Hannah, *who was the tallest girl in the class,* scored the goal.

  James entered the room *where his uncle was sitting.*

A clause must contain a verb and a subject:

  The river *flows* through the town.

  My aunt always *chooses* the best presents.

If a group of words does not contain a complete verb, it is not a clause but a phrase. So:

  The river flowing through the town

  To fly effortlessly through the sky

are not clauses, because they need another verb to tell us what is happening. Neither 'flowing' nor 'to fly' counts as a verb by itself, because there is not a particular act or event described.

  The river flowing through the town is full of fish.

  To fly effortlessly through the sky seems like a wonderful idea.

In the first sentence, 'flowing through the town' is an *adjectival phrase* describing the river, and in the second one 'to fly effortlessly through the sky' is the *subject* of the main verb.

It doesn't matter whether you know that a group of words is a clause or a phrase when you are modelling writing for children: the important thing is that you show them the principles of subordination so that they can make their writing more interesting and varied.

Activity

Can you decide which of the following are clauses and which are phrases?

1. Walking across the living room
2. I turned the television off
3. Out in the garden
4. The moon seemed very bright
5. Six surprisingly tall men
6. They walked across the lawn slowly
7. A mysterious man walked in front
8. A bunch of flowers in his hand
9. The sound of rushing traffic
10. Your supper is ready for you

Numbers 1, 3, 5, 8 and 9 are phrases. Numbers 2, 4, 6, 7 and 10 are clauses.

Complex sentences

A complex sentence has a main clause and one or more *subordinate clauses*, usually joined by subordinating conjunctions such as *because*, *while* and *although*. In the National Curriculum, children in Year 3 are expected to know and understand the term *subordinate clause*, which has certainly surprised some teachers. However, if the idea is explained carefully and through modelling and examples, there is no reason why most children shouldn't grasp the concept (the sentence you have just read has a main clause and a subordinate clause: can you identify which is which? Answer at the end of the chapter).

Begin by showing some examples of simple sentences and then model inserting or adding short clauses or phrases which provide additional information. For example:

Ryan finished his work.

Ryan, who had stayed in at playtime, finished his work.

Lauren went to the circus.

Lauren went to the circus, although she would rather have gone to the football match.

You can then discuss with the children what is the most important part of each sentence, and what could be left out but still leave the main part (or main clause) making sense. You could go on to show children a collection of main and subordinate clauses and ask them to see how many different complex sentences they can create from them. Try doing this yourself in the activity below.

Activity

Look at the clauses below and combine them in as many ways as possible to create complex sentences. Remember that a complex sentence has a main clause and at least one subordinate clause or phrase. Your sentences must be grammatically correct, but they could be nonsensical and still be grammatically correct!

Billy was the best player in the team	a person who was in an important position
David loved walking in the countryside	a player who scored a lot of goals
The magpie flew in front of the car	which looked beautiful in the sunshine
Chester is a very interesting city	who was often thought of as a balding lecturer
Michael was always making silly mistakes	where there was once a Roman camp

Some possible combinations are:

Billy, a player who scored a lot of goals, was the best player in the team.

David, who was often thought of as a balding lecturer, loved walking in the countryside.

Chester is a very interesting city, where there was once a Roman camp.

Michael, a person who was in an important position, was always making silly mistakes.

The magpie, which looked beautiful in the sunshine, flew in front of the car.

(There are several more possibilities.)

In the case study below you will see how a teacher planned to explore both compound and complex sentences with her class. Note how she uses the opportunity to reinforce their knowledge of metalanguage and provides opportunities for them to experiment with language. Note, too, the emphasis on oral rehearsal and discussion.

Case study: teaching multi-clause sentences to Years 3/4/5

Trish, a teacher in a small primary school, worked with a mixed Year 3/4/5 class and had planned a series of lessons on sentence types. She was keen to engage all three age groups at appropriate levels. Whole class shared reading and writing focused on texts which included good examples of a range of compound and complex sentences. For most Year 3 children and

→

some Year 4s she planned activities which involved creating compound and complex sentences, using commas and conjunctions to separate the clauses. The more able Year 4s and Year 5 were asked to look at specially chosen texts in which brackets and dashes had been used to separate some subordinates and additional pieces of information.

Trish ensured that all investigations were shared at plenary sessions so that younger children became aware of brackets, parentheses and dashes, and older children were able to revisit and revise the use of commas to separate clauses.

Each day, Trish used a different text for shared reading to show examples of brackets, parentheses, dashes and commas separating subordinates. She followed this up by asking children to help her to compose complex sentences in shared writing and then giving them opportunities to create their own individually or in pairs.

In the final lesson of the series, Trish asked children to compose simple sentences on mini-whiteboards and then pass them on to neighbours to add subordinates. They did this several times and, after each attempt, Trish asked children to read out examples, many of which had the class in fits of laughter, including:

Chelsea, who had a football team named after her, was good at netball.

Nick, who was an expert at blowing bubbles, ran out of the room rapidly.

Curriculum links

Children in Year 5 should learn how to use commas, brackets and dashes to indicate parenthesis, according to the National Curriculum (DfE, 2013, p.78). There will be opportunities across the curriculum to look at examples in texts and to make use of them in children's writing (see Chapter 6).

Changing word order in sentences

In English, unlike in some other languages, there is some flexibility in the way in which we can order words in sentences. For example:

Peter walked down the road.
Down the road walked Peter.

Jane climbed through the hole.
Through the hole climbed Jane.

Mustafa laughed when he heard the joke.

When he heard the joke, Mustafa laughed.

Ali kicked the ball into the goal as the crowd cheered.

As the crowd cheered, Ali kicked the ball into the goal.

But we cannot change the order of, for instance, the subject and the object; 'Leila likes Maria' is a different sentence from 'Maria likes Leila'. An adjective must be with the noun it is describing in English, for us to understand what the author means. Only in languages which use different endings to show case, number and gender (see below for explanation) is it possible to arrange words in a random order and still be sure that the meaning will be clear. We only have a few words in English which use different endings or spellings to show whether they are subject and object, and these are personal pronouns.

Subject	Object
I	me
he	him
she	her
we	us
they	them

So when using these words we could, for instance, say 'Him I saw' or 'Me she liked' and, although we might sound peculiar, the meaning would be clear. But with most of our words, the arrangement in a set pattern is necessary.

The house that the men lived in had a garden big.

What's big? The house, the men or the garden? Many other languages use markers to show agreement, which would solve the problem. In French, for example, the house would be *la maison* (feminine), the men would be *les hommes* (masculine and plural), and the garden would be *le jardin* (masculine singular). The adjective would agree with the appropriate noun, and would be *grande*, *grands* or *grand*, showing which noun it belonged with.

In ancient times, the oracles which foretold the future for the Romans and Greeks would often make their predictions by throwing out a handful of leaves, with one word written on each leaf; the grammar of the languages ensured that the message would be clear, no matter in what order the leaves fell.

Think of trying this in English. How many different messages could you work out from this set of words?

the	great	sea	will
overcome	before	the	pitiful
army	defeats	the	valiant
men	that	worship	gods.

It could get very confusing! But in an *inflected* language – one which uses agreements, such as some children may have met in German, French, Spanish, or other languages – the endings will make it clear whether, for instance, it is the sea, the men, the army or the gods which are pitiful.

Research focus: beginning sentences with conjunctions

As you saw earlier in this chapter, it is quite possible to begin sentences with conjunctions such as *and* and *but*, despite some people's misconception that this is grammatically incorrect. Crystal argues that *starting a sentence – or even a paragraph – with one of these conjunctions [and or but] is at the heart of English literary tradition. It was a major feature of Old English texts, and usage has continued without a break to the present day* (2004, p.29). Crystal provides examples from Chaucer, Shakespeare, Dickens and Churchill to reinforce the point. One example is of a new paragraph in Churchill's *A History of the English-Speaking Peoples*:

But this youthful, flourishing, immature civilization lacked any solid military defence.

Crystal asserts: *The effects are plain. A conjunction at the beginning of a sentence can mark a turning point in the narrative. It can make a dramatic contrast. The use of an opening monosyllable increases a sentence's narrative pace* (2004, p.30).

Why then do some teachers persist in telling children not to begin sentences with certain conjunctions? And are they always wrong to do so? The activity below may help you to decide.

Activity
Look at the 'sentences' below and decide which are acceptable without additions or adjustments:

> *And so, after a long journey, Fred finally arrived at his destination.*
>
> *Because I like bananas, I eat them every day.*
>
> *Because it would not work.*
>
> *But for Hart*

The first and second sentences can stand alone and convey clear meaning. However, when teachers tell children not to begin sentences with coordinating conjunctions, it is likely that it is examples like the third and fourth which they want to avoid.

Because it would not work doesn't tell us what wouldn't work and so we need to add another clause (a main clause) to help it to make sense. For example, *Because it would not work, Daniel took his watch back to the shop.* Now we have a sentence with a main and a subordinate clause.

But for Hart doesn't tell us much, but if we add *England would have lost by five goals to nil*, we have a complete sentence with a main clause and a subordinate phrase: *But for Hart, England would have lost by five goals to nil*.

When children are just beginning to write sentences, it may be justifiable to suggest they don't begin them with *and*, *but* or *because*, but as they develop as writers and read more challenging texts they will find that established authors frequently begin sentences with coordinating conjunctions. What children need then is guidance, through lots of modelling and guided writing, on how to do this successfully and grammatically accurately, rather than to have a dubious rule quoted to them. In a case study later in this chapter, you will see how a trainee teacher explores sentence development with children using shared writing to model. A first step in shared writing can be to encourage children to look for different ways of phrasing ideas, drawing upon examples from texts. They can also benefit from looking at examples of incorrect usage.

Don't dangle your participles!

A common problem when children are extending sentences by adding phrases is the *dangling participle* (sometimes known as the *hanging participle*). Look at these sentences:

> *Eating my tea, I found a slug in the salad.*
>
> *Closing the curtains, the moon seemed very bright in the sky.*
>
> *Walking on the hills, the day was bright and cold.*

Only the first of these examples is a correctly formed sentence, because only in the first one does the participle (the '-ing' word) refer to the subject of the main clause. The moon was not closing the curtains, and the day didn't walk in the hills. A present participle used in this way must always refer to the subject of the main verb, and it is important to explain to children why this makes sense and to help them to get it right.

Television commentaries on reality shows are often rich sources of this kind of phrasing. Look at these sentences and see if you can spot the problem:

> *Having chopped the onions, Dave's salmon now needs to be skinned.*
>
> *Expecting four guests, the beef will later be fried.*

Look at all the incorrect examples given above. How could they be rephrased to make them grammatically correct?

Making statements into questions

Word order, mentioned earlier, can also be important in English when we want to make a statement into a question. Sometimes we do not need to change the order at all. For example:

> *You want some tea.*
>
> *You want some tea?*

Here, the change from a full stop to a question mark at the end of the sentence changes the way we say the sentence and what it means.

In spoken language, we have, in recent years, become used to the so-called 'interrogative intonation', often through exposure to Australian soaps such as *Neighbours* and *Home and Away*. This means the way in which the voice rising at the end of a sentence can often make a simple declarative sentence sound like a question: 'I come from Sydney?' Interestingly, this pattern of rising tone is similar in many languages, including French, German, Spanish and dialects of Mandarin Chinese.

Tone, however, is no help in written language. We mark questions with an interrogation point (?) and also often by a question-marker word in the sentence: *who, where, why, when, how*. Where we do not have one of these words, we rearrange the word order:

> *That is a good idea.*
>
> *Is that a good idea?*

Or, in some cases, we change the form of the verb:

> *You saw the programme.*
>
> *Did you see the programme?*

If we think we know what the answer will be, we can use specific phrases to suggest this:

You ate the pie, didn't you? (Yes, of course I did!)

You didn't eat the pie, did you? (No, of course not!)

In the Latin language, there were actually different words to start a question according to the expected answer; *nonne* for the first example above, and *num* for the second one. The French language does something similar by forming questions with *n'est-ce pas?* (*isn't it?*) when they are expecting agreement. Perhaps in modern conversational English, *innit?* is starting to take on the same meaning?

Shortening sentences

It might seem from Trish's case study that there is always a virtue in lengthening sentences by making them compound or complex, but we do not always want to lengthen sentences. We may wish to shorten them if we wish to:

- summarise, i.e. reduce a text to its most important points, without going into details;
- make notes, i.e. taking the important information from a sentence and recording it in shorter form;
- edit, so that the sentence is more effective;
- avoid tautology – for example, *I myself personally* effectively says the same thing more than once;
- build up tension – for example, *He stopped. There it was again. Now it sounded closer.*

Activity
Look at the sentences below and see if you can shorten each of them, while retaining their essential meanings.

1. Although it rained throughout the day last Friday, we had a long period of sustained sunshine on Saturday.
2. In the long run, what really matters is that children acquire a high level of competence in writing accurately.
3. It is a truth universally acknowledged that a single man in possession of a good fortune must be in want of a wife. (This is the opening sentence of Jane Austen's *Pride and Prejudice*.)

These sentences are suggestions, but you may have written equally correct alternatives:

1. Although it rained all day last Friday, it was sunny on Saturday.

2. It is important for children to be able to write well.

3. Everyone knows that a rich bachelor needs a wife.

Research focus: sentence diagramming

In the USA, the accepted way to get children to understand sentence structure was, for many years, the technique called *sentence diagramming*, first formalised by Reed and Kellogg in 1877. Although it is no longer quite so widespread, it is still widely used and has many advocates; it is also the basis of a great deal of grammar theory. In the classroom, it can help children to look at the underlying structure of a sentence and decide what the main clause is and how all the other elements add to and refine the meaning of the whole structure. These can, of course, vary from the very simple to the elaborate. Here, for instance, is a simple example:

The sentence is: *Diagramming a sentence shows the structure behind the words.*

This diagram shows that:

- 'diagramming' is the subject;

- 'a sentence' is an adjectival phrase, describing (telling more about) the subject;

- 'shows' is the verb;

- 'structure' is the object;

- 'behind the words' is an adjectival phrase describing the object.

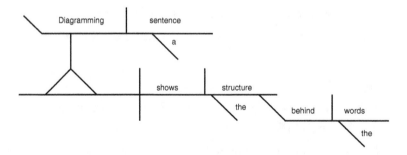

An example of how this kind of thing was taught in classrooms can be found in Laura Ingalls Wilder's *Little Town on the Prairie* (1941) in which a 15-year-old girl demonstrates the parsing of a complicated sentence in a school exhibition. Of course, we would not use this technique wholesale in our classrooms, but it is interesting to look at this kind of very formal *parsing* for comparison, and it could be used to demonstrate sentence-building, starting with a straight line of 'subject – verb' and seeing how the structure grows into a tree shape as more and more words, phrases and clauses are added.

And here is a diagram of the opening sentence of the US Constitution:

$\longrightarrow$

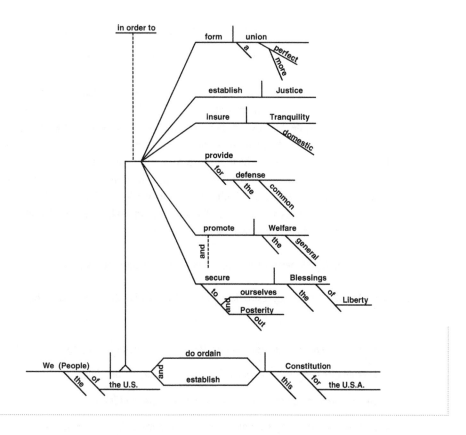

In the case study below a trainee teacher works with his class to develop their understanding that a range of different structures can be used in sentences to express the same ideas. Note how he makes use of published texts and his own writing to provide examples.

Case study: making sentences more interesting with Year 4

Nick, a PGCE trainee, devised a series of lessons for his Year 4 class to develop their knowledge and understanding of sentence structures. He began by showing the class some sentences he had written about recent snowfall:

The snow fell on the ground and covered the grass.

The snow fell on the ground and covered the grass with a white, soft carpet.

The lawn became a white carpet as the snow fell silently.

The lawn became a white carpet as the snow fell silently from a cold, grey sky.

Silently, from a cold, grey sky, snow fell and covered the lawn with a white, cold carpet.

The children had recently explored metaphors with their class teacher and some children were quick to spot examples, such as *white carpet*, in Nick's writing. He asked them to look at the sentences and decide which ones they liked the most and why. Nick encouraged the children to be critical and to pick out parts of the sentences which could be improved. One child said that she liked the sentence which began with *silently* the best because it was more interesting than the others and was 'a bit unusual'. Nick had anticipated that the sentence would attract interest and had prepared other sentences which contained adverbials so that he could ask children to discuss them and orally compose and rehearse possible alternatives which 'fronted' the adverbials. He showed them:

The cheetah galloped swiftly across the plain as it pursued its prey.

Nick asked his class to suggest different ways of expressing the same ideas. Children's suggestions included:

Swiftly, the cheetah galloped across the plain in pursuit of its prey.

Pursuing its prey, the cheetah galloped swiftly across the plain.

Swiftly galloping across the plain, the cheetah pursued its prey.

Pursued by the swiftly galloping cheetah, the gazelle dashed across the plain.

This led to children producing their own descriptive writing in which they were encouraged to compose orally before writing. Children were encouraged to discuss their sentences with writing partners and to help each other to develop varied and interesting sentences.

Curriculum links

Children in Years 3 to 4 are expected to draft and write by composing and rehearsing sentences orally (including dialogue), progressively building a varied and rich vocabulary and an increasing range of sentence structures. [1]

Research focus: sentence-combining

You have seen examples so far in this chapter of teachers and trainee teachers working with children to combine sentences. This is an established way of working in some countries, which Myhill et al. (2010, p.2) have examined in some detail:

→

A close reading of the research opens up new avenues of thinking. The US practice of sentence-combining, an activity in which young writers are shown different ways to combine simple sentences into more sophisticated sentences, using varieties of subordination and conjunction, has been the focus of numerous studies. Two recent large-scale reviews of writing research in the US (Graham and Perin 2007) and in England (Andrews et al. 2006) both argue that there is evidence of the effectiveness of this technique. It is very much a practical teaching strategy, rather than abstract, conceptual analysis, and Graham and Perin claim that 'teaching adolescents how to write increasingly complex sentences in this way enhances the quality of their writing' (2007:18). But there are two significant strands of criticism of the sentence-combining approach. First, simply producing longer, more complex sentences does not make better writing; they have to be used appropriately relative to form and purpose. Secondly, several critics have argued that it is not the sentence-combining strategy itself which works but the accompanying explicit discussion about language possibilities and how language works.

The English Review Group similarly concluded:

Taking into account the results and conclusions of the accompanying in-depth review on the teaching of formal grammar (Andrews et al., 2004), the main implication for policy of the current review is that the National Curriculum in England and accompanying guidance needs to be revised to take into account the findings of research: that the teaching of formal grammar (and its derivatives) is ineffective; and the teaching of sentence combining is one (of probably a number of) method(s) that is effective.

(Andrews et al., 2004, p.2)

When children are combining sentences they will be learning more about how to use coordinating and subordinating conjunctions effectively. It is worth noting the comment about the importance of discussing language. Shared and guided reading and writing offer excellent opportunities for this, with shared writing offering opportunities to work with the whole class to model and explore the effect that word order and the use of different conjunctions can have on the meaning and mood of the text. For example, *He went to the park* **because** *they were there* is very different from *He went to the park* **unless** *they were there* or **even though** *they were there*.

The role of shared writing

One reason for learning more about different types of sentence is that it helps us to understand different text genres and be able to use them. Key elements of shared writing which can help children to understand how sentences can be shaped and developed include:

- Rehearsing sentences orally before writing them down. So the teacher might invite children to suggest an opening sentence for a paragraph and then say it aloud and perhaps adjust it before writing it on the board.

- Modelling the automatic use of basic elements of writing such as punctuation and use of capital letters as writing takes place. Of course, this can be modified later and reviewed, but if the teacher thinks aloud as she writes on the board she can show children the importance of ensuring that they begin to develop an automaticity in their writing which will help them on occasions when their own writing is time-limited, such as in SATs tests.

- Repeatedly re-reading what has been written to check that it flows and is coherent.

- Discussing and explaining choices and inviting suggestions from children who can be encouraged to do the same.

- Checking for children's misconceptions, for example about punctuation, phrasing, subject-verb agreement.

- Occasionally making deliberate errors for children to identify and correct – apart from encouraging alertness this has the added benefit that you can intimate that any unintentional errors were deliberate!

- Modelling the use of terminology as you write, e.g. *Now, I could do with an adverb here to show how he did that …*

- Demonstrating how different grammatical features can be useful in different contexts.

It is worth considering how you might use shared writing to develop children's understanding of two different types of sentences.

Active and passive sentences

As we develop our knowledge about language and extend our reading, we become more aware of the different ways in which sentences can be written, even when they give the same information. For example, look at the sentences below and consider how they differ:

> *Michael stole John's ball.*
>
> *John's ball was stolen by Michael.*
>
> *Sara won a prize for her handwriting.*
>
> *The prize for handwriting was won by Sara.*

In the first sentence of each pair, the structure is the common 'subject/verb/object' sequence, in which the subject tells us who does the action of the verb and the object tells us what the action happened to.

Who's the subject?   Michael

What did he do?   He stole

What did he steal?   John's ball.

Sentences like these are called *active*, because the subject is the person or thing that does the action.

In the second sentence of each pair, the subject is the thing which receives the result of the action; this pattern is called *passive*. The person who did the action is now called the *agent*.

What's the subject?	John's ball
What happened to it?	It was stolen
By whom?	By Michael.

Why do we need to use a passive voice for some sentences?

1. We might not know the agent. A passive sentence can suggest that we do not know who the agent is:

   Some books have been taken from the library.

   My jumper has been moved from where I left it.

2. We might want to emphasise the action, rather than the agent:

   A magnificent prize has been offered by the governors.

3. Or we might want to sound impersonal: think of a politician saying:

   Mistakes have been made.

4. There are some situations when the passive is conventionally used, like, for instance, the writing up of research or experiments:

   The solution was heated over a Bunsen burner. The results were weighed again.

This suggests, perhaps, the clinical nature of the work and the detached nature of the results.

Research focus: active and passive

Trask (1994) explains that for hundreds of years the passive was only used in very simple sentences. He provides examples from Samuel Pepys with modernised spelling:

> I met a dead corpse of the plague, just carrying down a little pair of stairs.

> His picture is drawing for me.

Trask points out that before the nineteenth century this kind of phrasing was quite normal and that when writers began to change to the passive they were *bitterly attacked by linguistic*

$\longrightarrow$

conservatives, who called it 'clumsy', 'illogical', 'confusing' and 'monstrous' (1994, p.38). Today it is hard to imagine that *His picture is being drawn for me* could arouse such anger, unless you read the letters columns of *The Times*, *Daily Telegraph* or *Guardian*, where changes to our language are often the theme of angry letters.

In the case study below, a teacher helps her Year 6 class to understand passive and active sentences. Note how she encourages them to experiment with sentences and includes an exploration of real texts as part of the activities.

Case study: teaching active and passive voice to Year 6

Abi wanted to teach a Year 6 class the terms *active* and *passive*, and help them to understand the differences between the two forms. The class had been reading *Rooftoppers* by Katherine Rundell which offered a wide range of writing opportunities for the children. This included a crime report of the break-in at police headquarters, written by the Police Commissioner. To be able to write effectively, the children would need to use formal language and the passive voice.

Abi started by giving the class some examples of paired sentences:

I read the book.

The book was read.

Hanif broke the window.

The window was broken.

Abi asked the children to look at the sentences and then asked:

What don't the second examples tell us?

- When might we choose to say things in this way?

- How can we give the extra information?

*The book was read **by me**.*

*The window was broken **by Hanif**.*

Abi explained the term 'agent', and the class discussed why this might be included or omitted. Different types of phrases for completing sentences in this way were created and tried:

$\longrightarrow$

The prize was won by the best team.

The prize was won by sheer grit and effort.

The prize was won by cheating.

Working in pairs, the children then tried to work out a set of rules for changing the active voice into the passive, and vice versa. Each pair then tried out another pair's rules to see whether they worked satisfactorily.

Abi then provided individual sentences and short paragraphs written entirely in the active voice, and asked the children to change these into the passive. They then did a similar exercise the other way round, changing passive into active. They discussed differences in tone and meaning between the versions, and what kind of writing the alternative versions were best suited to. She also encouraged them to look at a range of texts to identify active and passive sentences. These included a formal police report of a burglary. Through the activities and discussion Abi provided, the children developed a secure understanding of the passive, and they were able to choose an appropriate voice when applying their knowledge in context.

Curriculum links

Children in Years 5 to 6 are required to understand how spoken language can be represented in writing by:

a) recognising vocabulary and structures that are appropriate for formal speech and writing, including the subjunctive;
b) using the passive voice to affect the presentation of information in a sentence;
c) using expanded noun phrases to convey complicated information concisely;
d) using modal verbs or adverbs to indicate degrees of possibility;
e) using relative clauses beginning with *who, which, where, why* or *whose* [152].

In addition, teachers should prepare pupils for secondary education by ensuring that they can consciously control the structure of sentences in their writing and understand why sentences are constructed as they are.

Conclusion

This chapter has explored a number of concepts which you may not have previously understood or been familiar with. You may wish to try out your ideas for lessons about phrases, clauses and sentences with colleagues before working with children. With so much terminology now expected to be used in the primary curriculum, it is easy to confuse terms if you have only just begun to use them.

Learning outcomes review

You should now be confident about the definitions of phrases, clauses and sentences, and understand the concepts of simple, compound and complex sentences. You should also have ideas for ways of working with children to help them to compose and refine sentences.

Self-assessment questions

Look at the sentences below and identify which are a) simple, b) compound and c) complex. Underline any subordinate clauses in the sentences.

1. David went out but Claire stayed at home.
2. Dawn broke.
3. Rosemary, who seldom slept in, was still fast asleep at ten o'clock.
4. The ball, which had begun to get very muddy, was booted into the net by Billy.
5. Nathan's sister ran home.
6. Michael, a polite and charming yet rather unpleasant man, made a mess of everything he did.

Look at the sentences again and decide which are in the active voice and which are in the passive voice.

Answer to question about sentence with a subordinate clause on p.150.
The subordinate clause is underlined. The rest is the main clause.

> *However, if the idea is explained carefully and through modelling and examples, there is no reason why most children shouldn't grasp the concept.*

Further reading

Crystal, D. (2005) *How Language Works*. London: Penguin.

This excellent book provides clear examples of language usage with simple explanations. The book is also full of interesting examples and provides an excellent starting point for studying language acquisition and development.

Horton, S. and Bingle, B. (2014) *Lessons in Teaching Grammar in Primary Schools*. London: Sage.

This book explains concepts in a simple and engaging way and provides lesson plans.

Waugh, D., Allott, K., Waugh, R., English, E. and Bulmer, E. (2014) *The Spelling, Punctuation and Grammar app*. Morecambe: Children Count Ltd (available through the App Store).

This app provides guidance and activities on all aspects of grammar, spelling and punctuation.

References

Andrews, R., Torgerson, C., Beverton, S., Freeman, A., Locke, T., Low, G., Robinson, A. and Zhu, D. (2004) The effect of grammar teaching on writing development. *British Educational Research Journal*, 32(1): 39–55.

Crystal, D. (2004) *Making Sense of Grammar.* Harlow: Pearson Longman.

DfE (2013) *The National Curriculum in England: Key stages 1 and 2 framework document*. London: DfE. Available from: **www.gov.uk/government/uploads/system/uploads/attachment_data/file/425601/PRIMARY_national_curriculum.pdf** (accessed 25.10.15).

Myhill, D., Lines, H. and Watson, A. (2010). *Making Meaning with Grammar: A Repertoire of Possibilities*. University of Exeter, UK. Unpublished.

Reed, A. and Kellogg, B. (1877) *Higher Lessons in English*. New York: Clark and Maynard.

Trask, R. (1994) *Language Change*. London: Routledge.

Wilder, Laura Ingalls (1941) *Little Town on the Prairie*. New York: Harper.

9 Putting it all together

Learning outcomes

By reading this chapter you will develop ideas for:

- creating cohesive texts with children;
- developing lessons which model writing;
- helping children to understand and use paragraphs effectively;
- constructing activities which will develop appropriate vocabulary for cohesion.

Teachers' Standards
This chapter will help you with the following Teachers' Standards.

3 Demonstrate good subject and curriculum knowledge:
- have a secure knowledge of the relevant subject(s) and curriculum areas, foster and maintain pupils' interest in the subject, and address misunderstandings;
- demonstrate a critical understanding of developments in the subject and curriculum areas, and promote the value of scholarship;
- demonstrate an understanding of, and take responsibility for, promoting high standards of literacy, articulacy and the correct use of Standard English, whatever the teacher's specialist subject.

Introduction

In previous chapters, you have seen how words can be created by building them from graphemes; and how we can then build words further by combining them to create compounds, or by adding prefixes and suffixes to modify their meaning. You have seen ways in which words can be brought together to create phrases, clauses and sentences. In this chapter, you will see how you can help children to bring together sentences to develop coherent, cohesive texts.

Of course, when we build texts we also need to know what whole texts look like and how all of the parts come together. This means that it is important that you share whole texts with children regularly through stories, poems and non-fiction. At the same time, you need to work with children to model writing, drawing upon their ideas and relating what you do to the whole texts with which children are familiar.

The Teaching Sequence for Writing illustrates the process (adapted from DCSF, 2011):

Teaching Sequence for Writing	
Stage in sequence	Activity and teacher's role
Familiarisation with the text/genre	Shared reading, exploring texts, discussing genre, identifying structure and language choices.
Capturing ideas	Developing ideas for content and inviting children for suggestions as to how to set out/ begin a piece of writing.
Teacher demonstration	Teacher models the writing process, for example thinking aloud while writing, talking about vocabulary, phrasing, presentation, etc. Increasingly, children are asked to make suggestions, perhaps by writing on mini-whiteboards and sharing ideas.
Supported writing	As children write, perhaps in pairs or small groups, teacher supports, prompts, shares ideas, etc.
Guided writing	Teacher works with a small group as they write, focusing on the particular aspect of writing the children need to strengthen, for example generating ideas, vocabulary, phrasing, spelling, punctuation, appropriate style, etc.
Independent writing	Children work independently of the teacher individually or in pairs.

Of course, the sequence may vary according to the children's needs, but key elements such as sharing examples of texts, modelling writing and moving towards independent writing will almost always feature. Even then, however, there may be room for flexibility.

In the case study below, the teacher begins a writing activity with a visual stimulus and then asks the children to make brief notes. These are then drawn upon in a shared writing activity in which she models writing for the children. Notice how, on this occasion, shared reading follows shared writing in order to broaden children's understanding of the genre in which they have written with the teacher, and to enable them to develop their writing further in a subsequent activity.

Case study: modelling cohesive writing

Heather wanted to encourage her Year 2 class to build coherent and cohesive texts, and decided to use descriptive writing as a starting point. She had hoped to use the weather as a theme and prepared by taking photographs of the school and its locality when heavy snowfall was forecast. These included scenes familiar to the children before snowfall; as snow began to fall; during a blizzard; thick snow in sunshine with children playing; and a snowy scene as darkness fell.

$\longrightarrow$

Heather put the photographs together in a PowerPoint presentation with space to add text beneath each photograph. She then talked with her class about the snow and their experiences of it, asking questions such as:

- When did you first know it was snowing?

- How did you feel?

- Have you played in the snow?

- Do you like the snow?

- Has the snow caused any problems?

She showed her class the PowerPoint pictures and asked children, in pairs, to use mini-whiteboards to jot down words which sprang to mind as they looked at each picture. Children were encouraged to share ideas with partners and to get their ideas written down without worrying about accurate spelling at this stage. (Do choose your words carefully when telling children that 'spelling doesn't matter' – it does, but accuracy is less important at some times than others.)

After showing the first picture, which depicted the school entrance before the snow fell, Heather asked children to hold up their whiteboards so that everyone could see what they had written. She wrote some of the children's ideas into PowerPoint. These included: no snow yet; waiting for the snow; sky getting darker. One pair had written 'anticipating the snow' and Heather took the opportunity to talk about what the word meant, citing examples such as anticipating Christmas, playtime, lunch and a birthday party.

By asking the children to write about one picture at a time and discussing and sharing their ideas, Heather built up an understanding in the class of ways of describing the scenes, and she found that children became more adventurous in their use of language with each successive picture.

Once all the pictures had been studied, Heather went back to her notes in PowerPoint and asked children to help her to turn them into sentences. She then wrote these on the board until a five-sentence piece had been created. Heather read this with the children and asked them to look at it critically and find ways of improving it. In particular, she asked them to look for ways to make links between sentences or ways to join some sentences together. The first draft was as follows:

The day is coming to an end as we anticipate the snow. Suddenly, fluffy white flakes fall from the sky, gradually covering the streets, houses and gardens. In the morning, children roll the snow to make snowmen and throw it at each other in the sunshine. By the time darkness comes, the snowmen shiver, with only their hats and scarves to keep them warm.

Heather followed up the work by reading a selection of poems about snow to the children and taking them out onto the school field to play in the snow. She then asked them to work in pairs and small groups to write in more detail about being in the snow.

Heather's work with her Year 2 class demonstrates the importance of providing visual stimuli for writing, as well as showing how writing can be modelled and developed from *observing* to *thinking* to *making notes* to *developing sentences* and then *cohesive paragraphs*. The quality of the writing produced in the shared writing activity is unlikely to be matched by many Year 2 children working independently, but it sets a standard for them and provides them with ideas for phrasing and structure.

Curriculum links

This way of working should not be confined to descriptive writing and might be used when writing in a range of genres. Rather than expecting children to produce a cohesive piece of writing at first attempt, we can help them to plan and structure their work so that they have an overview of a potential final product as they write. In history, this might involve making a timeline of events and adding brief notes about each, while in science notes can be made about key elements of an experiment, process or cycle, before children write in sentences and paragraphs.

A central theme of this chapter is cohesive writing, and this may seem to imply that this will generally involve creating longer sentences, perhaps by linking ideas together. However, it should be remembered that short sentences are also important and can be very powerful when used well. While children certainly need to understand how to build multi-clause sentences and ways to manipulate clauses and phrases to make their writing more interesting and varied, they should not be told that long sentences are always good and short sentences always bad (see Chapter 8).

Research focus: long sentences

Kuiper and Scott Allan (2004, p.9) pose the question: *What is the longest English sentence?* Their answer is as follows:

> There isn't one. You can keep adding to a sentence ad infinitum by using the little word *and*. Whenever you think you have reached the last sentence in the language, it is always possible to produce another by taking the last sentence, adding *and* to it and joining another sentence after the *and*. That way you get a new sentence. This means that there is no limit to the number of sentences which can be constructed in accordance with the rules of English.

Grammatically, Kuiper and Scott Allan are quite correct, but imagine what it would be like to read a long sentence which comprises a series of clauses joined together by a series of *ands*.

Of course, young children often write in a rather similar way by repeatedly using *and* or *then* to make links between their sentences, which suggests they understand the need to be cohesive. However, as they develop as writers they need to be aware of different ways of making links which will make their writing flow without it being repetitive. The term often used for these is *cohesive devices*.

Cohesive devices

There are four main types of cohesive device: *reference, substitution and ellipsis, connectives*, and *lexical*. In this section you will find descriptions and examples of each.

Reference

Look at the sentence below:

> *She told it to go away.*

The sentence is grammatically correct, but on its own it doesn't tell us very much. Who is *she* and what did she tell *to go away*? However, if we put another sentence before or after it, we begin to create cohesion:

> *The cat licked Alex's hand. She told it to go away.*

Or:

> *She told it to go away. Alex did not like it when the cat licked her hand.*

Now we have some cohesion, because one sentence refers to the other. We now know that the pronoun *she* refers to *Alex* and that the pronoun *it* refers to *the cat*. This device enables us to avoid repeatedly using a name, and helps make writing more varied and interesting.

Substitution and ellipsis

Look at the sentences below:

> *'Singing on stage can be very hard work,' said Adele.*
>
> *'Yes,' agreed Elliott, 'I can't understand why anyone would want to do that.'*

In Elliott's speech he substitutes *do that* rather than repeating *singing on stage*.

In the following sentence *so* is used to replace *it would snow heavily*:

> *John said that he hoped it would snow heavily the next day, and Sally said that she hoped so too.*

So we can substitute words or phrases for others to avoid repetition. We might also miss some things out altogether if our writing is sufficiently clear for the reader to understand what is missing. For example:

In one city there is an underground railway, but in another there are trams.

Here the word *city* is omitted in the second clause, but we have no difficulty in understanding that *another* refers to *another city*.

Activity

Look at the sentences below and decide what has been omitted in each:

On weekdays I eat a large plate of chips but on Sundays I never do.

One end of the pitch was muddy but the other was dry.

Possible solutions to the Activity are:

On weekdays I eat a large plate of chips but on Sundays I never do.

*On weekdays I eat a large plate of chips but on Sundays I never **eat a large plate of chips**.*

One end of the pitch was muddy but the other was dry.

*One end of the pitch was muddy but the other **end of the pitch** was dry.*

Connectives

The term *connective* has been used in the past as an umbrella term for words which help cohesion. This term is now regarded as being insufficiently precise and it no longer appears in the National Curriculum. We have used it here as an overarching term for cohesive or linking devices which may include *conjunctions*, *adverbs and adverbials*, *noun phrases* and *preposition phrases*. Children will need to be able to use these precise terms confidently for the GP&S tests, but more importantly, they need to know how to use them to provide signposts for their reader and ensure that their writing flows well. Regardless of whether or not the term *connectives* is used in the classroom, children need to understand the importance of drawing ideas together in their writing, as well as in separating them. They also need to understand the importance of using the most appropriate words and phrases when they want to relate things to each other and to show passage of time in their writing.

Conjunctions

Conjunctions join words, phrases and clauses within sentences.

The words *but* and *and* are both coordinating conjunctions. They link clauses with the same importance to create single, longer sentences.

> *There was a drought in spring 2012,* **but** *it ended with a heavy downpour.*

> *There are several popular crime dramas on television,* **and** Lewis, Inspector George Gently *and* Vera *are all watched by millions of people.*

As we saw in Chapter 8, subordinate clauses don't make sense on their own and need to be joined to the main clause by the subordinating conjunctions. In the following examples, the subordinating conjunctions are *where* and *even though*.

> *She walked to the end of the pier* **where** *the seagulls were already gathering.*

> *He knew he needed to get there* **even though** *it was getting late.*

Using subordination can strengthen cohesion by making the relationship between clauses more explicit, for example through such explanatory or causal links.

Adverbs and adverbials

We have already seen that adverbs are a word class. Adverbs can modify a verb, an adjective, another adverb or even a whole clause. They also include words that connect clauses to the content of the preceding text such as *meanwhile, however, moreover, altogether, therefore, consequently, otherwise* and *incidentally*.

An *adverbial* is the overarching category for words, phrases and clauses that act in the same way as an adverb. They often tell us when, how and where the verb is carried out and encompass many types of words and phrases – and not just adverbs! They can include preposition phrases such as *behind the dustbin*; noun phrases such as in the sentence: He finished work *this evening*; and subordinate clauses such as *until he had finished*.

Adverbials are highly versatile as they can be moved within a sentence. In the example, *He phoned her later that day*, 'later' refers back to something that happened earlier in the day. Note the change of emphasis if we write *Later that day, he phoned her*. When they come at the beginning of the sentence, they are usually followed by a comma and are known as fronted adverbials.

Adverbials also play an important role in connecting one part of the text with another and work across sentences. Examples include *in that case, on the other hand, several weeks later*.

Lexical cohesion

Lexical refers to words and *lexical cohesion* involves the use of synonyms or words which are related to each other semantically. For example:

*He used to own a **large dog**. The **huge hound** often barked all night.*

*Jade **kicked** the ball forward and then **hoofed** it into the back of the net.*

Here, *large dog* and *huge hound* are synonymous in the first sentence, while *kicked* and *hoofed* are synonymous in the second.

Activity

Look at the sentences below and consider different ways of making links between them to create a cohesive paragraph. This might involve using conjunctions to join some together or to begin sentences, or it might involve adding or changing words and presenting information in a different order.

Paul was good at most sports.

Paul loved football.

Paul hated rugby.

Rugby seemed to involve lots of pushing and shoving and mud.

Football seemed faster and more skilful.

You could still get muddy playing football.

Paul was not very tall or strong.

He could run very quickly.

Because of the huge variety of ways in which we can express ideas in English, it is unlikely than any two people working independently would rewrite the text above in exactly the same way. There is no correct answer, but there are many ways to make the text cohesive and coherent. As you saw in an earlier chapter, one strategy could be to use subordinate clauses to create longer complex sentences, or to use coordinating conjunctions to create compound sentences. Another could involve replacing nouns with pronouns to avoid repetition. One solution is presented below:

Paul was not very tall or strong, but he could run very quickly. He was good at most sports, and loved football but hated rugby. Rugby seemed to involve lots of pushing and shoving and mud, while football seemed faster and more skilful, although you could still get muddy playing football.

By combining and rearranging sentences and using subordinates and conjunctions such as *but*, *while* and *although*, we have made the text more coherent and cohesive.

In the case study below, Jerry, an experienced teacher, explores adverbials at the beginning of sentences in narrative writing with a Year 5 class. As you saw in Chapter 8, children can gain a great deal from oral work before writing takes place. Notice how Jerry draws upon a sample text first, then develops an oral activity, then models writing for the children, before asking them to work independently.

Case study: using adverbials to strengthen cohesion in a story

Jerry introduced children to some of the cohesive devices used by writers through shared reading. He talked to them about the words and phrases which he highlighted, before collecting these together on a flip chart to put on the working wall. They sorted the words and phrases by looking closely at how they signposted changes in direction (for example, *meanwhile*, *however*) and time (for example, *later*, *finally*, *eventually*) and talked about how they helped cohesion. Jerry explained that these were adverbials and asked the children to think about other sentences which might begin with some of the words. Finally, he organised a game in which a selection of words was given to children in pairs so that each pair had a card on which was written one of the following:

> *meanwhile, however, just then, next, in the end, after that, later, finally, eventually, at first, before, in the beginning, until then, up to that time, in the meantime*

Jerry invited suggestions for a story opening which would begin with one of the words or phrases. He asked the children to hold up their cards to suggest which could begin an opening sentence and which were unlikely to do so. Most agreed that *at first*, *before* and *in the beginning* were the most likely openers, but there was some debate about using some of the others where time shifts occur in stories and we read about an event that happens later.

Eventually, one pair began the story with:

> *In the beginning, Toby didn't like Sam.*

This was quickly followed by:

> *However, he soon changed his opinion.*
>
> *At first, Sam used to play on his own and never seemed to want to join in with Toby and his friends' games.*

At this point Jerry gave out mini-whiteboards and pens and asked children to write their sentences after they had said them aloud to the class. When everyone had taken a turn to

→

provide a sentence, he asked them to refine their sentences to make them more interesting, as well as to check spelling and punctuation.

After a few minutes, Jerry stopped the class and began to use the children's sentences to create a piece of shared writing, all the time encouraging children to read and re-read and offer suggestions for improvement. These included the use of subordinate phrases and clauses and adverbials. He encouraged them to think carefully about the best vocabulary to use. As a result, the opening lines became:

> *In the beginning, Toby didn't like the new boy, Sam.*
>
> *However, after the incident, he soon changed his opinion.*
>
> *At first, Sam used to play quietly on his own, on the other side of the playground, and never seemed to want to join in with the games Toby and his friends were playing.*

In subsequent lessons children developed the story independently or in pairs, and in guided writing groups with Jerry and his teaching assistant. Jerry drew the class together at least twice in each lesson to model writing, drawing upon children's suggestions and to share interesting vocabulary, phrasing and use of adverbials. A bank of these was created on the wall next to the board, and children were encouraged to 'magpie' some of them to include in their own writing if they wished.

You can see from the case study that by discussing children's ideas, sharing them orally and in writing, and modelling, it is possible to develop children's appreciation of the possibilities which exist for constructing writing and making it cohesive.

Curriculum links

In the National Curriculum (DfE, 2013, p.76,) children are introduced to *joining words and clauses* in Year 1, *subordination and coordination* in Year 2 (p.76), and *conjunction* in Year 3 (p.77). Here it states that children should develop their understanding by:

Expressing time, place and cause using **conjunctions** [for example, *when, before, after, while, so, because*], **adverbs** [for example, *then, next, soon, therefore*], or **prepositions** [for example, *before, after, during, in, because of*]

Year 6 children are expected to be able to link ideas across paragraphs using a wider range of **cohesive devices**: repetition of a **word** or phrase, grammatical connections [for example, the use of **adverbials** such as *on the other hand, in contrast,* or *as a consequence*], and **ellipsis** (DfE, 2013, p.79).

Cohesion within and between sentences

You may find it helpful, especially when working with older children, to provide a display of possible ways of combining information and developing cohesion for different situations. The table below shows different uses of conjunctions and provides examples.

Adding	Cause and effect
and	because
also	so
as well as	therefore
moreover	thus
too	consequently
Sequencing	**Qualifying**
next	however
then	although
first, second, third . . .	unless
finally	except
meanwhile	if
after	as long as
	apart from
	yet
Illustrating	**Emphasising**
for example	above all
such as	in particular
for instance	especially
as revealed by	significantly
in the case of	indeed
	notably
Comparing	**Contrasting**
equally	whereas
in the same way	instead of
similarly	alternatively
likewise	otherwise
as with	unlike
like	on the other hand

Activity

Look at the groups of words in the table above and try to construct a paragraph of sentences orally and then in writing, which use at least one conjunction in each sentence. Ideally, you should do this with a colleague. You may need to select some words from one group (for example, **Emphasising**) and some from another (for example, **Cause and effect**). Consider which genre or text type would be most appropriate for each paragraph. For example:

Although people often say that teachers have long holidays, it should be remembered that they work long hours. Indeed, some work for more than 60 hours a week, especially at the beginning of term. Consequently, many teachers are too tired to enjoy their holidays unless they can manage not to think about work at all.

Research focus: genres

Wilson (2005, pp. 31–2) maintains that problems arise when we try to define or count genres:

At times, some genre theorists have given the impression that examples of any given genre shared an identical structure. This implies that an individual writer, wanting to produce his or her own specimen of a genre – a business letter say – must have internalised the rules of production for this type of text and must strictly adhere to them . . . I have to say that to me genre counting sometimes seems akin to the medieval obsession with discussing how many angels can dance on the point of a needle because, though writers are operating within a social context and are aware of social pressures and expectations, the human mind is inventive and very few text types will stay fixed for long.

It is worth considering the implication of Wilson's views when examining the table below. There is often overlap between text types, and sometimes genres can be mixed within the same document. For example, instruction/procedural texts are often said to be characterised by having sentences that begin with imperative verbs (*mix the eggs, milk and flour; pour into a pudding tin; bake in a pre-heated oven*, etc.). However, some instructional texts include *adverbials of time* (adverbials that refer to time or sequence) such as *first, next* and *finally*, and new forms of texts are constantly being created electronically with hyperlinks and so forth. Nevertheless, the table may help you to consider typical purposes and cohesive devices for text types which feature in the curriculum and should become part of children's reading and writing repertoire.

Textual cohesion and different genres/text types

The table below examines non-fiction texts and shows how different types of non-fiction texts make use of different cohesive devices. Before looking at it, ensure you have read the cautionary note from Wilson (above) about defining and counting genres and text types.

Non-fiction text types and cohesive devices		
Text type	Purpose	Cohesive devices
Discussion	To present a reasoned and balanced overview of an issue or controversial topic. Usually aims to provide two or more different views on an issue, each with elaborations, evidence and/or examples.	Uses adverbials, e.g. *for example, therefore, however, on the other hand, in contrast.*
Explanatory	To explain how or why, e.g. to explain the processes involved in natural/social phenomena or to explain why something is the way it is.	Use of adverbials of time, e.g. *first, then, after that, finally.* Use of causal conjunctions, e.g. *so, because of this.*
Instructional/ procedural	Like all text types, variants of instructions occur and they can be combined with other text types. They may be visual only (e.g. a series of diagrams with an image for each step in the process) or a combination of words and images. Instructions and procedural texts are found in all areas of the curriculum and include rules for games, recipes, instructions for making something and directions.	Use of imperative verbs (commands), e.g. **Cut** the card . . . **Paint** your design . . . Instructions may include negative commands, e.g. *Do not use any glue at this stage.*
Persuasion	To argue a case from a particular point of view and to encourage the reader/listener towards the same way of seeing things.	Uses logical rather than adverbials of time, e.g. *This proves that . . . So it's clear . . . Therefore . . .* These are often fronted.
Non-chronological reports	To provide detailed information about the way things are or were. To help readers/listeners understand what is being described by organising or categorising information.	Uses the language of comparison and contrast, e.g. *Polar bears are the biggest carnivores of all. They hibernate, just like other bears. A polar bear's nose is as black as a piece of coal.*
Recounts	The primary purpose of recounts is to retell events. Their most common intentions are to inform and/or entertain.	Events being recounted have a chronological order so adverbials of time are common, e.g. *then, next, first, afterwards, just before that, at last, meanwhile.*

In the case study below, the teacher, Emily, works with a mixed Year 4/5 class to explore the use of conjunctions. Notice how the work leads towards a differentiated activity in which the older children create an exercise for the younger ones.

Case study: cohesive devices in non-fiction

Emily collected several different non-fiction texts and gave each of five tables of six children a selection of three. She asked them to look at the texts and find out different ways in which authors had linked and separated sections. For example, some texts included bullet points or subheadings, while others had adverbials of time such as *first, next, then* and *finally.*

→

Emily then looked at an example of a piece of instructional writing which used adverbials of time at the beginning of each sentence rather than beginning with an imperative verb. She read the text to and with the children and discussed the use of the adverbials, which were *first, after that, next, now* and *finally*. Emily then showed a similar piece of writing, but this time left spaces where the time words would appear. She read the text to the children and then with them, asking them to suggest suitable words to fill the spaces.

Subsequently, children produced their own instructions for making various foods (chocolate rice crispies, sandwiches, jacket potato and beans), making use of the adverbials they had discussed in previous lessons.

The Year 5 children were then asked to work in pairs to produce paragraphs of non-fiction texts which included adverbials. They could choose subjects which interested them and make use of books and websites to research the topics. Once they had produced a paragraph, they had to save a copy and then on a second copy take out the adverbials and leave underlines to replace the missing words. After Emily had read their work and corrected it where appropriate, the children then passed it on to the Year 4 pupils whose task was to select appropriate adverbials to fill the spaces.

The case study shows how language activities can be differentiated and children in mixed-age classes can develop activities for each other. A high proportion of schools in Britain have mixed-age classes, especially those with fewer than 200 pupils, so it is important that you develop strategies for engaging different groups.

Curriculum links

In the National Curriculum, Year 4 children are required to use paragraphs to organise ideas around a theme, and Year 5 children are required to use devices to build cohesion within a paragraph (e.g. *then, after that, this, firstly*) (DfE, 2013, pp.77–8).

Paragraphs

You have only to look at a page of solid unbroken prose to see why we have adopted the use of paragraphing in our writing. Many legal documents give a good example of this: the prose continues unbroken, often for several pages. In such documents, this is deliberate; where every word and every break can give rise to disputes about the exact interpretation, and vast amounts of money, prestige or reputation can rest on such disputes, it is important not to allow any accidental chance for a reader to say, 'This is a new paragraph and therefore the previous sentence does not apply to it.' Nevertheless, we usually need to read such documents several times before we can be sure we have understood them!

Paragraphs divide up a long text into manageable chunks, usually providing a new idea or event in each one, and make it easier for the reader to assimilate and understand the material which is being presented.

In fiction texts written for very young readers, it is not unusual to find almost every sentence starting on a new line – presented as a new paragraph, in other words. As the reader's attention span grows longer, each paragraph will also be longer. Any simple idea or statement will be expanded, described or commented on, and will generally continue until something else happens in the narrative. If the reader perseveres, she or he will eventually come to the solid structures of paragraphs which can follow a character's train of thought, or describe the details of a scene, for almost a whole page at a time undivided. A random choice of literature, with chapters chosen from different novels, showed that in a chapter from *Five Go to Billycock Hill* by Enid Blyton, there was an average of eight paragraphs to a page, with the average number of sentences per paragraph being two. In Daniel Defoe's *Robinson Crusoe*, the corresponding figures were two paragraphs to a page and twelve sentences to a paragraph. It is easy to draw conclusions about the reading ages expected for each! A similar exercise may be done by comparing editorial articles in, for example, the *Telegraph* and one of the 'red-top' newspapers such as the *Sun*.

When planning an essay or other piece of *discursive* writing (writing which is intended to present or discuss a point of view), we usually start with a rough plan. If using a computer, we often do this using bullet points which sum up each of the points we want to mention. We then expand these, making and explaining the point from each 'headline' in full expanded sentences, and giving evidence to support our points if this is relevant. For instance, a plan for this section of the chapter might have read:

- Statutory? documents etc.
- Why use paragraphs?
- Ease of reading:
  - Blyton vs Defoe
  - newspapers
- Planning with bullet points
  etc.

It is usual for the first sentence of a paragraph to introduce the idea which is about to be expanded, and not uncommon for the final one to sum up the point which has been made in the paragraph. This is similar to the way in which a good essay or composition will have an introduction and a conclusion, or the way a television or radio news programme presents the headlines at the beginning and the end. (As an early newsreader is alleged to have said, 'First you tell them what you're going to tell them; then you tell them; then you tell them what you've told them.') A well-structured paragraph should be readable on its own, although obviously the context would be needed for full understanding.

An activity to develop children's understanding and awareness of paragraphs

Shared reading of non-fiction texts can be used to draw children's attention to the reasons for changes of paragraphs and to promote discussion about their content. This can be followed by giving children examples of texts which feature a series of paragraphs. Ask them to:

- identify what each paragraph is about and describe this in notes or in a single sentence;
- suggest a title for each paragraph – this could be a subheading if the text is organised differently;
- state why each new paragraph has been started, for example, new time, place, topic.

They could go on to present the text in different ways, either using pens, pencils and paper or using charts and other presentational features on a computer. For example, a text which describes the life cycle of a frog might be presented in a flow chart or circular diagram or as a storyboard.

This process can also be done in reverse, if children are provided with charts and diagrams representing a sequence and are then asked to write a series of paragraphs on the topic. Exploring texts in this way not only helps children to understand textual features and become confident in using them, but also helps with note-taking through its focus on identifying key pieces of information in texts.

Conclusion

Teaching and learning how to construct cohesive texts need not be dull and can, in fact, involve lively discussion, oral work, modelling and creative activities. It might involve building texts or even taking existing texts and reshaping them.

One way in which we can develop our ability to use cohesive devices and our appreciation of different ways in which text can be restructured is through the once widely used practice of *précis*. As the word, which is French in origin, implies, this involves making something more precise and often requires pupils to take a passage of text and reduce it to a specified number of words while retaining its essential meaning. In doing this, we need to consider what are the key facts or details which need to be retained if the text is still to be useful and convey meaning, and we also need to experiment with different phrasing, word order and sentence structure. We will draw upon cohesive devices such as reference and omission to enable us to avoid repetition which would eat up valuable words, and we will make use of punctuation to draw clauses and phrases together, perhaps in place of conjunctions. For an example for you to try, see question 3 in the self-assessment questions below.

Learning outcomes review

You should now have ideas for creating cohesive texts with children which can be modelled through shared writing. In modelling writing and discussing cohesive devices such as conjunctions, you should be able to help children to understand and use paragraphs effectively.

Self-assessment questions

1. Name four cohesive devices.
2. What kind of cohesive devices are used in each of the following text types?

   - instructional/procedural;
   - recounts;
   - discussion.

3. Now draw upon all that you have learned from this chapter to attempt the following activity. Look at the information below, which is written in 150 words. Can you rewrite it in 80 words without removing any important information? Consider which cohesive devices you might need to help you to bring items together. How will you change punctuation? Which conjunctions might you use? (A possible solution is provided in Appendix 2, but your version will almost certainly be equally valid.)

   The Beatles were a very popular group in the 1960s. Millions of people all over the world bought their records and copied their hairstyles. Most of their songs were written by John Lennon and Paul McCartney, but some were written by George Harrison and Ringo Starr. The group came from Liverpool and some people even tried to talk with Liverpool accents to copy The Beatles. People screamed and fainted at their concerts. Ringo was the drummer and his real name was Richard Starkey. He was called Ringo because he wore so many rings. The other group members played guitars. John also played the mouth organ and Paul sometimes played the piano. The Beatles' songs are still heard today. They include 'I Want to Hold Your Hand', 'Yesterday', 'Let it Be' and 'Yellow Submarine'. Unfortunately, John Lennon was killed in 1980. Sadly, George died in 2001: Paul and Ringo still record.

   (Adapted from Waugh, 1996, p.146)

Further reading

Crystal, D. (2008) *Making Sense of Grammar*. Harlow: Longman.

This provides clear and interesting explanations of key aspects of grammar.

DCSF The National Strategies (2008) *Talk for Writing*. Nottingham: DCSF National Strategies.

This resource is no longer in print, but should be available in schools and in higher education libraries and resource centres. It provides excellent video material and other resources, which show experienced teachers working with children to devise and develop texts.

Horton, S. and Bingle, B. (2014) *Lessons in Teaching Grammar in Primary Schools*. London: Sage.

This book explains concepts in a simple and engaging way and provides lesson plans.

Waugh, D., Allott, K., Waugh, R., English, E. and Bulmer, E. (2014) *The Spelling, Punctuation and Grammar App*. Morecambe: Children Count Ltd (available through the App Store).

This app provides guidance and activities on all aspects of grammar, spelling and punctuation.

References

DfE (2013) *The National Curriculum in England: Key stages 1 and 2 framework document*. London: DfE. Available from: **www.gov.uk/government/uploads/system/uploads/attachment_ data/file/425601/PRIMARY_national_curriculum.pdf** (accessed 25.10.15).

DfEE (2001) *Literacy Across the Curriculum*. London: DfEE.

Kuiper, K. and Scott Allan, W. (2004) *An Introduction to English Language*. New York: Palgrave MacMillan.

Waugh, D. (1996) *Curriculum Bank Writing KS2*. Leamington Spa: Scholastic.

Wilson, A. (2005) *Language Knowledge for Primary Teachers*, 3rd edition. London: David Fulton.

Conclusion

We hope that, having read this book, you now feel more confident about your ability to teach grammar, punctuation and spelling. We hope, too, that you are convinced of the importance of developing children's knowledge about language in an engaging and meaningful way. The following checklist for developing children's knowledge about language may help you to keep in mind some of the strategies that will help them.

- Discuss words and their meanings and origins.
- Talk about morphemes and the way in which words are put together.
- Make collections of words, for example, homonyms, antonyms, synonyms, loan words, homographs and homophones.
- Read to children regularly from a range of genres and be prepared to discuss authors' use of language.
- Discuss phrasing, words and punctuation in the context of whole texts.
- Make use of children's writing as a resource for discussing grammar and punctuation.
- Develop a vocabulary for discussing writing and don't be afraid to use correct terminology – if children can differentiate between a diplodocus and a brontosaurus, they can distinguish between an adjective and an adverb!
- Use modelled, shared and guided writing to model and to discuss ways in which language can be presented.
- Don't over-use exercises. Use exercises to reinforce and check learning rather than to teach, and explain how applying their new learning will improve the writing children are doing.
- Make use of investigations into spelling patterns, etc. to help develop and reinforce learning.
- Talk with children about why it is useful to develop a good knowledge about language.
- Develop your own knowledge and understanding of language and show that you are enthusiastic about language.
- Read about language. There are many excellent and accessible texts, such as those by Bryson and Crystal, which provide fascinating insights into language, and you will find several websites which offer simple guidance on such issues as using apostrophes and the etymology of our words.
- Grammar, spelling and punctuation can be challenging for even the most sophisticated writers at times. Don't be afraid to say that you are unsure about something and to investigate it more deeply: doing so provides a good model for children.

One of us recently received an e-mail from a student on a Sunday evening, asking if we could settle an argument the family was having about possessive apostrophes. Far from being irritated by the intrusion into the remnants of our weekend, we were delighted that someone one of us taught was sufficiently interested in language use to send the message. We were also pleased to be able to tell our student that she was correct, and that *it's* doesn't have an apostrophe when used as a possessive pronoun. Our book will be a success if it not only provokes discussion about language usage, but also encourages teachers and trainee teachers to engage their children in talk about language.

David Waugh
Claire Warner
Rosemary Waugh
January 2016

Appendix 1: Glossary of terms

The National Curriculum for English is quite specific about what children should know about grammar and the terminology they *should learn to recognise and use ... through discussion and practice.*

In Year 1 this includes: *word, sentence, letter, capital letter, full stop, punctuation, singular, plural, question mark, exclamation mark.*

In Year 2: *verb, tense (past, present), adjective, noun, suffix, apostrophe, comma.*

Year 3: *word family, conjunction, adverb, preposition, direct speech, inverted commas (or 'speech marks'), prefix, consonant, vowel, clause, subordinate clause.*

Year 4: *pronoun, possessive pronoun, adverbial.*

Year 5: *relative clause, modal verb, relative pronoun, parenthesis, bracket, dash, determiner, cohesion, ambiguity.*

Year 6: *active and passive voice, subject and object, hyphen, synonym, colon, semi-colon, bullet points.*

In this glossary you will find definitions of the terms found in the National Curriculum, together with brief suggestions for ways of developing children's understanding. You will also find, where appropriate, chapter numbers to indicate where you can find out more. Some terms which do not feature in the National Curriculum are included for information, and these are shown in lower-case letters. We have tried to be as comprehensive as possible and have included:

- some words which are not in the National Curriculum document at all;
- some which are included in the glossary of the National Curriculum, but not in the programmes of study;
- others which are not defined in the National Curriculum, but are used as part of the definitions given;
- other terms which are in the programme of study, but not the terminology for pupils.

Term	Definition	How you might teach it	Chapter(s) in which you will find out more
		(NB This may be as a lesson, a game, an investigation or as a short warm-up activity at the beginning of a literacy lesson)	
Abbreviation	Abbreviations are shortened forms of words which include part of the longer word. We often shorten our first names or have them shortened by our friends, e.g. *Nick* for *Nicholas* and *Tom* for *Thomas*. We also abbreviate using some letters from words while missing others out between them as in *ltd* for *limited*, *cm* for *centimetre*.	Look at children's names – *Alex* for *Alexander* or *Alexandra*, *Kate* for *Katherine*, etc.	7
		Look at abbreviations which have come into common use, e.g. *pram*, *bus*, *i-* and *e-* (as in i-book and email), and abbreviations used only in writing such as *etc.*, *i.e.* and *e.g.*	
		Look at place names, for example when written on road lanes, e.g. *S'BORO*, *B'TON*.	
		Look at abbreviations in maths, e.g. *approx* for *approximately*, *mm* for *millimetres*.	
Acronym	An abbreviation made from the first letters of a group of words and sometimes said as a single word, e.g. WYSIWYG (What you see is what you get); and SATs for Standard Assessment Tests. Other acronyms tend to be said letter by letter, e.g. *RIP, MOD, TA* and *RSPCA*.	Look at texting – *LOL, OMG*, etc.	2, 3
		Explore well known acronyms – *BBC, NSPCC, QPR*.	
		Look at words which were created from acronyms – *nylon, radar, laser, scuba*.	
		Children can create acronyms for their names – *Kate* could be 'Kind and tremendously enthusiastic', or *Tim* might be 'Top in maths'.	
ADJECTIVE	Adjectives describe people and things, e.g. a *red rose*; *three dogs*; a *heavy weight*. They **modify** nouns.	Adjective-noun poems.	2
	Adjectives can also follow the verb *to be*, e.g.	Match adjectives to nouns in classroom and in pictures.	
	York is beautiful.	Take simple sentences and add adjectival/relative phrases or clauses.	
	David is happy.	Match adjectival phrases or clauses to simple sentences.	
	These are adjectival phrases and **complement** the verb. They provide more information about nouns and pronouns.		

(Continued)

(Continued)

Term	Definition	How you might teach it	Chapter(s) in which you will find out more
ADVERB	Adverbs are used to modify a verb, an adjective, or another adverb, e.g. She ran *quickly* – modifies a verb. York is *incredibly* beautiful – modifies an adjective. He drove *extremely* slowly – modifies another adverb. Fortunately, Rovers scored a *last-minute* goal – modifies a whole sentence. Usually (but not always), adverbs are created by adding the letters *ly* to the end of an adjective, e.g. *lucky* – *luckily*; *beautiful* – *beautifully*. Adverbs can be classified as adverbs of time, manner, frequency and so on, according to what kind of information they give. For instance: He arrived *later* – time. He arrived *noisily* – manner. He arrived *often* – frequency.	(NB This may be as a lesson, a game, an investigation or as a short warm-up activity at the beginning of a literacy lesson) A kinaesthetic approach can help children understand the function of adverbs. Try asking them to perform different actions such as walking, waving, smiling and talking in different ways (quickly, slowly, quietly, warmly, loudly, etc.). To show how adverbs can be placed at the front of a sentence, play 'fortunately/unfortunately', in which children take turns to make up a sentence which begins with one of the words, and tell a story: Fortunately, it's a very nice day. Unfortunately, there are clouds on the horizon and it looks as if it will rain. Fortunately, I have an umbrella. Unfortunately, it has a hole in it (etc.).	2
ADVERBIAL CLAUSE	An adverbial clause acts in the same way as an adverb but is a group of words which includes a verb, e.g. Billy kicked the ball *as if he was angry with it.*	Study of adverbial clauses can involve oral work, with children being given sentences to enhance. They might go on to try these in writing and to identify examples in texts.	8
ADVERBIAL PHRASE	Adverbial phrases add words before and/or after an adverb, e.g. *as quickly as possible.* Unlike an adverbial clause, an adverbial phrase doesn't include a verb.	Find examples of adverbial phrases in texts in shared reading. Ask children to take simple sentences and enhance them by adding adverbial phrases. Discuss the placement of adverbial phrases: they may follow the simple sentence or precede it (see **Fronted**).	8

Term	Definition	How you might teach it	Chapter(s) in which you will find out more
		(NB This may be as a lesson, a game, an investigation or as a short warm-up activity at the beginning of a literacy lesson)	
AGREEMENT	The subject and verb in a sentence must agree with each other in person and in number, e.g. I *am* at home – They *are* at home She *has* a cat – They *have* a cat. A few pronouns also change to agree with their role as subject or object in a sentence: I see them – They see me.	Provide lots of examples, both correct and incorrect, for children to discuss. For children who are learning a modern foreign language, this offers an opportunity to discuss the verb 'to be', which is often the most difficult for people to recognise as a verb. By looking at, say, *être* in French or *sein* in German, we can show how the most common verb changes to agree with its subject. Children who are speakers of other languages or learning a modern language may have met the idea of other agreements, such as that between nouns and adjectives – a point for discussion.	8
Antonym	Antonyms are opposites, such as *good* and *bad*, *high* and *low*, *hard* and *soft*.	Play simple opposites games with children. Make a set of cards with pairs of antonyms and ask them to play a snap game matching them. They can also play concentration games in which words are turned face down and turned over in pairs, with children trying to find pairs of antonyms. As children's knowledge of language develops, link work on antonyms with work on connectives to create compound and complex sentences with each clause having an antonym and being linked by a connective, e.g. Will's job was easy but his life was hard. Jo's idea was a good one, despite the bad feeling Tom had about it.	2
APOSTROPHE	Apostrophes can be used: • to show that letters are missing, e.g. *don't*, *shouldn't*, *can't*; • to show possession, e.g. *Abi's book*, *Sam's spade*.	Find and photograph examples of apostrophes in shops, etc. and include some which are incorrect. Show the examples to the children and discuss them. Why have apostrophes been used? Why should some not have been used?	7

(Continued)

(Continued)

Term	Definition	How you might teach it	Chapter(s) in which you will find out more
APOSTROPHE (Continued)	Possessive apostrophes are widely misunderstood, especially for plural nouns. Where a word is plural the apostrophe follows it, e.g. *the girls' toilets*, *the children's books*. In *girls* the plural is formed by adding -s so the apostrophe follows the -s. *Children* is the plural of *child* so we put the apostrophe after children – the -s is added to make it easier to say (but often difficult to punctuate!).	Show children examples of English from the past such as Chaucer's work, in which *-es* tends to be added to show possession (*The Nonnes Priestes Tale*). Talk about how the *e* has now been replaced by an apostrophe. Look at examples of sentences where an apostrophe is necessary for understanding, e.g. *Those things over there are my husbands.*	
AMBIGUITY	Sentences are ambiguous when it is unclear who is performing an action or what the action is, e.g. *Dogs must be carried on the Underground.* Does this mean that you must pick your dog up if you take a Tube train or is it compulsory to carry a dog? *Please sign up for a meeting on Monday.* Does this mean that you need to wait until Monday or that the meeting is on Monday?	Make a collection of potentially ambiguous sentences and ask children to discuss the different ways in which they might be interpreted.	6, 7
CLAUSE	A clause is a group of words that contains a verb – it describes someone or something actively 'doing or being', e.g. *when the boy watched the film* (*the boy* is the subject; *watched* is the verb); *she plays netball* (*she* is the subject; *plays* is the verb); *his fierce manner* is a phrase – there is no verb saying what the fierce manner did or what happened to it; *his fierce manner alarmed me* – this is a clause, because the fierce manner did something. A sentence is made up of one or more clauses:	Provide sets of clauses and ask children to find different ways of combining them. In shared writing, model sentence combining by showing how clauses can be brought together to create single sentences.	8

Term	Definition	How you might teach it (NB This may be as a lesson, a game, an investigation or as a short warm-up activity at the beginning of a literacy lesson)	Chapter(s) in which you will find out more
	It was raining.		
	It was raining *and the sky was grey* – two clauses, both main (equal, joined by *and*).		
	It was raining, *but we had a wonderful time* – main clause followed by a subordinate clause (in italics).		
	A main clause is complete on its own and can form a complete sentence.		
	A subordinate clause cannot be a sentence on its own, e.g.		
	I shall be late *if I miss this bus.*		
	Although we tried, we could not reach the branch.		
	Is this the dog *which bit the child?*		
	The house, *which was near the church,* looked deserted.		
COHESION	To be effective, text needs to be coherent and cohesive.	Look at sentences which are not coherent, and jokes which come from these, such as this example from the film *Mary Poppins*:	9
	Ideas in a text need to fit together and be relevant to each other so that the text is consistent and easy to follow for the reader. They need to be coherent.	*I know a man with a wooden leg named Smith.*	
		What's the name of his other leg?	
	Cohesion is created by using grammatical features such as connectives and punctuation to join ideas, e.g.		
	Ed wanted to be Prime Minister. Instead, he became Leader of the Opposition.		
	Instead links the two items together.		
	Jo loved bananas, so she bought a bagful.		
	So links two ideas.		

(Continued)

(Continued)

Term	Definition	How you might teach it (NB This may be as a lesson, a game, an investigation or as a short warm-up activity at the beginning of a literacy lesson)	Chapter(s) in which you will find out more
COHESION (Continued)	We can also use pronouns to make text cohesive, e.g. The dog was fierce. I had heard it barking the night before. *It* in the second sentence refers to *the dog* in the first. Nick loves his granny. He phones her every day. In the second sentence *her* refers to *granny* in the first.		
COHESIVE DEVICE	A cohesive device simply means any of the ways in which words or phrases may be connected with each other. A preposition, a conjunction, a connective adverb or a relative pronoun may serve as a cohesive device.	Give the children pairs or sets of simple sentences and see how many different ways they can join or connect them into longer structures.	9
Colloquial	Colloquialisms are used in everyday language rather than in formal speech or writing. These may be words, e.g. *telly* for *television*; *mum* for *mother*, or phrases, e.g. *doing your head in*, or *working your socks off*.	Explore the use of colloquialisms by children. Ask them to discuss with family and friends and make collections. Compare colloquialisms from different dialects and other versions of English, e.g. Australian, American. Get children in groups to act out a simple scene, once using completely formal language and once in colloquial language.	
COMPLEMENT	While many verbs have an *object* (e.g. Sharifa ate *the chocolate*, James fed *the dog*), the verb 'to be' is said to have a complement instead. This can be a noun or an adjective, e.g. The dog is a Labrador. The dog is brown. The complement gives more information about the subject, rather than telling us about an action. It is not the same as an object, because a complement is not something *affected by* the action of the verb. The subject and the complement can also be swapped around without the meaning being changed, e.g.	Model writing with children, encouraging them to look at how sentences might be restructured. Provide examples of sentences which include the verb 'to be', and ask children to suggest ways of changing their order.	8

Term	Definition	How you might teach it	Chapter(s) in which you will find out more
		(NB This may be as a lesson, a game, an investigation or as a short warm-up activity at the beginning of a literacy lesson)	
	My dad is the tallest man I know. The tallest man I know is my dad.		
COMPOUND WORD	A word made when two words are joined to form a new word, e.g. *toothbrush, football, toenail.* Hyphens are sometimes used to link the two parts of the word, e.g. *twenty-seven, self-audit, penalty-taker.*	Create a bank of words which can feature in compound words and ask children to match them. They could also invent new compound words, checking in a dictionary to see if they actually exist, and writing definitions, e.g. a *toebrush* for keeping toes clean; a *toothbag* for storing false teeth.	2
CONJUNCTIONS (see also Connectives)	These are words used to join words, phrases or clauses, e.g. *and, but* and *or.* There are two kinds of conjunction: **Coordinating conjunctions** (*and, but, or* and *so*) link statements of equal status, e.g. I ate the pizza and I drank the water. **Subordinating conjunctions** (*when, while, before, after, since, until, if, because, although, that*) link subordinate (less important) clauses to main clauses, e.g. *Before I went out, I combed my hair; I enjoyed the film, although it was rather violent in places.*	Look at compound sentences with children. Provide sets of simple sentences and ask them to combine them to make compound sentences linked by coordinating conjunctions. Ask children to write a series of short simple sentences which will form main clauses. Use some of these to model adding subordinate clauses, using conjunctions to link them to the main clauses, and then ask children to do the same.	2, 6, 8
Connectives	A connective is a word or group of words which connect words, phrases, clauses and sentences. This may be to help sequence ideas (*then, and finally*); to contrast ideas (*although, nevertheless, but despite that*); and to show cause and effect (*and due to that*). Connectives are often conjunctions, but adverbs and adverbial phrases and clauses can also work as connectives, e.g. *despite, eventually, in other words, that is to say.* The 2013 National Curriculum no longer uses the term connective, but it is still sometimes used in schools.	Find examples of connective phrases and clauses in texts and discuss them with children. Through shared writing, model ways of using connectives to join phrases, clauses and sentences. Emphasise in this, and all activities which involve expanding sentences, that sometimes short, simple sentences are the most effective way to express ideas, but that at other times writing becomes more interesting and informative if sentences are more complex. Look at how writers can use a combination of long and short sentences to make a passage interesting, or to achieve effects of drama, pathos, etc.	8, 9

(Continued)

Term	Definition	How you might teach it	Chapter(s) in which you will find out more
		(NB This may be as a lesson, a game, an investigation or as a short warm-up activity at the beginning of a literacy lesson)	
CONSONANT	Consonants are the sounds and letters which we make by touching parts of our mouth together. They are all the letters except 'a', 'e', 'i', 'o' and 'u', although 'y' can act as a consonant in *yes* and a vowel in *try*. See **Vowels**.	As children develop their understanding of and ability to distinguish between individual phonemes, look with them at common consonant clusters such as 'br', 'bl', 'sl', 'tr' and 'st'.	2, 4
CONTINUOUS TENSE	This term is used for the verb in a sentence when the action of the verb went on for a while. There is a present continuous, e.g. Hanif *is working*; and a past continuous, e.g. Anna *was travelling*.	Help children to understand the present continuous tense through activities such as taking on the role of the narrator during a role-play; provide opportunities for oral rehearsal prior to writing. Look with children at examples of text written in the continuous tense and ask them to help you to change it to the past tense, e.g. Hanif is working – Hanif worked. Anna was travelling – Anna travelled.	
COORDINATION	When a conjunction is used to link words or phrases as equals, they are coordinated, e.g. *Rome and Paris* are beautiful cities. We *ate and drank* all evening. John ate a *pear but Janet* ate an apple.	Link work on coordination to work on conjunctions and connectives, helping children to explore sentences in texts and asking them to produce their own examples.	9
DETERMINER	These are words used with nouns to help define them, e.g. *this* computer, *a* pencil, *the* book. The determiner limits, or determines, the reference of the noun in some way. Determiners include: • articles (*a/an*, the); • demonstratives (*this/that, these/those*); • possessives (*my, your, his, her, its, our, their*);	It tends to be the terminology rather than the concept which confuses people when they look at determiners, especially when they are referred to as definite and indefinite articles (*the* and *a/an*). Use the word *determiner* and play games in which singular and plural nouns are written on cards and children have to attach determiners to them: *that* dog, *this* dog, *a* dog, etc. Challenge them to see how many different determiners they can find for each word.	2

Term	Definition	How you might teach it (NB This may be as a lesson, a game, an investigation or as a short warm-up activity at the beginning of a literacy lesson)	Chapter(s) in which you will find out more
	quantifiers (*some, any, no, many, few, all, either, each*); • numbers (*one, two*, and so on); and • some question words (*which, what, whose*). Words used as determiners are followed by a noun (though not necessarily immediately), e.g. *Which black pen is mine?* *This book is yours.* Many determiners can also be used as pronouns. These include demonstrative pronouns, question words, numbers and most quantifiers. When used as pronouns, determiners are not followed by a noun – their reference includes the noun, e.g. *This is for you* (this book, this school, and so on).		
Dialect	All versions of a language are dialects and include words, phrases and clauses which may not appear in other dialects. Standard English is the dialect which is often accepted as 'correct' and is the version in which English should be written. Dialect should not be confused with accent. A dialect can be spoken with different accents. Our accent is the way we pronounce words, whereas our dialect has a grammatical structure, even if this is not written down as with Standard English.	Look for examples of regional dialect in the area where you teach. This could be phrases, clauses or individual words. Discuss the examples and compare them with Standard English forms. Look at examples of dialect in children's stories, e.g. Hodgson Burnett's *The Secret Garden*, books by Jan Mark, Dahl's *BFG* and *Danny the Champion of the World*. Look at texts written in dialect – for instance, poems by Robert Burns. See how much can be guessed or worked out. Make collections of different words for the same thing which are used in different areas and by different generations, e.g. the names of indoor shoes (*pumps, sandshoes, daps*, etc.); different ways of saying I am not (*I aren't, I bain't, I en't, I ain't*, etc.); or the words used in playground games when you are exempt from being 'had' (*fains, vainites, kings, crosses, pax*, etc.).	2

Term	Definition	How you might teach it (NB This may be as a lesson, a game, an investigation or as a short warm-up activity at the beginning of a literacy lesson)	Chapter(s) in which you will find out more
ELLIPSIS OR ELISION	The omission of one or more words from a sentence, especially when what is omitted can be understood from the context. Ellipsis is sometimes used to avoid repetition or give emphasis and it is a common feature of everyday conversation, e.g. Have Class 4 finished in the hall? Yes, break time this morning! (Yes, they finished in the hall by break time this morning.) Ellipses also occur in writing, e.g. The professor, although clever, was poor. The words *he was* are left out (*although he was clever*) but the sentence is still understood. Ellipses are also represented by three dots . . . to show that a number of words have been deliberately left out, or to show an unfinished thought at the end of a sentence.	Ask children to find examples of ellipsis in books and other texts. They will find examples in dialogue.	7
ETYMOLOGY	The study of words' origins and how they may have changed meaning or usage over time, e.g. *nice* originally meant something more like 'foolish', and *silly* meant 'simple'.	Encourage children to look in dictionaries to find the origins of words. Discuss etymology when talking about spelling and looking at morphology, e.g. looking at the origins of prefixes like *tele-*, *micro-* and *mega-* will help children interpret new words and provide strategies for reading them.	2
FINITE VERB	A finite verb is one which refers to a specific subject and action. Every sentence must have at least one finite verb. *The children read the books* is a sentence. *Reading books enthusiastically* is not, because it does not have a grammatical subject and *reading* is not a finite verb.	Provide examples of sentences and non-sentences and discuss with children which are complete and which need something else to complete them, e.g. in the definition *Reading books enthusiastically* would need a finite verb to make it into a sentence: The children *were* reading books enthusiastically.	8

Term	Definition	How you might teach it	Chapter(s) in which you will find out more
		(NB This may be as a lesson, a game, an investigation or as a short warm-up activity at the beginning of a literacy lesson)	
FRONTED	Sometimes we place words, phrases or clauses at the beginning of a sentence when they could equally well be placed after the verb, e.g. Mike ran a marathon, despite having sore feet. Despite having sore feet, Mike ran a marathon.	In shared reading, look for examples of fronted adverbials and discuss different ways in which sentences could be presented. Discuss why a writer might choose to construct a sentence this way, and what effects this can give to writing. Model fronting in shared writing and provide examples of sentences for children to create their own sentences and to look for opportunities when writing to vary sentence structures.	8
FUTURE TENSE	In English, references to the future are made using an auxiliary verb, usually *will* or *shall*. Tomorrow we *shall* go to the park. Class 4 *will* study the Romans next term.	Give children examples of sentences in the present tense and ask them to change them into the future tense, e.g. I am happy – I *will be* happy; John is a doctor – John *will be* a doctor.	8
GRAMMAR	A term used to refer to various aspects and levels of language as a system, e.g. the conventions which govern word formation and word order within sentences. More broadly, it covers the construction of larger units such as paragraphs and complete texts. Grammatical relationships within and between sentences are signalled by cohesive devices (see **Cohesion**). Grammar includes syntax (the study of sentence structure) and morphology (the study of word structure).	Discuss with children what is meant by grammar and provide examples of good and poor usage.	Introduction, 1, 2, 6, 8, 9
HOMOGRAPH	Homographs are words which are spelled the same as other words which mean something different and are pronounced differently, e.g. *sow* (spreading seeds) and *sow* (a female pig); *lead* (to take charge or something used to restrain a dog) and *lead* (a heavy metal), *row* (argue) and *row* (in a boat). Homograph means 'same writing'.	Ask children to make collections of homographs. Focus on the meanings to help them to see the difference between words.	2, 3

(Continued)

(Continued)

Term	Definition	How you might teach it (NB This may be as a lesson, a game, an investigation or as a short warm-up activity at the beginning of a literacy lesson)	Chapter(s) in which you will find out more
HOMONYM	Homonyms have the same spelling and pronunciation but different meanings, e.g. *left* (opposite of right) and *left* (departed). The term homonym is often used as a general term for **Homophones** and **Homographs**. Homonym means 'same name'.	Ask children to make collections of homonyms. Focus on the meanings to help them to see the difference between words.	2, 3
HOMOPHONE	Words which sound the same but have different spellings and meanings, e.g. *sea* and *see*; *sew*, *so* and *sow*; *blue* and *blew*; *great* and *grate*. Homophone means 'same sound'.	Ask children to make collections of homophones. Use mnemonics to distinguish between the homophones children find difficult, e.g. *practise* and *practice*: I practise singing; I go to cricket practice.	2, 3, 4, 5
Infinitive	The base form of a verb, usually used with 'to', e.g. *to read*, *to teach*. The infinitive is not a finite verb – it cannot be used on its own in a sentence. *To read a good book* is not a sentence.	Provide examples of the infinitive as a sentence opener in genres such as instructional or explanation text and ask children to suggest ways of continuing and completing sentences, e.g. *To drive a bus:* - you need a licence. - you need a lot of patience. - has been one of my ambitions for years.	8
INFLECTION	Inflection is a term meaning the changing of a word by adding prefixes of suffixes which change the meaning grammatically. Inflections in English include the genitive ('s); the plural (-s); the third person singular (-s); the past tense (-d, -ed or -t); the negative particle (-n't); -ing forms of verbs; the comparative (-er); and the superlative (-est).	Discuss ways in which words are made into plurals and ask children to investigate them to find patterns and probabilities, e.g. look at words which end with -sh, -ch and -tch which tend to have the inflection -es added for the plural. Ask children to look at texts to find other plurals and to decide which are the most common inflections for creating plurals.	2, 6

Term	Definition	How you might teach it	Chapter(s) in which you will find out more
		(NB This may be as a lesson, a game, an investigation or as a short warm-up activity at the beginning of a literacy lesson)	
Loan words	Loan words are words whose origins are from another language, but which have become widely used in English, such as *en route*, *etcetera, kindergarten*.	Loan words don't need to be specifically taught – there are so many of them – but you can extend children's fascination with words by drawing attention to word origins right across the curriculum. Ask children to investigate the origins of a selection of loan words. Talk about the way in which they are pronounced and the clues which this gives us about their origins, e.g. *ciabatta* and *cappuccino* from Italian have unfamiliar pronunciations of *c* and *cc*, while *hamburger* and *frankfurter* are named after the German cities where they originated: Hamburg and Frankfurt. It can be interesting to discuss the way in which *burger* has come to be a general term for a type of food and has been made into a compound according to what it is made from (*beefburger, beanburger, turkeyburger*).	3
MODAL VERB	Modal verbs are the verbs which change or modify the meaning of another verb; for instance, to refer to the future. In English, the main modal verbs are *will, would, can, could, may, might, shall, should, must* and *ought*. These verbs cannot stand alone in a sentence, although in conversation they are often used alone when the main verb is elided, e.g. Will you go to visit him? I should – I must – I shall!	Display modal verbs and talk about the function they have in a sentence, i.e. what they are there to tell us. Have modal verbs on card, a washing line and pegs. Sort out the modal verbs on a certainty/uncertainty continuum.	1
MODIFY	Modify means to give more information about a word in a sentence, to make it more specific or to tell how it is done. An adverb *modifies* a verb. A modifier may be a word, a phrase or a clause, e.g. He wandered aimlessly. He wandered, lonely as a cloud. He wandered as if he had all the time in the world.	Create short sentences for the children to extend with modifiers – adverbs, phrases or clauses.	8
MORPHEME	A morpheme is the smallest unit of language that can convey meaning. It cannot be broken down into anything smaller that has a meaning. A word may consist of one morpheme (*need*), two morphemes (*need/less, need/ing*) or three or more morphemes (*un/happi/ness*). Suffixes and prefixes are morphemes.	Make lists of familiar words which can be broken into morphemes, and look at patterns; use these to create new words.	2

(Continued)

Term	Definition	How you might teach it	Chapter(s) in which you will find out more
		(NB This may be as a lesson, a game, an investigation or as a short warm-up activity at the beginning of a literacy lesson)	
NOUN	Words used to identify people, places, things and ideas. The suffix 's' is often added to nouns to indicate a plural (more than one).	Make collections of collective nouns. You can find lots of examples on websites. Find interesting examples, e.g. *a murder of crows; a charm of goldfinches*. Discuss common collective nouns. Ask children to invent their own collective nouns for things which do not usually have them (*caravans, teachers*).	2
	Collective nouns		
	These are nouns that refer to a group of things or people, e.g. *collection, family*. Collective nouns may either have either singular or plural agreement with a verb, depending on the intended meaning, e.g. *his family is large* but we say *his family are all elderly* because we are eliding the members of his family.	For proper nouns, start with children's names and the names of places they know. Ask them to look for examples in texts.	
	Proper nouns		
	These nouns refer to the name of people, places or things that are unique and are normally written with an initial capital letter. Brand names of products and companies are proper nouns.		
	Noun phrases		
	These are groups of words doing the work of a single noun, e.g. *the chairman of the board of governors*.		
PARAGRAPH	A distinct division of text which begins on a new line and consists of one or more sentences, usually dealing with a single thought or topic, time or place, or quoting one speaker's continuous words.	Look at texts within shared reading and ask children to suggest reasons why paragraphs change. Provide examples of texts without paragraphs and ask children to mark where the paragraph should begin and end.	9
		Demonstrate how to 'box up' the text. This strategy helps children to gain a sense of structure when planning writing – it can be a paragraph planner, or each box may represent a number of paragraphs.	
PARENTHESIS	When writers wish to separate a word or phrase from the rest of the sentence we use devices such as brackets or dashes, known as parentheses (the plural of parenthesis), e.g.	Show children examples of parentheses in texts and discuss why they have been used. Explain that parentheses are useful devices but that, if used excessively, they can make the reader's task challenging as the text becomes disjointed.	6, 8
	He stepped from the train (he thought he must have been here before) and looked for the exit.		

Term	Definition	How you might teach it (NB This may be as a lesson, a game, an investigation or as a short warm-up activity at the beginning of a literacy lesson)	Chapter(s) in which you will find out more
	Brackets – which can be rounded or squared ( ) or [ ] – are often also called parentheses.		
PARTICIPLE	A verb form derived from its infinitive or base form and which can be used as an adjective. There are two participles in English: the present participle and the past participle. The **present** participle is formed by adding -ing to the base form of a verb: *working, reading, going,* and so on. The *-ing* ending is also used for a verb functioning as a noun, e.g. *Teaching is my chosen career.* This form is sometimes called a verbal noun or a gerund. The **past** participle often ends in *-ed*, but many common verbs are irregular and have other endings. Past participles are used after parts of *to have* to make the perfect tense (e.g. I *have* taught), and after parts of the verb *to be* to make the passive form (e.g. the papers *are* read, he *was* pushed). Participles, present and past, are sometimes used as adjectives: *falling* leaves, *stolen* goods. They can also be used to introduce participle verb phrases, e.g. *Being a teacher,* I work with young people. A **dangling** participle means that the subject of the participle is not the same as the subject of the main clause, e.g. *Reading my paper,* the afternoon passed slowly.	Look at examples of 'dangling participles' and help the children to see why these do not make grammatical sense.	8
PAST TENSE	A past-tense verb (a verb in the past tense) normally has a suffix *-ed,* and refers to an event or situation in the past.	Make a list of verbs which do not follow the regular pattern, e.g. *go, think, have.* Ask children to find more examples.	8
PERFECT	In grammar, perfect means 'completed', and the perfect form of a verb generally refers to an action which has happened once. It is formed by taking the past participle of the verb (e.g. *shown, taken, helped*) and adding the verb *have* before it (e.g. she *has* helped). It can also be combined with the continuous (e.g. he *has been* reading).	Look at examples of writing in the perfect tense and ask children to explore and discuss ways of changing tenses in a range of texts.	1

(Continued)

Term	Definition	How you might teach it (NB This may be as a lesson, a game, an investigation or as a short warm-up activity at the beginning of a literacy lesson)	Chapter(s) in which you will find out more
PHONEME	A speech sound. In writing, words are made up of letters and in speech they are made up of phonemes. There are roughly 44 phonemes in standard English, 20 vowels and 24 consonants. Phonemes can be represented by a single letter, pairs of letters (digraphs) such as *sh*, *ea* and *ll*, three letters (trigraphs) such as *tch*, and even four letters (*ough* as in *though*). English has 44 phonemes but more than 150 common ways of representing them, with many irregularities resulting from the language's development from a range of other languages. Thus *ch* can be pronounced as in *chip*, *chef* and *school*, while there are at least eight ways of representing the *c* sound in *cat*: *c, k, ck, q, que, cc, ch, kk*.	Children will probably have learnt phoneme-grapheme correspondences through a systematic programme in Key Stage 1. However, older children who continue to struggle may need additional tuition. They can also benefit from being given reinforcement activities at their maturity level: try activities such as 'football matches' in which children look for phonemes teams have in common and match them, e.g. Manchester City and **Chelsea**; Southampton and Sunderland.	4
PHRASE	A group of words not containing a verb, that acts as one unit. Some phrases act as nouns, e.g. *a newly qualified teacher*; some as adjectives, e.g. she is *utterly determined*; and some as adverbs, e.g. he goes to the gym *every now and again*. Many phrases are prepositional phrases (see **Preposition**), e.g. *on top of the cupboard*, *in a country far away*.	Encourage children to look for appropriate opportunities to incorporate subordinate phrases into their writing to add information. Discuss how these can be punctuated.	8
PLURAL	The plural forms of words show that they refer to more than one item. This usually involves adding an -s (*cats, books*) or -es (*matches, buses*); but some plurals are irregular, e.g. *child* becomes *children*, *mouse* becomes *mice*, and *goose* becomes *geese*. Some nouns remain the same in their plural form as in their singular form, including *sheep* and the names of many fish (*one haddock, two haddock; one salmon, two salmon*).	Make collections of plurals and look at them with children to work out common rules, e.g. adding -s, -es, changing medial vowels.	2
POSSESSIVE	A word which shows the possessor (owner) of a noun, e.g. *my book* shows that I am the owner of the book, and *the teacher's book* shows that the teacher is the owner. In these cases, the possessives are also determiners. However, if you omit the noun, you would use a possessive pronoun, e.g. *mine, yours*.	Look at examples of possessives and discuss with children when apostrophes should be used and how. Ask children to find examples in texts and sort these according to use of apostrophe and non-use of apostrophe.	7

Term	Definition	How you might teach it (NB This may be as a lesson, a game, an investigation or as a short warm-up activity at the beginning of a literacy lesson)	Chapter(s) in which you will find out more
PREDICATE	The predicate is all of a sentence except the subject – it gives information about the subject, e.g. *Asif went to Filey for his holidays. Asif* is the subject and *went to Filey for his holidays* is the predicate.		8
PREFIX	Prefixes are morphemes which are placed at the beginning of a word to modify or change its meaning, e.g. *dis*/like, *micro*/scope, *tri*/cycle.	Play a morpheme game in which children have to match root words with prefixes to create words. Look at the use of prefixes in the environment, e.g. in *supermarkets* and *hypermarkets* we find *multibuy* offers. Ask children to create new words and define their meanings, e.g. *ungo* (to stay), *multifun* (lots of fun).	2
PREPOSITION	Prepositions are usually attached to a noun or noun phrase, showing the position or relationship of one thing to another and include words such as *at*, *over*, *by* and *with*. When a prepositional phrase is formed, it usually does the work of an adverb or adjective.	Play an I-spy game in which you give the initial letter or sound of a word and add a prepositional phrase to provide a clue as to where the item might be found, e.g. I spy with my little eye something beginning with L which is above all of us (*light*).	2
PRESENT TENSE	A present-tense verb (a verb in the present tense) is the simplest form of the verb, and refers to an action or situation happening now. It normally has either no suffix or -s (depending on the subject), and is a finite verb.	Look with children at examples of early reading books, especially those from some of the older reading schemes where the text was presented in the present tense (e.g. Tom is in the garden. Julie is up the tree.). Ask them to use the pictures and the text to create a story in the past tense.	8
PRONOUN	A word used in place of a noun, a noun phrase or several nouns, e.g. • personal pronouns: *I/me, you, he/him, she/her, we/us, they/them, it*; • possessive pronouns: *mine, yours, his, hers, ours, theirs, its*; • reflexive pronouns: *myself, herself, themselves*; • indefinite pronouns: *someone, anything, nobody, everything*;	In shared reading, look at text in which a noun or proper noun is used repeatedly and could often be replaced by pronouns. Ask children to read it with you and to comment on ways in which it could be improved, e.g. Tom was very clever but Tom did not understand long division. Tom tried hard to learn and Tom's dad helped him at home, but Tom just could not understand. One day Tom's friend Tim helped Tom and showed Tom how to do long division.	2

(Continued)

Term	Definition	How you might teach it (NB This may be as a lesson, a game, an investigation or as a short warm-up activity at the beginning of a literacy lesson)	Chapter(s) in which you will find out more
PRONOUN (Continued)	• interrogative pronouns (used in questions): *who/whom, whose, which, what;* • relative pronouns: *who/whom, whose, which, that.*		
PUNCTUATION	Punctuation marks are used to separate sentences, phrases and clauses; to help separate items in lists (commas, semi-colons, bullet points); to guide readers on intonation, e.g. More tea? More tea! Shoot, Rooney! Shoot Rooney! Shoot Rooney? The word punctuation derives from the Latin *pungere*, 'to prick' (think of 'puncture'); this gives *punctus* – 'pierced' – as the participle (see Waugh and Jolliffe, 2012).	Let children try reading passages from which all the punctuation has been removed, to show how punctuation helps understanding. See if they can make sense of old punctuation exercises such as: I would rather be looked after by a red cross nurse than a red cross nurse. Or: Caesar entered on his head A helmet on each foot A sandal in his hand he had His trusty sword to boot.	6
RELATIVE CLAUSE	A relative clause is a subordinate clause that modifies a noun by using a relative pronoun, e.g. *That is the house. I told you about the house*, can become: *That is the house which I told you about.* Formal grammar uses *whom* for the object case of *who*: There is the man *whom* I saw yesterday. However, many writers nowadays use *that* instead.	Model the use of relative clauses as part of modelled writing. Give children pairs of simple sentences to join by using relative pronouns.	8
ROOT WORD	A root word is a word which contains only one idea or unit of meaning and cannot be split into smaller units, e.g. *need, walk, penguin.*	Look with children at words with more than one morpheme and ask them to find the root word. Look at the origins of the root words	2

Term	Definition	How you might teach it	Chapter(s) in which you will find out more
		(NB This may be as a lesson, a game, an investigation or as a short warm-up activity at the beginning of a literacy lesson)	
		and find other words with these roots in them. This will reinforce children's understanding of morphemes as well as broadening their vocabularies, e.g. look at the following words: *design, resign, signature, designate, assign, disrupt, bankrupt, erupt, interrupt, telegraph, grapheme, autograph*. The roots are *sign* (seal, mark, sign, tell something), *rupt* (break) and *graph* (write). Find other examples of roots within words and their origins. There are several websites which you will find useful.	
SENTENCE	The items in a sentence are linked by grammatical rules concerning the order of words and the type of words included. A **simple sentence** contains just one clause, e.g. Mrs Peacock laughed. A **compound sentence** contains two or more main clauses joined by *and, or, but* or *so*, e.g. Mrs Peacock laughed but Mr Peacock smiled drily. A **complex sentence** contains a main clause plus one or more subordinate clauses, e.g. Although Mrs Peacock laughed, she wasn't amused. Sentences can be: • *declarative:* The lesson finished on time. • *interrogative:* Is that your book? • *imperative:* Give me that book! • *exclamatory:* The book's fallen into the sink!	See research on sentence combining in Chapter 8. Use shared writing to model and discuss sentence combining. Often, children's understanding of the concept of a sentence can best be developed through looking at examples of non-sentences and asking them to make changes or additions in order to create complete sentences, e.g. what is needed to complete each of the following? *He was a . . . A large dog . . .*	8

(Continued)

Term	Definition	How you might teach it	Chapter(s) in which you will find out more
		(NB This may be as a lesson, a game, an investigation or as a short warm-up activity at the beginning of a literacy lesson)	
SINGULAR	A word form used to refer to one of something. When more than one is referred to, a plural form is used. Nouns can be singular or plural (see **Agreement**).	Look at examples of singulars and plurals with children. Provide them with examples of plurals and ask them to work out what the singulars are. For words which form the plural by adding -s, this will be simple, but for those with irregular endings they can use dictionaries.	2
STANDARD ENGLISH	The variety of English used in public communication, particularly in writing. It is sometimes referred to as 'BBC English'.	Approach teaching Standard English in three key ways: • incidental reflection on language used in the classroom/playground; • regular planned opportunities for more focused study; • occasional extended language investigations. Invite children to record the occasions when they have spoken to different people in different ways over a couple of days/a week. Provide examples of non-standard English and ask them to consider how they need to be changed, e.g. We wasn't there. Why is you doing that? This can lead to discussion about use of negatives, subject-verb agreement, etc.	1
SUBJECT	This refers to the person or thing performing the action of the verb in a sentence, e.g. His father attended the meeting. In this sentence, *His father* is the subject (see also **Predicate**).	Give children cards and ask them to write common, proper or abstract nouns on them. Ask them to think of sentences which have their words as the subject. Go on to ask them to pass cards on to others to create new sentences. Encourage them to develop their sentences by adding subordinates, when appropriate.	8

Term	Definition	How you might teach it	Chapter(s) in which you will find out more
SUBJUNCTIVE	Subjunctive verbs indicate 'unreality', uncertainty, wish, emotion, judgement, or necessity. They are not widely used in modern English, and are usually only met in very formal writing. It can express a wish about the way things ought to be: many children will be familiar with *Hallowed be thy name* or *Britannia rule the waves.*	(NB This may be as a lesson, a game, an investigation or as a short warm-up activity at the beginning of a literacy lesson) Look at the difference between *If I were* and *If I was.* *If I was* refers to something that really happened: If I was late for school, I was punished. *If I were* refers to an unreal/hypothetical situation: If I were Prime Minister, I'd ban motorbikes!	
SUBORDINATE CLAUSE	A subordinate clause is subordinate to (i.e. less important than) some word outside itself: it may modify this word (as a relative clause or as an adverbial), e.g. *I saw the tree which you told me about.* *Jack won the race, although he had hurt his foot.* Or it may be used as a verb's object, e.g. *Hannah believed her puppy knew the sound of her voice.*	Look at examples of subordinate clauses in texts and ask children to identify them and suggest alternatives. Encourage them to look for opportunities to add subordinate clauses to their writing in appropriate places.	8
SUBORDINATION	Subordinate to means 'less important than', and in a sentence the relation of subordination means that a word, phrase or clause gives more precise detail about some other part of the sentence. In a sentence such as: *The powerful black horse galloped swiftly over the wide meadow towards its master, its mane rippling like water.*	Subordinate phrases and clauses can be introduced during a range of sentence-level activities including making human sentences. Have words, phrases and punctuation marks written on card. Give one card to a child and invite him/her to swap places. Model how you can play with a sentence to give differing effects. Invite the children to write a description starting with a simple sentence such as *the boy wore bright red kneepads.* Demonstrate how to add a subordinate, e.g. *The boy, nervously holding his skateboard, wore bright red kneepads.*	8

(Continued)

Term	Definition	How you might teach it (NB This may be as a lesson, a game, an investigation or as a short warm-up activity at the beginning of a literacy lesson)	Chapter(s) in which you will find out more
SUBORDINATION (Continued)	*powerful* and *black* are adjectives subordinate to *horse*; *swiftly* is an adverb subordinate to *galloped*; *over the wide meadow* and *towards its master* are prepositional phrases subordinate to *galloped*; *its mane rippling like water* is an adjectival phrase subordinate to *horse*.		
SUFFIX	Suffixes are morphemes added to the ends of words to modify their meanings, e.g. *use* and *useful* or *useless*; *look* and *looking*, *looks* or *looked*.	Look at a range of root words and suffixes and ask children to see how many words they can modify using the suffixes. Encourage them to use dictionaries to check spellings. Discuss spellings when suffixes are added and words change, e.g. doubling consonants in *run* and *running*, dropping the *e* when changing *hope* to *hoping*.	2
SYNONYM	Synonyms are words with the same or similar meanings, such as *big* and *large*, *quick* and *rapid*, *tall* and *high*.	Create synonym charts (sometimes known as semantic maps) with children to encourage vocabulary development, e.g. challenge them to find synonyms for *good*, *happy*, *large* and *frightened*. Ask children to find alternatives to *said* when writing dialogue and create charts to provide ideas.	1
Tautology	The same information is repeated unnecessarily in different words in the same sentence, e.g. He did his daily jog every day. She baked a great big huge enormous cake.	Provide examples of tautological sentences and ask children to discuss ways of simplifying them to avoid repetition. Look, in particular, at some of the phrases people commonly use and consider how these might be simplified, e.g. I myself personally . . . At this present moment in time . . .	8
TENSE	Tense is the grammatical term for the time referred to by a verb – usually present or past. Present and past tense forms are both single words in English; other tenses involve the use of *modal verbs*.	Ask children to change pieces of writing from the present to the past tense and from the present to the future tense. Look with them at what happens to verbs when they change from present to past and present to future tenses.	8

Term	Definition	How you might teach it	Chapter(s) in which you will find out more
VERB	A 'doing' or 'being' word that expresses an action or a state. Verbs change their form, or tense, according to when the action takes place. So verbs may be in the past, present or future tense. Modal verbs are ones such as *can, may, might, will*, which are used to express different degrees of certainty. See also **Participle, Infinitive** and **Agreement.**	(NB This may be as a lesson, a game, an investigation or as a short warm-up activity at the beginning of a literacy lesson) In PE, make use of action verbs to encourage children to create sequences of movement (*run-leap-crumple; jog-sprint-amble; dash-jump-roll*, etc). This will help internalise the meanings of the words and enables you to link work in PE with literacy.	2
WORD	A word is a unit of grammar that can be selected and moved around relatively independently of other such units. In punctuation, words are normally separated by word spaces. When word divisions are unclear we may be able to show this uncertainty by using hyphens. Apostrophes for omitted letters show where two words are treated as one.	Create word banks for each activity in each lesson and encourage children to be adventurous in their use of vocabulary. Ensure that at Key Stage 2 children have access to a thesaurus so that they can look for alternative vocabulary. Word webs/maps can help children to see the links between different words, e.g. *sign* and *signature.*	1, 2, 3, 4, 5
WORD FAMILY	Words related to each other, such as *child, children, childish, childlike; field, fielding, fielder.*	Word families can be studied in conjunction with morphemes and plurals. When teaching spellings, talk to children about the ways in which prefixes and suffixes can be added to modify them or change their meaning.	2
VOWEL	The letters *a, e, i, o, u.* See also **Consonant.** There are roughly 20 vowel sounds in English. We sound vowels without stopping air flow – we don't bring parts of our mouth together as we say them. Long vowel sounds include all the letters when said as their names plus the sounds *air, ar, ear, ir, oy, oo* (cook), *oo* (boom), *oo* (poor), *or* and *ow* and the *schwa* sound in teacher, doctor, etc. Short vowel sounds are *a* in *hat, e* in *bed, i* in *it, o* in *log* and *u* in *bun.*	Discuss how the different vowels are pronounced in different accents or dialects of English. If the children are speakers of other languages, or learning another modern language, discuss the sounds of this language.	2

Reference: Waugh, D. and Jolliffe, W. (2012) *English 5–11.* London: Routledge.

Appendix 2: Model answers to self-assessment questions

Please note that answers are only provided for activities which enable you to check your knowledge and understanding. Some activities in chapters are open-ended and it is not possible to provide definitive answers.

Chapter 1: Teaching grammar

1. You were asked how you would ensure that all children have a wardrobe of voices that includes Standard English. Your answers to this question will vary but you are likely to consider ways of explicitly focusing on the difference between spoken and written language through:

- incidental reflection on language in daily use in the classroom;
- regular planned opportunities for more focused study;
- occasional extended language investigations, for example exploring a wardrobe of voices.

Possible pedagogical approaches may include:

- whole-class interaction and dialogue to model and develop speaking and listening;
- the use of language games, role-play and drama to support children to use Standard English in formal spoken and written contexts.

2. You were asked what you saw as the key features of an effective pedagogy for teaching grammar. Your answers to this question will vary, but are likely to draw on the findings of Myhill, Lines and Watson (2011) outlined on pp.11–12 and include:

- experimentation and playful engagement with language;
- explicit teaching and application using the texts children are already using as part of a unit of work;
- explicitly teaching meta-language and the reasons for using it;
- deconstructing how grammar is used in different texts and encouraging children to use this knowledge in their own writing;
- experimenting with and playing with grammar rather than teaching grammar out of context as a discrete lesson.

3. There is not a specific answer to this question.

Chapter 2: Words

1. Which of these words have prefixes: *ready*, **reaction**, **disappear**, *press*, **precaution**? In each prefixed word, the prefix can be removed to leave a root word: *re+action*, *dis+appear*, *pre+caution*. This is not possible with *ready* and *press*.

2. How many new words can you create from the word *play* (the words must actually exist in a dictionary)? Your choices might include *replay*, *playful*, *replay*, *playable*, *playing*, *unplayable*, etc.

3. What is a homophone? Words which sound the same but have different spellings and meanings are homophones – for instance, *slay* and *sleigh*.

4. What is a homograph? Homographs are words which are spelled the same as other words which mean something different and are pronounced differently – for instance, *lead* piping and *lead* the way.

5. *Good* and *nice* are antonyms – true or false? False – they are synonyms because they have similar meanings.

6. *High* and *low* are synonyms – true or false? False – they are antonyms because they have opposite meanings.

7. In the word *unusually*, which parts are bound morphemes? *Un-* and *-ly* are bound morphemes because they cannot stand alone and have meaning. *Usual* is a free morpheme because it can stand alone.

8. Choose the free morphemes in each of these words: *discoloured*, *unpainted*, *bicycle*. *Colour*, *paint* and *cycle* are free morphemes because they can stand alone and have meaning.

9. What is an inflectional ending? Use inflectional endings to modify these words: *pass*, *table*, *plant*. Inflectional endings change words by adding suffixes which change the meaning grammatically. *Pass* can become *passable*, *passing*, *passed*, *passer*, etc.; *table* can become *tables*, *tabled*, *tabling*, etc.; *plant* could become *plants*, *planting*, *planter*, etc.

10. Look at the sentences below and identify in each the verbs and nouns:

- The chair fell over. (*Chair* is the noun, and *fell* the verb.)

- Dogs bark at strangers. (*Dogs* and *strangers* are nouns, and *bark* the verb.)

- Girls are clever. (*Girls* is the noun and *are* is the verb – from the verb 'to be'.)

11. Now add an adjective to each sentence. Your choices might include:

- The (*brown/wooden/comfortable/broken*, etc.) chair fell over.

- (*Horrid/vicious/useful/well-trained*, etc.) dogs bark at (*noisy/tall/most*, etc.) strangers.

- (*Modern/older/blonde/happy*, etc.) girls are clever.

12. In the sentences below, identify the determiners, prepositions and adverbs:

- The jolly old man walked slowly along the dusty road.

  (determiners – *the* (twice), preposition – *along*, adverb – *slowly*)

- A sneaky snake slithered slyly into the soft sand.

  (determiners – *a* and *the*, preposition – *into*, adverb – *slyly*)

- Those people who drop litter on the ground carelessly should be put into prison.

  (determiners – *those* and *the*, prepositions – *on* and *into*, adverb – *carelessly*)

Chapter 3: Why spelling matters

1. You were asked to consider your approach to teaching spelling. Your answers will vary, but you will know that teaching spelling goes beyond sending word lists home to be learned. You will be aware that if children are to become confident spellers you will need to teach spelling strategies systematically and explicitly and provide opportunities for children to apply these in their writing.

2. Successful spellers are able to draw on and integrate many different kinds of knowledge. Good spellers draw on the four key aspects of spelling addressed in this chapter:

- phonemic knowledge and analogy making;
- morphological knowledge;
- semantic knowledge;
- visual knowledge.

  A good spelling programme will help children to draw on a range of strategies and recognise that they can use them to improve their spelling.

3. Creating a classroom environment where children actively investigate words, their origins and their meanings is likely to include:

- strengthening your own knowledge of the origins of words so that you have a wealth of knowledge to draw on;
- encouraging the children's curiosity in words – taking every opportunity to investigate the relationship between word origins and their spelling, using planned and incidental opportunities across the curriculum to investigate and discuss meanings;
- making sure you have access to etymological dictionaries; challenging children to find out how different words have entered the English language;
- considering how the learning environment will support children's interest in words – for example, your working wall may include word webs focused on a word root.

Build up word banks with a root, such as *aquatic, aquarium, aquamarine,* and invite the children to deduce the meaning of *aqua.* The webs can be added to over days or weeks, as additional examples are found in their reading and writing.

You will have your own ideas to add to this list, and will find further suggestions in Chapter 5.

Chapter 4: Spelling and phonics

1. The four key concepts that are important for teaching the simple and complex code are:

   a) Sounds/phonemes are represented by letter/graphemes.

   b) A phoneme can be represented by more than one letter.

   c) The same phoneme can be represented in more than one way.

   d) The same grapheme can represent more than one phoneme.

2. The position of phonemes:

   a) **ai** and **oi** do not occur at the end of English words.

   b) The **w** special occurs when an /o/ sound follows a /w/ sound and is spelled with the letter **a** (e.g. *was, wallet, want, wash, watch, wander*).

   c) When an /ur/ sound follows the letter **w** (but not **qu**) it is usually spelt **or** (e.g. *word, worm, work, worship, worth*). The one important exception is *were.*

   d) The /or/ sound before an /l/ sound is frequently spelled **al** (*walk, talk*).

   e) If a word ends in a /v/ sound, the letter **e** has to be added.

   f) When deciding whether to use **ant** or **ent**, **ance** or **ence**, consider whether there is a related word where the vowel sound is more clearly pronounced. When deciding, for example, between *referance* or *reference*, the related word *referee* may help.

Chapter 5: Teaching spelling rules, generalisations and tricky words

1. You were asked to review your current classroom environment. What might you change or add to ensure that it is a positive environment for learning spellings? Your answers will vary, but the activity that considers a classroom where there is a high interest in words will provide a good starting point.

2. The four key aspects of the teaching sequence for spelling are:

- Revisit, explain, use.
- Teach, model, define.
- Practise, explore, investigate.
- Apply, assess, reflect.

3. Four key memory strategies for learning tricky words are: using syllables, base words, analogy and mnemonics. You were asked to consider how to use memory strategies to help children remember the spellings *some*, *their/there*, *people* and *resign*. Your answers will vary, but may include:

some	Using analogy: *come* and *some*.
their/ there	Looking at words within the word – the word *heir* is in *their* (their son and heir); *here* is in *there* (remember the phrase 'here and there').
people	Inviting children to devise a mnemonic such as **people** eat oranges, pigs like eggs.
resign	Making a word web around the base word sign. Words are likely to include signature, design, assign, signal, and, of course, resign.

4. You were asked to consider how you will make spelling lists an effective and worthwhile task for the children if your school sends these home each week. Refer back to the list of suggestions under the heading 'Spelling lists' (p.97) and choose three or four of these to try out.

Chapter 6: Punctuation

You were asked to punctuate sentences. The following are suggested answers. You may have punctuated them in a slightly different way.

1. David, Julie, Rosemary and Gill sat in Trafalgar Square.
2. Sam, who was thirty-two, had thinning, blond hair.
3. 'Oh no!' cried Sue, as she saw the damage Bill had done to her new BMW.
4. 'You,' shouted the teacher, 'have the manners of a two-year-old!'
5. Rimmer sat miserably in the control room of Red Dwarf.

The punctuation marks which are used for each of the given purposes are as follows:

1. To separate the different parts of a sentence and provide clarity for the reader: *comma*.
2. To separate two main clauses in a sentence: *semi-colon*.

3. Before a second clause that expands or illustrates the first: *colon*.

4. At the end of an interjection to indicate strong feeling or emotion: *exclamation mark*.

5. In informal writing to replace brackets and some other punctuation marks: *dash*.

Chapter 7: Apostrophes

Activity (p.125) You were asked to place apostrophes in the correct places:

1. The dogs aren't used to their kennels.

2. The snow's been falling all day but there still isn't enough to make snowballs.

3. Jack's mother didn't send him out to swap the cow for some beans.

4. The men's team lost to the women's team by three goals to two.

5. The Joneses' roof had a hole in it.

End of chapter self-assessment questions:

1. The **children's** work **wasn't** as good as that of their teachers.

2. **Jill's shoes** were covered with mud and the **twins'** jackets were little better. (It is assumed here that there are two twins each of whom has a jacket. If one twin owned more than one jacket you would write *the twin's jackets*.)

3. The **pupils'** desks were dreadfully untidy and their attitude to the teachers' (or *teacher's* if it was one teacher) **instructions was** poor.

4. The **government's** concern for education is illustrated by **its** commitment to maintaining **teachers'** salaries at their present level.

5. The **boys'** toilets were a haven for **smokers'** nefarious activities.

6. The **ladies'** cloakroom was full of expensive fur **coats** belonging to the **party's** guests. (If you wrote *the parties' guests* this would mean that more than one party was taking place.)

7. The **greengrocer's** shop window bore signs advertising potato's, carrots', tomato's and onion's (apostrophes not needed, but that was probably what was in the window!).

8. 'It's unlikely that you will pass your course if you miss my **lectures**,' announced the balding academic.

9. The **Rovers'** goal was being bombarded by shots from **United's** eager **forwards**. (The team is called Rovers and so the apostrophe comes after Rovers, just as the opposition is United and so an *apostrophe s* is added.)

10. The **trout's** eye seemed to be looking at me as I prepared to take a forkful of his body.

Chapter 8: Phrases, clauses and sentences

You were asked to look at the sentences below and identify which are a) simple, b) compound and c) complex, and to underline any subordinate clauses in the sentences.

1. David went out but Claire stayed at home. (Compound – each clause has equal weight)
2. Dawn broke. (Simple)
3. Rosemary, <u>who seldom slept in</u>, was still fast asleep at ten o'clock. (Complex)
4. The ball, <u>which had begun to get very muddy</u>, was booted into the net by Billy. (Complex)
5. Nathan's sister ran home. (Simple)
6. Michael, a polite and charming yet rather unpleasant man, made a mess of everything he did. (Simple – there is only one verb)

All but number 4 are active sentences. Number 4 is a passive sentence because the action was performed upon the ball rather than the ball performing the action.

Chapter 9: Putting it all together

1. Name four cohesive devices:
- reference;
- substitution and ellipsis;
- conjunction;
- lexical.

2. What kind of cohesive devices are used in each of the following text types:
- instructional/procedural – imperative verbs;
- recounts – temporal connectives such as *then, next, first, afterwards, just before that, at last, meanwhile*;
- discussion – connectives such as *therefore* and *however*.

3. Possible solution: précis.

> *Liverpool musicians The Beatles were very popular in the 1960s. People copied their accents and hairstyles and screamed and fainted at their concerts. Guitarists John Lennon and Paul McCartney wrote most of the songs, but guitarist, George Harrison, and drummer, Ringo Starr, whose real name was Richard Starkey, wrote some. Their songs, which include 'I Want to Hold Your Hand', 'Yesterday', and 'Let it Be' can still be heard. John was killed in 1980, and George Harrison died in 2001.*

Appendix 3: The Grammar, Punctuation and Spelling tests

In this book we have stressed the importance of teaching grammar in engaging ways, and provided a range of examples to show how new learning can be applied in authentic contexts. The case studies show how trainee and experienced teachers are successfully doing this to good effect in the classroom. The approaches that we have described allow teachers and children to develop a shared meta-language, to see how language works and describe and discuss the way texts are designed and constructed. As we explore and discuss how writers use language to create the impact they want to have on their readers, so we can empower children to see themselves as creating rather than *doing* writing. As creators of writing, they are far more likely to take ownership of their writing and take responsibility for deciding the best form to use for their particular purpose and audience. We have been clear that being able to spot an adverb and identify a multi-clause sentence is of little intrinsic worth; it does not lead to better-quality writing.

When schools adapted their long- and medium-term planning to meet the demands of the 2014 National Curriculum, many chose to take a fresh look at units of work in English – and across the curriculum – in order to identify the best place for particular aspects of grammar to be taught. Pat Hutchins's *Rosie's Walk*, for example, is a text that is ideal to refer back to when looking at prepositions. In *Leon and the Place Between*, Angela McAllister and Graeme Baker Smith have created a wonderful picture book for lower KS2, rich in descriptive, almost poetic language that provides a natural place to explore adverbials and multi-clause sentences. The simplicity of the opening of Louis Sacher's novel *Holes* enables older, more sophisticated writers to see how single-clause sentences can be used to great effect to draw the reader in. We need to be clear that we are not suggesting that these books should be read in order to teach grammar. They deserve to be read, savoured, enjoyed and responded to. But as we take a deeper look at the author's craft close up, so we can explore the way the text has been created and this is where we can look at the grammar in context.

Exploring language in different contexts across the curriculum can be particularly helpful for looking at levels of formality. Information texts and formal reports may allow authentic opportunities to use the passive voice. Discursive texts in history or geography can be a good place to introduce and explore a wide range of adverbials.

Where the curriculum is carefully planned and taught in this way, children will be familiar with the meta-language they need to be successful in the Grammar, Punctuation and Spelling (GP&S) tests at the end of Key Stage 1 and Key Stage 2. This is not to suggest that the tests do not need to be prepared for. The stakes are high. From 2016, National Curriculum tests are reported using a scaled score, comparing children against the national cohort by decile. The GP&S score will be combined with teacher assessment of writing. The DfE (2015a) makes clear that we *should not use the frameworks to guide teaching and learning. They do not provide information on how the new national curriculum should be taught.* There is no suggestion that curriculum delivery should be regarded as a 'tick list'.

Most of the test content at Key Stages 1 and 2 is drawn from the statutory appendices of the 2014 National Curriculum (*Appendix 1: Spelling* and *Appendix 2: Vocabulary, grammar and punctuation*), although there are some areas of content from across the programme of study for English at KS1. The DfE (2015b) has produced full, detailed guidance for schools on the content domain in the English Grammar, Punctuation and Spelling Test Framework and these are available on the **www.gov.uk** website. The content is demanding – at the end of Key Stage 2, children need to recognise and explain the use of ambiguity and double negatives, subjunctive mood, subject and object, and passives with and without agents. This may be challenging for many adults.

At the end of Key Stage 1 there are two papers:

Paper 1: the spelling task. This will use picture and/or dictated sentences as prompts. Children will be expected to spell simple monosyllabic and polysyllabic words, including common exception words and homophones and near-homophones.

Paper 2: short questions where children will be asked to identify grammatical terms and punctuate sentences. The test is likely to ask them to put in appropriate coordinating and subordinating conjunctions (referred to as *joining words*), demonstrate their knowledge of tense agreement, know about the past tense subject-verb agreement and recognise different types of words.

At the end of Key Stage 2 there are two papers:

Paper 1: grammar, punctuation and vocabulary questions including grammatical terms, the functions of sentences, words, phrases and clauses, verb forms, tense and consistency, punctuation, vocabulary, standard English and formality. Most questions on the paper will be short answers, with some sentence answers towards the end of the paper.

Paper 2: spelling questions. Each spelling will be contained in a contextualised sentence.

Sample papers can also be downloaded from: **www.gov.uk/ search?q=sample+grammar+tests**.

There are many ways in which we can enable children to be successful other than giving them endless practice papers, and we have suggested some below.

1. Be clear about what the children already know, understand and are able to do, so that you are clear about their misconceptions. Remember that it is not just about plugging gaps in knowledge – all grammar is interrelated, so it is important to make sure that understanding is based on a firm foundation. In addition to whole-class teaching, use guided sessions to work with groups of children who share the same misconceptions.

2. Do use the correct terminology throughout the school. Some of the terms we have become used to have changed: for example, make sure you talk about adverbs, adverbials, progressive verbs, prepositions and conjunctions rather than the generic term *connectives*. Be careful to be precise. Verbs are commonly talked about as *doing words* – but they also include *to be* and *to have*. Some schools have chosen colours for different word classes (for example, green for adjectives, blue for nouns) and used these consistently across the school. This approach can be helpful, but remember that words can belong to different word classes according to how they are used (see Chapter 2 and below).

3. Use language which avoids suggesting that words have a fixed 'class', and show that it depends on the job they do in the sentence. The word *green*, for example, can be an adjective, noun or verb. Encourage a problem-solving approach. If children are unsure about the job the word is doing, suggest that they swap in other words to help them to work out what it might be.

    Make sure children know why as well as what, so that they can answer questions such as *Why do the underlined words start with a capital letter?* (DfE, Key Stage 1 sample test).

4. Try to have a short grammar/punctuation/vocabulary/spelling warm-up session every day where children can play with language in creative and imaginative ways. Use drama to help children take on more formal 'voices' – at Key Stage 1 this will really help with Standard English. Integrate these sessions with your units of work so that there are opportunities to practise and apply new learning in English and across the curriculum.

5. Use precise meta-language when modelling writing yourself and when modelling the redrafting process, focusing on the impact that you want to have on your reader. Use it selectively and appropriately in your marking, always taking care to respond to the text as a whole first and not just to words and sentences.

6. Encourage children to use language precisely when peer- and self-assessing. Make sure you have modelled how to do this. If you have a visualiser, use it to discuss the writing of one of the children or to point out how authors have used the particular aspect of grammar or punctuation that the children have been learning during shared reading.

7. Make sure you don't just test spelling and punctuation, but teach it too. Challenge children to come up with 'rules' themselves rather than simply telling them – this approach can be used for punctuation and spelling. There are suggestions for ways of doing this in the earlier chapters.

Preparation for the tests

It is clearly important to prepare for the end of Key Stage tests and to make sure that children are familiar with the layout and the type of questions that will be asked. They will need to be introduced, discussed and practised.

There is a variety of question types, which will reflect the range of the cognitive demand scales. The tests use a three-point taxonomy, based on Bloom's taxonomy. As far as possible these appear in order of difficulty:

1. Knowledge and comprehension questions, such as:

    What is the name of the punctuation mark below?

    Circle two {verbs} in this sentence.

2. Application and analysis questions, such as:

    Complete the sentence below with an {adjective} that makes sense.

    Categorise these {types of sentence}.

    Rewrite the sentence below {using Standard English}.

3. Synthesis and evaluation questions, such as:

    What would be the effect of replacing this {full stop} with a {semi-colon}?

Synthesis and evaluation are not used in the Key Stage 1 test.

The questions in both the Key Stage 1 and Key Stage 2 tests are categorised into two broad formats:

*   *selected response* – where children select the correct answer;
*   *constructed response* – where children write a short answer themselves.

Children will need to be familiar with both these formats and the different ways that the information may be required. Being asked to write a sentence using the past progressive will, of course, be more cognitively demanding than ticking a box or underlining it in a sentence.

An ideal opportunity for introducing the test questions is when you have been exploring a particular aspect with children. If you have been focusing on a particular aspect of grammar or punctuation, show children what the test question which assesses this will look like. For example, in Year 2 you may have been telling recounts orally using the past tense. If you then show the test question below, the children will be able to write the verbs in the past tense confidently.

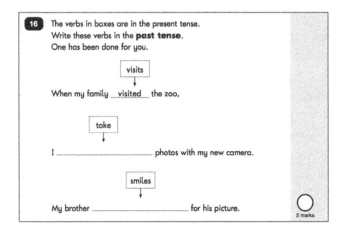

(DfE (2015c))

At Key Stage 2, you may have been looking at the impact of using a range of subordinating conjunctions and discussing how these can change the overall mood and meaning of a piece of writing. In the test question below, the children would be able to recognise that *after* is used as a subordinating conjunction in the final sentence.

38 Tick one box in each row to show whether the word <u>after</u> is used as a **subordinating conjunction** or as a **preposition**.

Sentence	<u>after</u> used as a subordinating conjunction	<u>after</u> used as a preposition
He moved here <u>after</u> the end of the war.		
Entry is free <u>after</u> 5pm in the evening.		
I went to the cinema <u>after</u> I had eaten my dinner.		

1 mark

(DfE (2015d))

References

DfE (2015a) *Guidance for Test Developers Working on Key Stage 1 and Key Stage 2 National Curriculum Tests*. Available from: **www.gov.uk/government/collections/national-curriculum-assessments-test-frameworks** (accessed 1.8.15).

DfE (2015b) *Key Stage 1: English Grammar, Punctuation and Spelling Test Framework*. Available from: **www.gov.uk/government/publications/key-stage-1-english-grammar-punctuation-and-spelling-test-framework** (accessed 1.8.15); *Key Stage 2: English Grammar,*

Punctuation and Spelling Test Framework. Available from: **www.gov.uk/government/uploads/ system/uploads/attachment_data/file/439645/2016_KS2_EnglishGPS_framework_ PDFA.pdf** (accessed 1.8.15).

DfE (2015c) *2016 Key Stage 1 English Grammar, Punctuation and Spelling: Sample Test Materials, Mark Scheme and Test Administration Instructions*. Page 13. Available from: https://www.gov.uk/ government/uploads/system/uploads/attachment_data/file/439447/Sample_ks1_EnglishGPS_ paper2_questions.pdf (accessed 22/11/2015).

DfE (2015d) *2016 Key Stage 2 English Grammar, Punctuation and Spelling: Sample Test Materials, Mark Scheme and Test Administration Instructions*. Page 22. Available from: https://www.gov.uk/ government/uploads/system/uploads/attachment_data/file/439299/Sample_ks2_EnglishGPS_ paper1_questions.pdf (accessed 22/11/2015).

Hutchins, P. (1968) *Rosie's Walk*. London: Bodley Head.

McAllister, A. and Baker Smith. G. (2008) *Leon and the Place Between.* London: Templar Publishing.

Sachar, L. (1998) *Holes.* New York: Bloomsbury.

Index

Added to a page number 'g' denotes glossary.